AZUSA STREET AND BEYOND

D0064369

Azusa Street and Beyond

Pentecostal Missions and Church Growth in the Twentieth Century

L. Grant McClung, Jr., Editor

Bridge Publishing Inc.
Publishers of:
LOGOS • HAVEN • OPEN SCROLL

#14522243

© 1986 by Bridge Publishing, Inc.
All rights reserved
Printed in the United States of America
ISBN 0-88270-607-1
Library of Congress catalog number 86-70742
Bridge Publishing, Inc.
2500 Hamilton Blvd.
South Plainfield, NJ 07080

Affectionately dedicated
to Janice—professional secretary,
anointed musician, committed wife and
mother—for her partnership
in matrimony and ministry

About the Author

Lloyd Grant McClung, Jr. graduated from West Coast Christian College in 1972. He received a master's degree from California Graduate School of Theology in Glendale, California, and was an instructor at the European Bible Seminary in West Germany. The Seminary is operated by the Church of God (Cleveland, Tennessee), the denomination in which he is an ordained minister.

Subsequently he completed the Master of Divinity at the Church of God School of Theology in Cleveland, Tennessee, and was accepted into the Fuller Theological Seminary School of World Mission. He is currently a Ph.D. candidate and holds the Doctor of Missiology from Fuller, where he formerly served as teaching assistant to C. Peter Wagner. In 1984 he was awarded the Paul Yonggi Cho Church Growth Award for his work on pentecostal missions and church growth.

At present, he is Assistant Professor of Missions and Church Growth at the Church of God School of Theology in Cleveland, Tennessee. He is married to the former Janice Leach of Tampa, Florida. They have two sons, Matthew and Joel.

Table of Contents

Table of Contents

Permissions

Foreword

When compared to other significant Christian traditions, pentecostals have majored in being *doers* of the Word, much more than just *hearers* of the Word or even *writers* of the Word. This task-oriented approach to serving God has resulted in the most rapidly growing movement of our day. Estimates in the mid-eighties put the number of pentecostals (including charismatics) at 120 million worldwide, and the rates of growth far surpass those of any other Christian group.

The early pentecostal leaders were men and women so consumed with the passion for making the gospel message known to unbelievers that they could not bring themselves to prioritize formal education and scholarly pursuits. A change has come in the second and third generation of leaders, however. While no less fervent in preaching the gospel, some of them are paving the way in documenting and analyzing just how this extraordinary work of the Holy Spirit has developed through the years.

Grant McClung is one of this new breed. He combines the attributes of an evangelist, a missionary, a pastor, a teacher, a prophet, and a scholar. His heart beats for the evangelization of the world, and in this book he sets out to shed new light on how the pentecostal movement has generated such an awesome growth dynamic around the globe. In order to do this he undertook an extensive research project searching out all that pentecostal leaders had written about their movement. He allowed the cream to come to the top and skimmed it off by selecting outstanding contributions to the literature and including them in this book. Each section is introduced by McClung's own integrating comments, reflecting his personal creativity and his scholarly grasp of the contents.

The result is an outstanding book which is a gift to the church as a whole. While most of the contents are written by pentecostals, it is a book that will fascinate non-pentecostals as well. We live in an age of The Third Wave in which growing numbers of non-pentecostals are experiencing God's supernatural power in ways common to pentecostals. It is a book that they will read with great enthusiasm and appreciation.

McClung's book will also serve to encourage today's pentecostals to get back to their roots. As in any religious movement, there is a danger that today's more sophisticated and more respectable pentecostalism will cool off the fire and fervency of past generations. This must not happen, and it will not if pentecostals read this book with the prayer that God will continually renew and revive their movement for His glory and for the evangelization of the world.

C. Peter Wagner
Fuller Seminary School of World Mission
Pasadena, California

Preface

This project began when, as a pentecostal missionary, I began to look for one central sourcebook on pentecostal missions and church growth. Though many pentecostal missiologists had reflected upon the reasons and methods of their growth in a variety of scattered sources, there was nothing to be found that brought it all together at a glance. I discovered this after reviewing scores of dissertations, theses, books, and articles, which finally came to be produced as an Annotated Bibliography of Pentecostal Missions and is found at the concluding section of this book.

What has been produced, then, for researchers and students of pentecostal church growth in seminaries, Bible schools, denominations, and missions is a reader, a compendium of pentecostal writings from four broad perspectives: history, theology, practice, and the future of pentecostal missions. A separate section has been reserved for the interaction of outsiders from the perspective of the Church Growth Movement.

Personal insights from my review of the literature are found as the introductory chapter to each section. In addition, the interpretations of other authors are edited together in contributing articles.

Part One, Historical Perspectives, gives a glimpse into the early dynamics that God converged to bring about the initial thrust of pentecostal missions. There is an opportunity to "visit" Azusa Street and interact with original participants through their eyewitness accounts. It also contains the historical analysis of subsequent products of the movement.

Part Two, Theological Motivations, attempts to capture the motivating beliefs that propelled pentecostals into worldwide expansion. It traces the eschatological urgency, sense of destiny, and high regard for the supernatural working of the Holy Spirit that have been at the heart of pentecostal missions. It will be seen that, though not always academically articulated and systematized, pentecostals *have* had a missions theology.

Part Three, Strategic/Practical Issues, looks at what pentecostals have actually been doing and the reasons for their methods. It will be seen that they have combined a "spontaneous strategy of the Spirit" with calculated forethought in finding the best ways to reap the harvest.

Part Four, Pentecostals and the Church Growth Movement, is a parenthesis of sorts. It traces some of the most significant literary commentaries by proponents of the Church Growth Movement on the missionary beliefs and practices of the Pentecostal Movement. Here are insights from Donald M. McGavran, the father of the Church Growth Movement, and his colleagues. It will be seen that the two parallel movements (the Pentecostal Movement and the Church Growth Movement) have both informed and instructed each other.

Part Five, Future Cautions and Challenges, observes that as they near their centennial, pentecostals now have a history. The question is posed, however, whether pentecostals will have another one hundred years and what will be their direction into the future. It will be seen that pentecostals are committed to future challenges, but there are some cautions to take into consideration. This section concludes with major declarations by the two leading North American pentecostal denominations on their commitment to and vision for the future.

The final section is an extended bibliography on pentecostal missions. It is an extensive review of related literature with more than three hundred entries for the benefit of future researchers. It includes all of the references cited in the book plus additional listings for research purposes. Bibliographic references are placed in the body of the text. The references immediately follow the quotations and are placed in parentheses. For example, (Orr 1973:184). This means that the reference is from Orr's book or article dated 1973, and it is quoted from page 184. To find this reference refer to the Annotated Bibliography in the final section of the book. If the author of the quotation (or the person referred to) is clear in the text, then just the year and page number are provided. For example, the text may refer to Donald Gee, introduce a quotation from him, and then close with (1949:3). This means you should look in the final bibliography for Gee's name, followed by the date. The quotation is from page 3 of his 1949 book.

I gratefully acknowledge the interest and encouragement of my mentor, Dr. C. Peter Wagner, and all of the School of World Mission faculty at the Fuller Theological Seminary; the godly heritage of my pentecostal parents, Lloyd and Pauline McClung; the love and support of my family—Janice, Matthew, and Joel; and the grace and forgiveness of a loving God expressed to me in the person of His Son, the Lord Jesus Christ, whose servant I am.

L. Grant McClung, Jr.
Church of God School of Theology
Cleveland, Tennessee

Part One
Historical Perspectives

Introduction

Explosion, Motivation, and Consolidation: The Historical Anatomy of a Missionary Movement

L. Grant McClung, Jr.

It began with the scorn and opposition of clergymen and the secular press:

> Breathing strange utterances and mouthing a creed which it would seem no sane mortal could understand, the newest religious sect has started in Los Angeles. Meetings are held in a tumble-down shack on Azusa Street, near San Pedro Street, and the devotees of the weird doctrine practice the most fanatical rites, preach the wildest theories and work themselves into a state of mad excitement in their peculiar zeal. (*Los Angeles Times* 1906:1)

Estimates of its size in 1906 ranged from 13,000 (Corum, 1981, Volume 1, Number 1:1) to 15,000 (Orr 1973:184). By the mid-1920s it had, in the United States alone, increased ten-fold (Orr 1973:184). By the time of its "Golden Jubilee" it had reached a count of at least ten million worldwide (du Plessis 1958:200) and had become known as "The Third Force in Christendom" (Van Dusen 1958:113-124).

Within eighteen years of the end of this century, the secular press again reported on this phenomenon. Using the figures in David B. Barrett's *World Christian Encyclopedia* (1982 Oxford University Press) *Time* magazine's Richard Ostling reported that this movement had fifty-one million adherents (1982:66), along with "another eleven million charismatic fellow-travelers . . . within the major Christian bodies" (Spittler 1983:13).

What is the historical anatomy of this missionary awakening known as the Pentecostal Movement? What happened to men and women at the turn of this century to cause a veritable explosion of worldwide evangelistic activity around the globe? Not all of the answers are offered in the following introductory essay, but the reader should be able to gain something more of an "inside view" by tracing some of the historical elements of the movement and reading some of the accounts of first-hand participants.

Explosion

The "Pentecostal Explosion" at the advent of the twentieth century was not an isolated event. Although Azusa Street seemed to be a focal point, especially from 1906 to 1908, the movement cannot be said to have been centered in any one place. Bloch-Hoell asserted, "As the Pentecostal Movement spread in the United States, the importance of both Azusa Street and Los Angeles decreased. After the first formative years, the Movement had no joint headquarters" (1964:53).

Leaderless leadership. In addition, no main personality can be said to be the originator of the movement. This, said widely respected pentecostal spokesman Donald Gee, is:

> ... one highly significant feature of the Movement that distinguished it in a striking way from most of those that have gone before. The Pentecostal Movement does not owe its origin to any outstanding personality or religious leader, but was a spontaneous revival appearing almost simultaneously in various parts of the world. We instinctively connect the Reformation with Luther, the Quakers with George Fox, Methodism with Wesley, the Plymouth Brethren with Darby and Graves, the Salvation Army with William Booth, and so on. But the outstanding leaders of the Pentecostal Movement are themselves the product of the Movement. They did not make it; it made them. (1949:3)

One well-known product of the movement, David du Plessis, (known as "Mr. Pentecost," 1977 Logos) emphasized the leadership of the Holy Spirit in the twentieth century as in the first-century church, and underlined Gee's emphasis that "there is no man who can claim to have been the founder of this great worldwide Christian revival" (1958:194).

A God to be experienced. This phenomenon of "leaderless leadership" and "denominationless dynamics" was not the result of a "new emphasis on any special doctrine. Rather, the emphasis is upon an experience" (du Plessis 1958:194). Pentecostals have been known for their insistence upon the necessity of experiencing God through the Holy Spirit. They have historically seen the Holy Spirit himself as the originator and impetus for world mission. Gee said that the central attraction of the movement:

> ... consisted purely of a powerful individual spiritual experience. The stress was not on any system of doctrine, for Arminians and Calvinists found themselves on the same platforms, and teachers with diverse views upon Holiness and Eschatology were conscious of a new, deep fundamental unity in spirit. Neither was the emphasis upon any ideas about Church government, for Episcopalians, Methodists, Brethren, Salvation Army members, and indeed some from practically every section of the Church, participated in the Movement. There was no particular cult or method practiced, for if there was one thing above another that marked the meetings it was their amazing diversity. (1949:30)

4

Pentecostal ecumenism. Researcher John Thomas Nichol agreed that "the early Pentecostals emphasized an experience rather than a system of doctrine or church government" (1966:55). Thus, he observed in his oft-quoted *Pentecostalism:*

> . . . Arminians and Calvinists, Holiness folk who believed in a "second work of grace" and Baptists who adhered to the theory of "the finished work at Calvary," Methodists, Brethren, and Anglicans—all of whom represented variant forms of church doctrine and polity—all met around the same altar to pray and expect the impartation of the Holy Spirit and his charismatic gifts. (1966:55)

The explosion that temporarily resulted in a "pentecostal ecumenism" was later to solidify into more neatly marked doctrinal and governmental boundaries, but for the meantime, says Larry Christenson, "Pentecostal Christianity in its formative period had strong ecumenical tendencies. The spontaneity and vitality of its experience spread without too much regard for denominational boundaries" (in Synan 1975:31).

A student movement. But if the explosion could be said to be ecumenical, cross-cultural, and missionary in nature, it could also be described as a "student movement" of sorts. The event that preceded Azusa Street by five years and actually precipitated the revival in Los Angeles began at the outset of the century in a student atmosphere (Corum 1981, Volume 1, No. 2:1). Was it not in a Bible School in Topeka, Kansas, where Charles Parham's students searched the Scriptures for evidences of a pentecostal experience? Was it not a student (Agnes N. Ozman) upon whom the Holy Spirit came during that prayer/study vigil? Was it not also a student who later came to Parham's second school in Houston, Texas? (Synan 1975:31) This student

> . . . was destined to become another key figure in the story of the Pentecostals: W.J. Seymour, an ordained Negro minister. It was Seymour who carried the Pentecostal message to California, to one of the most famous addresses in Pentecostal history: 312 Azusa Street, Los Angeles. (Sherrill 1964:38-39)

Internal elements. Additional reading from two main sources can inform us as to the inner dynamics that made this explosion possible. One of them, Christenson, delineates four basic elements that were present in early pentecostalism. First, he says, was the priority of event "Pentecostal Christianity tends to find its rise in events which are heralded as a demonstration of supernatural power and activity." There was, in the second place, a mood of expectancy. Pentecostal Christianity, he notes, "is Christianity standing on tiptoe, expecting something to happen." The third element was fullness of life in the Holy Spirit, a fullness in which "the Holy Spirit is the initiator of rich and varied Christian experience. No personal testimony is adequate, no worship service complete, without clear-cut evidence of the presence and activity of the Holy Spirit." Finally, already introduced earlier, there was the paradox of ecumenism and exclusivism. Though ecumenical at the outset, the movement developed "exclusivistic tendencies" ("Pentecostalism's Forgotten Forerunner" in Synan 1975:25-31).

A second source for further study is Chapter 5 of Nichol's *Pentecostalism* in which he articulated some fifteen "Causes for the Initial Success of Pentecostalism." In summary form they are:

1. A world conditioned to expect the supernatural.
2. Christians previously prepared to expect manifestations of the Spirit.
3. Emphasis upon experience rather than doctrine or church government.
4. Pentecostals' self-image as a revitalization movement within the Christian Church.
5. An early thrust toward nominal Christians and lethargic believers rather than to the unconverted.
6. An appeal to the lower strata of American society.
7. Taking initiative in going to people rather than waiting for them to come to them.
8. The use of mass meetings to create a sense of belonging to a community.
9. The effective use of newspapers/periodicals to disseminate the pentecostal message.
10. A democratic tendency which drew people of all classes with no discrimination.
11. Emphasis upon divine healing.
12. Meeting psychological felt-needs of people.
13. The conviction of early adherents that God had raised them up for a special work.
14. A tremendous spirit of sacrifice.
15. The principle of establishing indigenous churches.

(1966:54-69)

Motivation. To say that early pentecostals were motivated and driven by a power beyond themselves would be a classic understatement! Their lifestyle and message proceeded from a conviction that God was in their midst and had chosen them for a special work. It was this certainty, "the sense of reality that emanated from them, which undoubtedly attracted people. The Pentecostals were convincing, someone has said, because they themselves were convinced" (Nichol 1966:66). Their conviction is measured on at least three levels of their experience: theological motivation, evangelistic zeal, and supernatural recruitment.

Theological motivation. Early pentecostals were marked by their exactness in following a literal interpretation of Scripture. They sought to be people led by "The Book" and by the Holy Spirit. They saw themselves in the midst of a literal fulfillment of Joel 2:28-32. Whatever criticism is offered against their subjective interpretation of Scripture and their high value upon experience,

6

pentecostals have always valued Scripture as God's Word for today. One of the earliest Azusa Street alumni, Frank Bartleman, recalled, "In the beginning of the Pentecostal outpouring I remember preaching for three hours one evening in the heart of New York City. And then the people wanted more. Those were days of great hunger for the Word of God" (n.d.:7). A Church of God minister, C.M. Padgett, wrote in the December 14, 1918, issue of the *Church of God Evangel* about the "Results of Sanctification." One of them, he said, will be:

> The Word of God will be prized above all reading, to your soul it will be the book of books; other reading matter will be secondary. The newspaper will not be allowed to crowd out the Word of God. (Tomlinson 1918:1)

Agnes Ozman, whose baptism in the Holy Ghost on January 1, 1901, signaled the beginning of the modern Pentecostal Movement in America, was deeply motivated by the Scriptures. During her active involvement in mission work—visiting the elderly, praying for the sick, preaching and testifying—she realized:

> . . . a need within. And for about three weeks my heart became hungry for the baptism of the Holy Ghost. I wanted the promise of the Father more than ever I did food or sleep. On New Year's night, January 1, 1901, near eleven o'clock, I asked that prayer be offered for me and hands be laid on me to fulfill all scripture, that I might receive the baptism which my whole heart longed to have. (LaBerge n.d.:27-29)

Immediately after her controversial baptism in the Holy Ghost and its surrounding publicity, Agnes Ozman and her Bible school colleagues went to the Scriptures:

> So we blessed God and gave thanks for all things, made a study of the outpouring of the Holy Ghost. We found the sign given when the former rain of the Spirit was poured out was talking in tongues and magnifying Jesus as in Acts 2:4. (n.d.:30)

But if their experience was informed by the Word, their passion was fired by the Spirit. They followed the precedent of holiness teachers such as Torrey, Moody, and Simpson who saw that "the divine purpose in the baptism in the Holy Spirit was an enduement with power for witnessing and service" (Gee 1961:30). The pentecostals believed that the new experience of the Holy Spirit was more than and separate from their experience of sanctification. The original statement of faith from the first issue of *The Apostolic Faith* (Seymour's paper from the Azusa Street Mission) had a statement to that effect:

> The Baptism with the Holy Ghost is a gift of power upon the sanctified life. . . . Too many have confused the grace of Sanctification with the enduement of Power. (Corum 1981, Volume 1, No. 1:2).

Numerous testimonies match the story of pioneer preacher Aaron A. Wilson, who "felt the call to preach from a child, but when filled with the Spirit such a burden for lost souls came upon me!" (in Warner 1978:78).

Motivation for lost souls and the preaching of the gospel to all the world flowed from a life in the Spirit and the literal instruction and modeling of Scripture, particularly the book of Acts. It was also literal words of Scripture and the prevailing mood of premillennialism that provided yet another theological motivation: an eschatological urgency.

Eschatological urgency is at the heart of understanding the missionary fervor of early pentecostalism. Damboriena has accurately observed, "Understood as the theology of 'last things,' eschatology belongs to the essence of Pentecostalism" (1969:82) and other analysts, both sympathetic and non-sympathetic, have documented the symbiotic relationship between premillennialism, dispensationalism, and the Pentecostal Movement (Bloch-Hoell 1964; Sheppard in Hunter 1983).

The early pentecostal preachers believed that they were proclaiming the "End Time message" (Nichol 1966:66). Their early records revealed:

> . . . a close and abiding association between the baptism in the Holy Spirit as evidenced by speaking in tongues for an enduement of power in Christian witness, a fervent belief in the premillennial return of Christ and His command to evangelize to the uttermost parts of the world. This Baptism, viewed as the fulfillment of Joel's prophecy for "the last days," seemed to heighten the imperative for world evangelism. (McGee 1983:6)

These pioneers envisioned a revival that was going to touch and inspire every part of the Christian Church, for they were representative of so many of its sections. Above all things, says Gee, "their hearts glowed with the expectation and conviction that this was destined to be the last revival before the coming of the Lord, and that, for them, all earthly history would soon be consummated by the 'Rapture' " (1949:2). In telling the story of the West Central Council of the Assemblies of God, Eugene N. Hastie takes note of a number of early missionaries from the council who went before the formation of a missions board. One group, the Crouch family, left in 1912 for Egypt on a one-way trip! "The Crouch party," says Hastie, "went mostly at their own expense, expecting to remain there until the rapture, which they believed was very near at hand" (1948:143).

A look inside the Azusa Street paper, *The Apostolic Faith,* reveals interesting glimpses of the urgency reflected in their times. Though somewhat lengthy, the following quotations provide observers with the eschatological worldview of early pentecostals. This series covers a time period from September 1906 to January 1908:

> Many are the prophesies spoken in unknown tongues and many visions that God is giving concerning His soon coming. The heathen must first receive the gospel. One prophecy given in an

unknown tongue was interpreted, "The time is short, and I am going to send out a large number in the Spirit of God to preach the full gospel in the power of the Spirit."(Corum 1981, Volume 1, No. 1:1)

Similarly, another instance seems to be typical of the messages given in those early days. Headlined under "The Second Chapter of Acts," it reads:

A preacher's wife, who at first opposed Pentecostal truth, went home and read the second chapter of Acts, and while she read, the Spirit fell upon her and she began to speak in tongues. . . . As she was on the way to the church she met a brother whom she had been instrumental in leading to the Lord. He is a foreigner and as soon as she saw him, she began to pour out her soul in French. He was amazed and said, "When did you learn French?"

"What did I say?" she asked.

"You said: 'Get ready! Get ready! Jesus is coming soon!' " (Volume 1, No. 2:2)

Others have come from the Atlantic coast and from Colorado and different states and they have received a Bible Pentecost, evidenced by speaking in tongues, and from other centers workers are going out to the ends of the earth, till we cannot keep track of them. The Lord is speedily preparing His people for His coming. (Volume 1, No. 6:1)

Following the summer camp meeting of 1907 (in Hermon on the outskirts of Los Angeles) a reporter said:

Many were the heavenly anthems the Spirit sang through His people. And He gave many beautiful messages in unknown tongues, speaking of His soon coming, invitations to come to the Lord, and exhortations from the Word. (Volume 1, No. 10:1)

A sense of immediacy is found in this final quote:

There is no man at the head of this movement. God Himself is speaking in the earth. We are on the verge of the greatest miracle the world has ever seen, when the sons of God shall be manifested, the saints shall come singing from the dust (Isaiah 26:19) and the full over-comers shall be caught up to meet the Lord in the air. The political world realizes that some great crisis is at hand, the scientific world, the religious world all feel it. The coming of the Lord draweth nigh, it is near, even at the doors. (Volume 1, No. 11:1)

Twenty years later one of the most remembered of the early Pentecostal pioneers, T.B. Barratt, wrote in the preface to his *When the Fire Fell*, "I am convinced that this Movement is the last call to all ere Christ comes!" (1927:3). As the reader will note in Part Two (which deals more at length with theological motivations, the eschatological factor) though somewhat diminished, is still at work among pentecostals today.

Reflecting back near the forty-year mark of the movement, Donald Gee noticed that on the British scene, the early sense of urgency tended to keep things from being too well organized:

> The strong expectation of the soon return of our Lord prevented any great expectation of perpetuity in the home assemblies. . . . Evangelistic zeal mostly expended itself in open air preaching and missionary fervour. (1949:63)

A sense of the imminency of Christ's return caused other things, like theologizing, to be postponed. Responding to the criticism that pentecostals have produced little literature, Church of God historian Charles W. Conn noted at the movement's fifty-year mark:

> Another factor that must be considered is the Pentecostal sense of urgency. The belief in the imminent second-coming of Christ has been so great that more emphasis has been placed on the present than on the future. Our message has been one of immediacy—to reach as many of the lost with the message of Christ as is possible before His return. For that reason we have preached, prayed, fasted and urged much, but have written little. (1956:34)

Evangelistic zeal.   Early pentecostal missionaries, as Gary B. McGee's informative article illustrated, were characterized with the watchword, "They went everywhere preaching the gospel" (1983:6). McGee, Associate Professor of Theology and Church History at the Assemblies of God Theological Seminary, claimed, "The history of Pentecostalism cannot be properly understood apart from its missionary vision." Evangelism and missions typified the movement, said Assemblies of God historian Stanley H. Frodsham who asserted, "This Pentecostal revival has also been decidedly missionary from the beginning" (1946:50).

Azusa Street participants were flung from Los Angeles and other centers of pentecostal worship into the far corners of the world. In the years 1906-1908 pentecostal missionaries began pressing "to the regions beyond" (McCracken 1943:8):

> Whole families volunteered for the Word, sold their possessions, and started for the field. They were possessed with a passion to go to the ends of the earth for their Lord, and no sacrifice seemed too great for them that the gospel might be proclaimed and the coming of the Lord might be hastened. (McCracken 1943:8)

This early evangelistic zeal was characterized by a spontaneity in sending forth personnel without prearranged financial help. Missionaries went strictly "by faith." This was still before consolidation and the structural "means" of missions. The following story of an early Pentecostal Holiness missionary typifies scores of stories which could be recounted:

> Soon Miss Almyra Aston was also ordained by the Oklahoma Conference which met at Oklahoma City August 25, 1911, and sent

to India. She had only ten dollars toward her fare when she started for California, but God miraculously supplied her need and on January 3, 1912 she sailed for Hong Kong. Here she intended to stay until God saw fit to provide passage to India, which He did, and in due time she arrived at her destination where she labored for several years. (Campbell 1951:346)

Supernatural recruitment. As one reads the book of Acts, he is amazed at the surface simplicity with which the early Christians obeyed the leading of the Holy Spirit. For example, the evangelist Philip was preaching in Samaria (Acts 8) and a great revival ensued. In the midst of this turning to God, Philip was instructed to leave and go to the road that led from Jerusalem to Gaza (8:26). With like simplicity, he obeyed the Holy Spirit who told him to approach the Ethiopian eunuch in the chariot (8:29-30). In fact, he was so eager to obey the Lord that he ran to the man! The same impression is conveyed by the spontaneity in the sending forth of early pentecostal missionaries.

These early evangelists were supernaturally recruited in a variety of ways: dreams (Ingram 1938:12); visions (Burton in Gee 1949:100); prophecy (Corum 1981:6); tongues and interpretations (Durasoff 1969:69-70); words/inner impressions (Lindsay 1972:20); and the direct voice of God (Lindsay 1972:17; Cook 1955:20). Others had this calling initiated or confirmed by the Lord "customizing" certain portions of Scripture to them during their Bible reading (Warner 1978:140-141; Frodsham 1946:145).

These leadings of the Holy Spirit not only characterized pentecostal missions in the early stages but continued on through the years (du Plessis 1977:1-6; Richards 1972:41; Sumrall 1977:24-30). Of interest is the experience recorded by many of being in prayer, hearing the name of a place which they had never heard of before, and later having to find the place on a map:

It was during this period, whilst I was in prayer, that the Holy Spirit impressed a word upon my soul. It was the name of a town that I had never visited and knew nothing about. . . . I felt that God was speaking to me to go to this particular town to establish another church. (Richards 1972:41)

Subsequently this English author went to Slough, in Buckinghamshire, and established a church that later grew to more than five hundred members.

Robert F. Cook was an Azusa Street recipient who went to India as an independent missionary and later joined the Church of God through the efforts of J.H. Ingram. He tells the unusual account of how God confirmed his leading to India. In order for Cook's wife to be assured of the Lord's leading:

He gave her the name of a town in South India, of which she was quite ignorant at the time.

She and a friend, Esther Lampert, were sitting on the floor while Esther was tuning Wife's guitar; suddenly Wife spoke out, "Bangalore."

Sister Esther looked up and said, "Did you say 'Tune lower'?"

"No," said Wife, "I heard a voice saying 'Bangalore' and I repeated it."

When I came home, they told me of this, and I said, "Why, that is the town where the missionary with whom we are going has lived." (1955:20)

Recently, in discussing intercession for "hidden people," Foursquare pastor Jack Hayford said, "One man I know was given the name of a province in China which he had never heard of. He had to find it on the map to verify it existed, yet the Holy Spirit had whispered it to his heart while he prayed" (in Pedersen 1981, Volume 18, No. 2:14).

Though in the early stages when there were no mission boards, denominations, or special organizations, there was still a spiritual sending forth, a sense of belonging to a group which was "sponsoring" one, even if only pledging to pray and send whatever finances that could be raised by faith. In Fred T. Corum's *Like as of Fire* (a collection of Azusa Street papers) one notes a picture of a group of twelve which formed part of the original "leadership" at the mission. These, says Corum:

. . . were the twelve selected to examine the candidates for licenses as missionaries and evangelists. The licenses were signed by the Pastor W.J. Seymour, and Elder Hiram W. Smith, who had formerly been a Methodist Pastor. These twelve acted as the Credential Committee and after a candidate had been approved they laid on their hands and prayed as did the Apostles of old. People were told where to go on the mission field through visions and prophecy and results followed wherever they went. (1981:6)

One of the early earmarks of the movement was a practice which has received both negative and positive commentary even within the Pentecostal Movement. In order for it to be understood, the backdrop of the events surrounding the baptism of Agnes Ozman needs to be retold from another angle. In her own words:

The next night after I received the Holy Ghost . . . I with others went to a mission downtown in Topeka and my heart was full of glory and blessings. I began to pray in English and then in tongues. At the close of the services a man who is a Bohemian said he understood what I said in his own language. . . . When my husband first heard speaking in tongues at a street meeting in Oklahoma City, Oklahoma, two women spoke in tongues and he thought they had learned the language they were speaking. And it was a sign to him, then it made him hungry. (La Berge n.d.:32)

As reports circulated about the events at Parham's Bible school,

. . . reporters, government interpreters, and language experts converged on the school to investigate the new phenomenon . . .

a remarkable claim made during these meetings was that the students, Americans all, spoke in twenty-one known languages. . . . (Synan 1971:102)

Pentecostal historian Vinson Synan says that Parham began to take these events at face value and

. . . immediately began to teach that missionaries would no longer be compelled to study foreign languages to preach in the mission fields. From henceforth, he taught, one need only receive the baptism with the Holy Ghost and he could go to the farthest corners of the world and preach to the natives in languages unknown to the speaker. . . . Very few pentecostal leaders accepted this premise, although Parham held to it until his death. (1971:102-103)

The phenomenon recorded in Ozman's testimony is known as *xenolalia,* "speaking in a known language which the person has not learned by mechanical methods" (Hunter 1983:13). Norwegian researcher Nils Bloch-Hoell (an outside observer) has related this activity to pentecostal missions in his *The Pentecostal Movement* under the subtopic "Xenolalia and The Resulting Urge to Open Foreign Missions":

In December of the year 1906 a headline in a New York newspaper announced that "FAITH GIVES QUAINT SECT NEW LANGUAGES TO CONVERT AFRICA." There followed an account of Pentecostals on their way to Africa and other distant fields because they believed that they had received, together with the gift of glossolalia, a call to the missionary field. This case is by no means unique. There are many reports from the early Pentecostal Movement claiming that immigrants were converted when the persons who spoke with tongues used a language which they had never learnt, the native language of the immigrant. It was on this account that Pentecostal believers went from America in 1906, believing that the gift of speaking with tongues which they had received would enable them to preach the gospel to the heathens in their own languages. A source from January 1908 reports eighteen cases from China, Japan, and India, all of which were unsuccessful. (1964:87)

What Bloch-Hoell calls *xenolalia* is referred to by Assemblies of God researcher Ralph W. Harris as *xenoglossolalia* (1973:6) and by anthropologist/ linguist William J. Samarin (*Tongues of Men and Angels*) as *xenoglossia* (1972:109ff). Technically, says Church of God of Prophecy theologian Harold D. Hunter:

Glossolalia is a form of speech which does not directly correspond to any known language, while akolalia can be used to describe that phenomenon in which the speaker uses one language and the audience "hears" the words in a different language(s).

> Xenolalia refers to one speaking in a known language which the person has not learned by mechanical methods. It would be possible to use the term heteroglossolalia for what I have labelled xenolalia. (1983:13)

That Azusa Street missionaries were influenced by Parham's teaching is evidenced in the first issue of *The Apostolic Faith:*

> Many are speaking in new tongues, and some are on their way to the foreign field, with the gift of the language. We are going on to get more of the power of God. (Corum 1981 Volume 1, No. 1:1)

The practice was further undergirded by such accounts as that of A.G. Ward, a pioneer minister among the Indians in Canada. One day while preaching to them through an interpreter, "he began to speak in other tongues under the power of the Spirit. His interpreter suddenly exclaimed, 'Why you are now speaking to us in our own language' " (Gee 1949:14).

Without discounting the practice altogether, most pentecostal writers have later interpreted xenolalia to be the exception rather than the rule. Frodsham, however, devotes an entire chapter to it in his *With Signs Following* (1946:229-252) and takes a rather positive view of the practice. Harris, who has devoted an entire book to the subject *(Spoken By the Spirit* 1973), says that the phenomenon is characteristic of *contemporary* pentecostalism as well as that reported from the earlier days of the movement. He collected instances of "xenoglossolalia" from more than sixty languages. His informants were from a wide spectrum of participants who responded to his query for actual, verifiable instances (1973:8).

McGee notes that early in the movement many Pentecostals had begun to question the missionary use of tongues and emphasized that the Baptism of the Holy Spirit was for an avenue of praise and intercession to God. "Early periodicals," he said, "began to emphasize the need for language study before commencing overseas evangelism" (1983:6). Donald Gee has also attempted a correction by pointing to the use of tongues primarily in worship and personal devotion:

> Although its chief purpose was for communion with God in prayer and praise, yet it could also provide an arresting sign to unbelievers if any were present. Divine providence could add to the impressiveness of the sign by causing the language uttered to be the mother tongue of the unbeliever, as on the Day of Pentecost. This was apparently incidental, however, and was not inherent in the gift. (1972:62-63)

While this is not the place for a lengthy treatment of the subject in itself, it should be seen as a central element in the missionary fervor and practice of the first pentecostal missionaries. They were theologically motivated by literal biblicism and the dynamic personal working of the Holy Spirit; they were full of evangelistic zeal and spontaneous missionary sending; and they were recruited supernaturally. Such were the characteristics of the pentecostal explosion and motivation.

Consolidation. The early explosive years of the movement and the fiascos associated with doctrinal naiveté (Synan 1971:111) and financial immaturity (Conn 1959:24-25) began to demonstrate the need for sound financial support, overall strategizing, and proper preparation for work on foreign fields (McGee 1983:7). Conn suggests that two words typify the missionary efforts of the "primitive Pentecostal movement . . . vague and simple . . ." (1959:15):

> In order to understand the situation of this primitive period, one must understand something of early Pentecostal missions. There were no strong denominations or wealthy mission funds. So universal was the Pentecostal revival that there were few clear-cut sectarian lines. Even those bodies that were identifiably organized, such as the Church of God, were too poor or too small to accomplish a great deal alone. Pentecostal missionaries went to all parts of the world, to be sure, but they usually went as emissaries of the entire Pentecostal fellowship, without sponsorship of any specific church or missions board. They went forth, as they call it, "by faith," expecting to be kept on the mission field by whatever support might be sent to them. They were the true pioneers of the Pentecostal faith, souls who bore a burden to carry the message of Christ to distant shores, who labored without certainty of provision and accepted even occasional aid as a gift from God. (1959:14-15)

Our discussion of the maturation and consolidation of pentecostal missions will be guided by three considerations. There will be a look at three kinds of pentecostal missionaries, a pentecostal faith mission (case study), and the subsequent denominations.

Three kinds of missionaries. McGee has helped the process of sorting out the maze of missionary types from the early days of the movement by suggesting that there are at least three different groups of missionaries in early pentecostalism:

1. Those who had been called, but due to their feelings about the urgency of the hour and their belief in the missionary purpose of tongues, took little or no time to gather financial resources or study the history, culture, or language of the country where they were going to minister.

2. The newly Spirit-filled veterans of other missionary agencies.

3. Men and women who had received Bible institute education in preparation for overseas endeavors (1983:6-7).

McGee notes that the second group of missionaries figured prominently in early pentecostal missions. These were persons of experience who brought to the movement accumulated years of experience in missionary structures (1983:6-7). In some cases, the work of newly formed denominations and mission boards was as much that of consolidating and amalgamating *existing* works started by independent pentecostals as that of initiating new advances in missions.

Such was the case of a Church of God missionary, J.H. Ingram, who, "More than any other person before him (in the Church of God) . . . personified missionary zeal and dramatized the missions cause"(Conn 1959:28). Ingram not only served as a missionary himself but embarked on several around-the-world "good will tours" for his denomination, intending to "contact independent missionaries around the world who were interested in affiliating with the Church of God" (Conn 1959:29). As with the Church of God so with others: consolidation had begun.

A Pentecostal faith mission. As the North American scene was still in the explosion phase (ca. 1906-1911) the British were busy putting together a faith mission: The Pentecostal Missionary Union.

A conspicuous result of the fervor and motivation stirred by the expanding Pentecostal Movement was the kindling of a new zeal and interest in foreign missions. In Great Britain, says Donald Gee:

> . . . the need became apparent for some kind of Pentecostal missionary organization. Young men and women were coming forward in an increasing stream who evidently needed some kind of training before they left; whilst experienced missionaries connected with existing Societies were finding themselves forced out on account of coming into fresh blessing through the Pentecostal Movement. (1949:46)

Thus, on January 9, 1909 (less than a decade after the Ozman baptism in Topeka, Kansas, and only three years following the initial events at Azusa Street), a small company gathered at All Saints' Vicarage in Sunderland to form the "Pentecostal Missionary Union." Alexander A. Boddy was the first chairman, but at a later meeting on October 14, when the first official minutes began, records show that Cecil Polhill was elected president, "a post which he retained until the Pentecostal Missionary Union became merged with the Assemblies of God in 1925"(Gee 1949:46). Cecil Polhill had already distinguished himself as a veteran missionary, having gone to China twenty years before as one of the now famous "Cambridge Seven" (C.T. Studd was another of that early group). Polhill had subsequently visited the outpouring in Los Angeles and was baptized in the Holy Spirit at a prayer meeting in a private house there. Gee tells us that Polhill brought experience and instruction to the fledgling young pentecostal mission:

> The principles of the Pentecostal Missionary Union were very largely formulated upon the model of the China Inland Mission. This is not surprising in view of the fact that Cecil Polhill was also a member of the Council of the China Inland Mission. It was therefore what is generally known as a "faith mission," and the Directors did not guarantee any fixed amount of support to workers, but sought faithfully to distribute the funds available. It was undenominational in character; and missionaries were at liberty to adopt whatever form of church government they

personally believed to be most scriptural in any churches formed by the blessing of God through their ministry. (1949:47)

The PMU did not waste any time in appointing their first missionaries. Four months later, two single women, Kathleen Miller and Lucy James, sailed for India on February 24, 1909. Miller had previously been in India but was now returning under pentecostal auspices. Miss James was a first-term appointee. The first four missionaries actually trained by the PMU went out in 1910. One of them was John C. Beruldsen, who ministered for over thirty-five years in North China (1949:47-48).

Of interest is that fact that the PMU was organized and sending forth board-sponsored missionaries at least fifteen years *prior* to the establishment of boards and departments by the two largest North American pentecostal bodies—the Assemblies of God and the Church of God. The Assemblies of God did not formalize their "Missionary Department" until 1919 (Menzies 1971:131) and the Church of God established a standing Foreign Missions Board in 1926 (Conn 1959:25). One year after the PMU sent Miller and James, Church of God missionary R.M. Evans sold his possessions in Florida and landed with his wife and another self-supporting missionary, Carl M. Padgett, in Nassau, Bahama Islands, on January 4, 1910 (Conn 1959:50). Evans, however, had gone totally at his own expense.

The following year (in September, 1911), some of the earliest Assemblies of God missionaries (the Clyde Millers and Vivian Waldron) left Des Moines, Iowa, for British East Africa. Eugene N. Hastie tells us they were the first pentecostal missionaries from the West Central District Council. Since there was no organized body to stand behind them, "a local missionary board was formed in Des Moines to send them support and encouragement" (1948:142).

Many ideals and models could be drawn from the PMU before it later merged with the Assemblies of God. At least one main emphasis of the mission should be quoted in our day in which mission agencies and denominational boards are awakening to the challenge of "unreached peoples":

> . . . the particular emphasis of the Pentecostal Missionary Union was always upon China, and reaching the closed land of Tibet. A specially urgent emphasis was placed upon taking the gospel to the last few lands that had never heard, and a further party went to the North-West Frontier of India, in an attempt to reach Afghanistan. (Gee 1949:48)

Frontier missions and focus upon the unreached was a part of pentecostal missions as early as 1909 with the vision of the Pentecostal Missionary Union.

Elsewhere in Europe, the Norwegian foreign mission work was sending missionaries to India, South Africa, and South America by 1910. About the same time the Swedish pentecostal churches were initiating an aggressive missions program (Woodford in Greenway 1952:42-43).

The North American denominations. Back on the North American scene, as Woodford observed, most pentecostal denominations were making initial efforts at some type of missions organization within ten years of the first spontaneous events associated with Azusa Street and other indigenous missions (in Greenway 1952:42).

It appears that the Pentecostal Holiness Church was one of the earliest groups to begin the consolidation process. Joseph E. Campbell, one of their earliest historians, says that the earliest record of a "missionary board" in the Pentecostal Holiness Church was at the Fayetteville Convention in 1904. There may have even been some type of earlier activity, but "there is no concrete evidence to warrant such a conclusion" (1951:344). In 1906 at the Lumberton, North Carolina Convention, a Reverend T.J. McIntosh was received as an ordained minister in the organization. McIntosh went to China in 1907 and traveled on around the world. In 1909 he circled the world a second time. Though he was the first missionary to receive financial support from the Pentecostal Holiness Church, he did not go out officially under the church's board. "There were no official missionaries sent out by the Pentecostal Holiness Church," says Campbell, "until after the consolidation with the Fire-Baptized Holiness Church in 1911" (1951:344).

The Pentecostal Holiness Church elected a Foreign Missionary Board in 1911. By the time of their General Convention in 1913 they had some eleven missionaries on the field, some partially supported while others received no support at all (1951:347-348).

The Church of God (Cleveland, Tennessee) which, as is typical of most North American pentecostal groups, has more members *outside* of North America than on the continent, was founded on August 19, 1886, with nine members (Conn 1959:11). As such, it has the distinction of being the oldest pentecostal church in America, pre-dating the Topeka outpouring and the Azusa Street revival. It should be noted, however, that the Church of God was not a pentecostal church at its inception. It was ten years from the founding of this movement before they experienced supernatural signs and wonders during the "Shearer Schoolhouse Revival" of 1896. It remained static until it became fully pentecostal (McClung 1983b:8-9; Conn 1959:11-12).

As early as the General Assembly of November, 1913, "a systematic raising of foreign missions finances was introduced" to the Church of God (Conn 1959:23). The following year the first "Committee to Consider Plans for Foreign Mission Work" met and

> . . . submitted some resolutions providing for state treasurers and a general treasurer, and for tithes of freewill offerings and special mission offerings, taken by evangelists at their convenience, to be forwarded to Headquarters. This was modified slightly the next year, a committee of five being appointed, who urged that a special offering be taken at least once a month and that the pastors present the matter to their people oftener. (McCracken 1943:13)

By 1917 there was a bimonthly special missions page in the Church of God *Evangel* that announced special "mission-day" offerings. Historian Horace McCracken observed, "The increase between 1916 and 1919 is partly traceable to these 'mission days' " (1943:13). The Church of God eventually instituted a standing Foreign Missions Board in 1926 (forty years after their founding in 1886) and created a full-time office of Executive Mission Secretary in 1942 (1943:15).

April 2, 1914 was the date of the first gathering of a new pentecostal denomination, which has become the largest and best known of all North American pentecostal movements: The Assemblies of God. There is agreement among Assemblies of God historians that one of the powerful motives and initial reasons which brought the Assemblies of God together was the cause of world evangelization (Kendrick 1961:96; Hodges 1974:31; Menzies 1971:94, 106). In a sense, the denomination was founded as a missions organization.

The December 20, 1913, issue of a pentecostal tabloid *Word and Witness* carried a formal call for a "General Convention of Pentecostal Saints and Churches of God in Christ" (Menzies 1971:93). The same issue enumerated five subjects to be considered at the forthcoming meeting. Two of those subjects directly addressed the need for consolidation and coordination of foreign missionary efforts (1971:94).

The need had come, says Kendrick, for a "clearing agency":

> . . . one that could receive and forward funds, make appeals, and publicize the work of missions. The Assemblies of God became just such an agency. The first council directed the chairman to serve as "missionary secretary" and to administer all missionary contributions. The Executive Presbytery was also considered a "missionary presbytery" and as such assisted the chairman with the missionary problems of the new group. (1961:96)

At the initial General Council in part of a second resolution which later became part of a document entitled "Preamble and Resolution on Constitution," there was an appeal "to be more scriptural and legal in transacting business, owning property, and executing missionary work at home and foreign lands" (Menzies 1971:100).

The strong missions flavor present at the founding meeting carried over to the third council in 1915. At that time a definite missionary policy was desired. Accordingly, says Kendrick, the following written plan was "adopted as the basis of the missionary practices of the church":

> *Resolved.* That this Council exert all its powers to promote the evangelization of heathen lands according to New Testament methods, viz:
> First. In the proper testing of those who claim to be called to the foreign work. Rev. 2:2; Acts 13:1-4.
> A. As to a personal experience of full New Testament salvation.
> B. As to a definite call to foreign work.
> C. As to physical, mental and spiritual fitness for the work.

Second. In the proper sending, supporting and supervision of those approved.

A. Every Assembly ought to have a definite part in it, either sending or maintaining one or more missionaries of its own, or sharing the burden of one or more missionaries with one or more other assemblies.

B. Missionaries receiving the baptism on the field ought to be brought in touch and supported by the assemblies having no missionaries of their own.

C. Missionaries who fail on the field ought to be brought home by assemblies concerned.

D. Missionaries are responsible to the assemblies supporting them for all funds entrusted to them and should give a periodical report.

E. No missionary should return home without the approval of his or her supporting assemblies except in extreme circumstances.

Third. Missionaries home on furlough should be maintained and supervised by their assemblies the same as while on the field. Every opportunity should be afforded to present the needs of their field and of mission work in general, not only to their own assemblies, but the Assemblies of God everywhere.

(1961:96-97)

In 1919, J. Roswell Flower was appointed to a newly developed position, Missionary Secretary. This was followed by the establishment of the "Missionary Department" that same year and a reorganized Foreign Missions Board in 1955 (Menzies 1971:131, 246).

Other North American groups followed suit. The Pentecostal Assemblies of Canada consolidated their position between 1919 and 1921 (Woodford in Greenway 1952:43) and the Open Bible Standard Churches between 1927 and 1932 (Mitchell 1982:105). Within twenty years of its birth the pentecostal explosion, though not losing its momentum and fire, was consolidated and ready to move into further organized expansion. "From this time," says Woodford, "advance was registered all along the line . . ."(Greenway 1952:43).

20

World pentecostalism cannot be understood without a "visit" to Azusa Street, scene of the widespread beginning of the Pentecostal Movement. Thankfully, a return to Azusa Street is made possible because of the foresight of early pentecostals who published and preserved for history *The Apostolic Faith* magazine. The following report is the lead article from the very first issue of the Azusa Street paper, dated September, 1906. It is taken from *Like as of Fire: A Reprint of the Old Azusa Street Papers,* privately compiled by Fred Corum in 1981 (160 Salem Street, Wilmington, MA 01887).

1
Pentecost Has Come
The Apostolic Faith Magazine*

Los Angeles Being Visited by a Revival
of Bible Salvation and Pentecost as
Recorded in the Book of Acts

The power of God now has this city agitated as never before. Pentecost has surely come and with it the Bible evidences are following, many being converted and sanctified and filled with the Holy Ghost, speaking in tongues as they did on the day of Pentecost. The scenes that are daily enacted in the building on Azusa Street and at missions and churches in other parts of the city are beyond description, and the real revival is only started, as God has been working with his children mostly, getting them through to Pentecost and laying the foundation for a mighty wave of salvation among the unconverted.

The meetings are held in an old Methodist church that had been converted in part into a tenement house, leaving a large, unplastered barn-like room on the ground floor. Here about a dozen congregated each day, holding meetings on Bonnie Brae in the evening. The writer attended a few of these meetings and being so different from anything he had seen and, not hearing any speaking in tongues, he branded the teaching as third-blessing heresy and thought that settled it. It is needless to say that writer was compelled to do a great deal of apologizing and humbling of himself to get right with God.

In a short time God began to manifest His power and soon the building could not contain the people. Now the meetings continue all day and far into the night and the fire is kindling all over the city and surrounding towns.

* *Apostolic Faith* was published from the Azusa Street Mission by William J. Seymour and Florence Louise Crawford. Five thousand copies of the first issue were distributed. Only thirteen issues were published from Los Angeles before Crawford moved to Portland, Oregon, to establish with the Apostolic Faith movement in the Northwest. The last issue was dated May, 1908.

Proud, well-dressed preachers came in to "investigate." Soon their high looks are replaced with wonder, then conviction comes, and very often you will find them in a short time wallowing on the dirty floor, asking God to forgive them and make them as little children.

It would be impossible to state how many have been converted, sanctified and filled with the Holy Ghost. They have been and are daily going out to all points of the compass to spread this wonderful gospel.

The Old Time Pentecost

This work began about five years ago last January, when a company of people under the leadership of Charles Parham who were studying God's word, tarried for Pentecost in Topeka, Kansas. After searching through the country everywhere, they had been unable to find any Christians that had the true Pentecostal power. So they laid aside all commentaries and notes and waited on the Lord, studying His word, and what they did not understand they got down before the bench and asked God to have wrought out in their hearts by the Holy Ghost. They had a prayer tower from which prayers were ascending night and day to God. After three months, a sister who had been teaching sanctification for the baptism with the Holy Ghost, one who had a sweet, loving experience and all the carnality taken out of her heart, felt the Lord lead her to have hands laid on her to receive the Pentecost. So when they prayed, the Holy Ghost came in great power and she commenced speaking in an unknown tongue. This made all the Bible school hungry, and three nights afterward, twelve students received the Holy Ghost, and prophesied, and cloven tongues could be seen upon their heads. They then had an experience that measured up with the second chapter of Acts and could understand the first chapter of Ephesians.

Now after five years something like 13,000 people have received this gospel. It is spreading everywhere, until churches who do not believe backslide and lose the experience they have. Those who are older in this movement are stronger, and greater signs and wonders are following them.

The meetings in Los Angeles started in a cottage meeting, and the Pentecost fell there three nights. The people had nothing to do but wait on the Lord and praise Him, and they commenced speaking in tongues, as they did at Pentecost, and the Spirit sang songs through them.

The meeting was then transferred to Azusa Street, and since then multitudes have been coming. The meetings begin about ten o'clock in the morning and can hardly stop before ten or twelve at night, and sometimes two or three in the morning, because so many are seeking, and some are slain under the power of God. People are seeking three times a day at the altar and row after row of seats have to be emptied and filled with seekers. We cannot tell how many people have been saved, and sanctified, and baptized with the Holy Ghost, and healed of all manner of sicknesses. Many are speaking in new tongues, and some are on their way to the foreign fields, with the gift of the language. We are going on to get more of the power of God.

Pentecostal church history has revealed that a common thread runs from Azusa Street through contemporary pentecostal denominations and their missionary expansion. The following story, related in the Fall 1983 issue of *Assemblies of God Heritage,* illustrates how the revival went through the process of explosion, expansion, and eventual consolidation into denominational missions structures. It also demonstrates how the pentecostal fire has touched the social needs of suffering humanity.

2
When the Pentecostal Fire Fell in Calcutta

Maynard Ketcham
and Wayne Warner*

Images of poverty, starvation, disease, and death come to mind when the city of Calcutta is mentioned. But then we are also reminded that the situation is not entirely hopeless as long as the loving ministries of people such as Mother Teresa and Mark and Hulda Buntain continue.

These compassionate ministries might seem so small when the need is so great. But the success stories flowing from these gallant efforts are filling volumes![1]

To chart the ministry of Pentecostals in Calcutta one must go back to 1907 when the Holy Spirit was poured out in two separate locations about five miles apart. These revival fires later merged and gave a foundation to the work of the Assemblies of God in Calcutta, Eastern India, and Bangladesh.[2]

The first fire started when Alfred G. and Lillian Garr arrived in Calcutta, fresh from the Azusa Street meetings in Los Angeles.

Garr was pastor of a Burning Bush congregation in Los Angeles in 1906 when the pentecostal outpouring shook Los Angeles and transformed believers around the world. When he received a mighty enduement of power, Garr spoke in Bengali—a language he did not know. As a result of this unusual experience, the Garrs felt a strong call to service in India; so in the fall of 1906 they left their Los Angeles congregation in the hands of others and set out for New York and eventually India.

---

* In 1910 a Spirit-filled Methodist missionary, Fanny Simpson, laid her hands on the head of five-year-old Maynard Ketcham and claimed him as a missionary to the Bengali-speaking area of Eastern India. In 1926 Maynard and Gladys Ketcham arrived in India to begin a missionary career with the Assemblies of God. He later became their Field Director of Asia. Ketcham is now retired and lives in Springfield, Missouri. Wayne Warner is the Editor of *Assemblies of God Heritage* and the Director of the Assemblies of God Archives. He is the editor of *Touched by the Fire* and has authored numerous articles on early pentecostalism.

Enroute to New York City the Garrs stopped at Burning Bush congregations in Chicago and Danville, Virginia, telling of their recent experience at the Azusa Street Mission. Consequently, many of these people received the Pentecostal experience.[3]

While they were still in this country Garr wrote to William J. Seymour, pastor of the Azusa Street Mission, concerning the Pentecostal revival in Danville. He closed his letter with a note of faith for their mission to India: "We are expecting God to give us a good revival in India." [4]

God honoured their faith in a greater way perhaps than they could have imagined.

After arriving in Calcutta, the Garrs met a sincere and dedicated minister, Pastor Hook of the Bow Bazar Baptist Church—the same church which had rung to the impassioned eloquence of William Carey 100 years earlier!

Pastor Hook invited Garr to conduct services at the church, and it wasn't long before another Pentecostal fire was burning in the world—this one more than 8,000 miles from the Azusa Street Mission.

Missionaries and nationals alike were touched by the fire. Many were convicted of sin. Some were impressed to make restitution. It was a genuine move of the Spirit which was reported in Pentecostal periodicals around the world.

One of the reports was published in *The Apostolic Faith,* Seymour's periodical in Los Angeles. Mrs. Garr wrote:

> God is spreading Pentecost here in Calcutta, and thirteen or
> fourteen missionaries and other workers have received it. . . . We
> are among Bible teachers, and they have the Word so stored away;
> but now the Spirit is putting life and power into it, which is
> wonderful to behold.[5]

Lillian Garr also reported that Miss Susan Easton, head of the American Women's Board of Missions, had been baptized in the Spirit and "is a power for God." [6]

So the fire that had started in Los Angeles was now burning in Calcutta.

But a second fire was about to start some five miles from the Bow Bazar section of Calcutta. Apparently this revival effort was independent of the Garr meetings.

Fanny Simpson, a Methodist missionary from Boston, directed a girls orphanage on Elliot Road which was sponsored by the Methodist Women's Union Missionary Society.

Little did Miss Simpson know that the revival which would start in her orphanage would be the means of her dismissal from the orphanage.

One day Fanny heard about fervent morning prayer meetings among the girls. Then she heard about girls who were confessing wrongs, returning stolen rice and soap. A chapel service was interrupted when several girls were slain in the Spirit. Some of the girls began to prophesy. Others began to speak in unintelligible languages.

Fanny was a very proper Bostonian with impressive missionary credentials.

But this was all new to her. She didn't really know how to handle the demonstrations. It was evident, however, that lives were being changed. There was no doubt about that, and girls whose lives were revolutionized were making a deep impression on their director.

Finally Miss Simpson's doubts began to disappear, and she too sought God—right alongside the former street urchins who had been praying down the blessings of God. When the girls saw their beloved leader praying, they joined her and "prayed her through" to the baptism in the Holy Spirit.

News soon circulated around Calcutta that some unusual things were happening at Sister Simpson's orphanage over on Elliot Road.

Unfortunately, the bishop had apprehensions about what was going on in the orphanage. He warned Fanny that something had to be done. "Sister Fanny, you are highly regarded and respected," the bishop began in his effort to stop the revival, "but this emotion, these manifestations, they are unseemly for mature and respectable Christians."

Fanny would have to stop the manifestations or take the prayer meetings to a back room.

But Fanny had seen enough of the outpouring to know that it was of God and that pushing it to the back of the orphanage would be wrong. And she told the bishop so.

Despite the bishop's respect for Fanny's life and ministry, he felt he must dismiss her as the orphanage leader. But even after Fanny packed her bags and returned to America, the orphanage revival continued. The girls who had received the baptism in the Holy Spirit knew the experience was real and should not be quenched. Many of the girls later married and reared Christian families, some of whom went into the ministry.

One of the ways God used to keep the fire burning in Calcutta was through the Chandra family.

Rai Bahadur Chandra was a Brahmin of the highest rank, the "collector," or highest government official. The British government had made him a Rai Bahadur, which is equivalent to being knighted. He gave up Hinduism and became a devout Christian under the ministry of Dr. Alexander Duff, a famous Scottish Presbyterian missionary. Rai Bahadur Chandra reared a remarkable family of three boys and two girls. The boys became judges and magistrates, and the girls became directors of Christian institutions.

When the Chandra family heard of the Spirit's outpouring at the meetings conducted by the Garrs and the Elliot Road orphanage, they became interested. On a trip to England they came in contact with Elim Pentecostals and received the baptism in the Holy Spirit.

They returned to India and constructed a small chapel and residence next door to their house in Baniapuker. Here in the House of Prayer and Good News, as it was called, English and Bengali services were conducted by the Elim missionaries. Later, because the Elim organization was limited in personnel and finances, the work was transferred to the American Assemblies of God.[7]

Now, what happened to Fanny Simpson?

Some believed her ministry was finished when the bishop dismissed her from the orphanage in 1907. But that was hardly the case.

She was already blessed with a dynamic personality, eloquent speech, and music skills. Now that she had received the baptism in the Holy Spirit, she became an effective evangelist during the early years of the Pentecostal movement.

One of the meetings in 1910 in a little Methodist church in Eastport, Long Island, would play a part in the missionary call to Maynard Ketcham—a 5-year-old boy at that time. Maynard's mother received the baptism in the Holy Spirit under Fanny's ministry in one of the Eastport meetings. Then Miss Simpson turned her attention to young Maynard at his mother's side. She laid her hands on Maynard's head and claimed him by faith as a missionary to the Bengali-speaking area of Eastern India.

Fanny Simpson would live to see that prayer answered when in 1926 Maynard arrived in India as a missionary. He and his wife Gladys became the first Assemblies of God missionaries to the Bengali-speaking area of Eastern India which includes Calcutta and what was then called East Bengal.[8]

The burden Fanny Simpson carried for India could not be shelved. In 1920 she returned to the country—this time to Purulia—where she established an orphanage and mission work which would later become the hub of the Assemblies of God work in Bengal. Miss Simpson purchased the land with her own money (about $2,650) which she had received from her mother's estate.

And Fanny Simpson's ministry in India continues to this day—34 years after her death. Nationals still carry on the work she started in Eastern India. And one of her successors, Maynard Ketcham—who is now retired in Springfield, Missouri—had an important role in the origin of one of the most dynamic Christian ministries in the entire country.

In 1955 Maynard, now field director for Asia, invited a young evangelist to consider becoming a missionary to Calcutta. The young evangelist had received another offer of ministry elsewhere, but he agreed to pray about Calcutta.

After prayer the young man accepted the Calcutta challenge. He is still here, and his name is Mark Buntain.

And here is something else that gives the Pentecostal work in Calcutta an interesting twist. Mark Buntain built a church building almost across the road from the orphanage Fanny Simpson was forced to leave in 1907!

Maynard Ketcham is thrilled at what God has done in Calcutta, and he imagines that others are also looking on: "The Garrs, Fanny Simpson, and Neville Chandra are looking down on the city of Calcutta from the battlements of heaven and are rejoicing."

The same Holy Spirit who touched lives in 1907 continues to use dedicated men and women to reach Calcutta's suffering masses.

The fire has never gone out.

Footnotes

1 For more information on Mother Teresa, see *Teresa of Calcutta,* by Robert Serrou (McGraw-Hill). Doug Wead's *The Compassionate Touch* (Bethany House) is the story of Mark and Hulda Buntain's ministry in Calcutta.

2 Today the Assemblies of God has 37 missionaries, 513 credentialed national ministers, and 70 lay workers ministering in India. There are 487 churches, 456 outstations, eight Bible schools, and nearly 100,000 believers. Buntain's Calcutta Christian Mission Hospital annually cares for some 80,000 outpatients plus the inpatients. Thousands are fed daily through a church-operated program.

3 At this time, Garr and other Pentecostals believed the gift of tongues was for preaching to foreigners in their own language. Later they realized that whenever this experience took place it was the exception, not the rule. (See Gary McGee's "Early Pentecostal Missionaries" in the Summer 1983 *Heritage.*)

4 A.G. Garr, "Pentecost in Danville, Va.," *The Apostolic Faith,* October, 1906, p. 2.

5 Lillian Garr, "In Calcutta, India," *The Apostolic Faith,* April, 1907, p. 1.

6 Lillian Garr, "In Calcutta, India," *The Apostolic Faith,* April, 1907, p. 1. Susan Easton became an Assemblies of God missionary and served on the Foreign Missions Committee. Alfred G. Garr founded the Carolina Evangelistic Association in 1930. Alfred C. Garr, Jr., now pastors the church his father founded in Charlotte, North Carolina.

7 Maynard and Gladys Ketcham were the first Assemblies of God missionaries in charge of the Bengali services. They were followed by Dan and Esther Marocco. Some of the outstanding Assemblies of God missionaries who ministered in the English branch of this ministry included the Hillarys, Cawstons, Barricks, Bryants, Wollevers, John Lewis, and others. One of the outstanding nationals trained here was David Roy Chowdhury.

8 The pentecostal message reaching Bangladesh is a thrilling story in itself. Abdul Munshie, a Baptist preacher and convert from Islam, discovered Aimee Semple McPherson's book, *This Is That,* in a library. He wanted to know more about the pentecostal experience, so he wrote letters to India, one of which was addressed to "The Pentecostal Missionaries in Eastern India." After bouncing around several post offices, the letter arrived at the Purulia mission. Here Munshie heard more about the pentecostal experience. Just before Maynard and Gladys left Purulia for their first furlough, a great outpouring of the Spirit stirred the area. The entire Munshie family received the baptism in the Holy Spirit. Abdul, despite severe persecution, returned to his homeland as the apostle of Pentecost. Today his son Daniel is the superintendent of the Assemblies of God work in Bangladesh.

Early pentecostal missionaries were a breed of men and women unlike any before them. They carried a burden for lost souls and were marked by the sacrificial self-giving of their predecessors. But they were also the recipients of a new move of God in their time. They saw their pentecostal baptism with its resulting supernatural signs as evidence that the last days had come upon them and that God's hour of reaping was at hand. Their character, their mistakes, and their dedication is captured in this excellent article by Gary B. McGee. It was first published in the Summer, 1983 issue of *Assemblies of God Heritage*.

3

Early Pentecostal Missionaries—
They Went Everywhere Preaching the Gospel

Gary B. McGee*

When the Pentecostal movement emerged at the beginning of this century, many participants felt called to overseas evangelism. The early records of the revival speak of a close and abiding association between the baptism in the Holy Spirit as evidenced by speaking in tongues for an enduement of power in Christian witness, a fervent belief in the premillennial return of Christ and His command to evangelize to the uttermost parts of the world. This Baptism, viewed as the fulfillment of Joel's prophecy for "the last days," seemed to heighten the imperative for world evangelism. The history of Pentecostalism cannot be properly understood apart from its missionary vision.

Many of the early Pentecostals believed that speaking in tongues had a unique missionary function. According to this perspective, the new tongues were actually spoken languages to be used by the Pentecostals in the proclamation of the Gospel in foreign lands. Charles F. Parham, leader of the revival in Topeka, Kansas, and later participant in the Azusa Street Revival, firmly believed in this special missionary role of tongues. Two items in *The Apostolic Faith,* an early publication from Azusa Street, reported:

> The gift of languages is given with the commission, "Go ye into all the world and preach the Gospel to every creature." The Lord has given languages to the unlearned, Greek, Latin, Hebrew, French, German, Italian, Chinese, Japanese, Zulu and languages of Africa, Hindu and Bengali and dialects of India, Chippewa and

---

* Gary B. McGee is Associate Professor of Theology and Church History at the Assemblies of God Theological Seminary in Springfield, Missouri. He is the author of *This Gospel Shall Be Preached,* a history and theology of Assemblies of God foreign missions.

other languages of the Indians, Esquimaux, the deaf mute language and, in fact, the Holy Ghost speaks all the languages of the world through His children.[1]

God is solving the missionary problem, sending out new-tongues missionaries . . . without purse or scrip, and the Lord is going before them preparing the way.[2]

Before long, however, many Pentecostals questioned the missionary use of tongues and emphasized that the Pentecostal Baptism was an avenue of praise and intercession to God provided by the Holy Spirit. Early periodicals began to emphasize the need for language study before commencing overseas evangelism.

At least three different groups of missionaries went overseas as a result of the Spirit's outpouring.

(1) The first group represented those who had been called, but due to their feelings about the urgency of the hour and their belief in the missionary purpose of tongues, took little or no time to gather financial resources or study the history, culture, or language of the country where they were going to minister.

While many shared their testimonies and witnessed the mighty power of the Holy Spirit, their overall impact appears to have been short-lived and disappointing. Disillusionment crept in as the harsh realities of the foreign fields surfaced: the need for language and cultural studies, the importance of dependable financial support from the home churches to meet expenses and expand activities, in addition to the need for a long-term strategy for the development of indigenous churches.

Information about the activities and successes of these early missionaries is limited. One glimpse comes from a contemporary and not-too-sympathetic observer, A.B. Simpson, the founder of the Christian and Missionary Alliance. Since the Alliance was experiencing a Pentecostal revival in some quarters at home and abroad, Simpson reported to the 1908 convention of the organization that one of the unfortunate results of the fledgling Pentecostal movement was

. . . the sending forth of bodies of inexperienced and self-appointed missionaries to foreign lands under the honest impression of their part that God had given them the tongue of the people to whom they were to minister the Gospel. Without preparation, without proper leadership, and without any reasonable support, several of these parties have gone out to heathen lands only to find themselves stranded upon some foreign shore without the ability to speak any intelligible tongue, without the means of support, or even of returning home. These unhappy victims of some honest but mistaken impression, have been thrown upon the charity of strangers, and after the greatest sufferings have in most cases with much difficulty, been compelled to return to their homes, disappointed, perplexed and heart-broken.[3]

Although accurate to a considerable degree, Simpson failed to take into account that some of the early missionaries did persevere in their overseas ministries. The A.G. Garrs and Lucy Leatherman were noteworthy exceptions to Simpson's observation. The sufferings of many of these individuals must have been heroic; while we have learned from their mistakes, we can nevertheless be inspired by their devotion to the cause of Christ.

(2) The second group of missionaries that figured prominently in early Pentecostal missions was the newly Spirit-filled veterans of other missionary agencies. One prominent veteran missionary who received the Pentecostal Baptism was Miss Susan Easton, the head of the American Women's Board of Missions in India. Miss Easton had attended the important Ecumenical Missionary Conference at New York City in 1900 and represents the prominent role of women in 19th century Christian missions and in the later Assemblies of God foreign missions program. Shortly after the General Council was organized in 1914, Miss Easton received nomination to serve on the Foreign Missions Committee. She served in that post for several years.

Another missionary who had served with distinction overseas since 1892 was William W. Simpson of the Christian and Missionary Alliance (no relation to A.B. Simpson). Born in the Tennessee mountains in 1861, Simpson eventually surrendered his life to Christ and felt called to serve in overseas missions. Attending the New York Missionary Training College (later Nyack College) founded by A.B. Simpson in 1891, he headed for the Far East the following year with other Alliance missionaries. Receiving instructions and encouragement from J. Hudson Taylor, William Simpson and his colleagues headed for Tibet—considered by many to be the "uttermost" part of the world! These early Alliance missionaries witnessed the protective power of God as they penetrated the Tibetan border with the Gospel.

Attending a convention of missionaries in Taochow, China, in 1912, Simpson received the Pentecostal Baptism. Many received this experience on that occasion. Due to his uncompromising belief that the baptism in the Holy Spirit was evidenced by speaking in tongues, he was dismissed from the Alliance and eventually joined the Assemblies of God. Simpson continued as a missionary with the latter organization in China and Tibet for many years.

Unlike many other missionaries in the early part of this century, the Pentecostals were rarely trained in universities and Christian colleges before they entered their missionary activities. The Pentecostals quickly adopted the new Bible institute approach in theological education. Shorter than the traditional program of ministerial preparation, the Bible institute offered the student an intensely biblical education, dynamic spiritual atmosphere through daily chapel services and prayer meetings and a speedier entry into the ministry.

New schools, such as the Rochester Bible Training School, Bethel Bible Training Institute of Newark, New Jersey, and Central Bible Institute, Springfield, Missouri, became prominent in the preparation of missionaries. Other schools emerged in the early decades of this century to share the responsibility.

(3) These institutions prepared a third group of missionaries: men and women who had received Bible institute education in preparing for overseas endeavours. Examples include Marguerite Flint (India), Eric Booth-Clibbourn (Africa), John Burgess (India), Margaret Felch (India), Grace Walther (India),

Ralph Riggs (Africa) and Edgar Pettenger (Africa). The Bible colleges in the Assemblies of God continue to play a very prominent role in the training of Assemblies of God missionary personnel.

As the Pentecostal Movement matured, more attention was placed on preparation for the foreign fields, sound financial support, and the necessity of an overall strategy to fulfill the Great Commission. This was particularly true with the developing Assemblies of God foreign missions program.

The dedication of the early Pentecostal missionaries to the proclamation of the Gospel is truly impressive to this modern-day observer. Let us never depart from that vision.

Footnotes

1 *The Apostolic Faith,* September, 1906, p. 1.
2 *The Apostolic Faith,* November, 1906, p. 2.
3 *The Eleventh Annual Report of the Christian and Missionary Alliance* by A.B. Simpson, President and General Superintendent (May 27, 1908), pp. 11-12.

Through the initial explosive years of the Pentecostal Movement there were significant events happening simultaneously in rapid-fire succession around the world. Later, during the 1920s and 1930s there seemed to be a time of consolidation. The movement had a future but was not yet old enough to have a history. Finally there was a time to stop, reflect, and celebrate. That is the tone which David du Plessis sets in his mid-century appraisal of worldwide pentecostalism. It was a conspicuous article since it appeared in the *International Review of Missions* (April, 1958) and was written by a well-known pentecostal who was gaining prominence in ecumenical circles.

4
Golden Jubilees of Twentieth-Century Pentecostal Movements

David J. du Plessis*

Receiving the Holy Spirit
During the closing days of the last century when serious-minded Christians began to feel that the revival of the 1850s had cooled off, many began to speak and pray about the need of another *Pentecost* for the Church of the twentieth century. Teachers and Bible students began to ask, "What is the Bible evidence of the Baptism in the Holy Spirit?" A study of the *Acts of the Apostles* brought the answer: "Speaking in unknown tongues as the Spirit gives utterance" is the Scriptural confirmation of the fact that the Holy Ghost had been received. . . .

The Holy Spirit assured the entire control and leadership of the Church, the Body of Christ, and the Lord continued His mighty works through its members. . . . The Holy Spirit continued in control until the close of the first century, when He was largely rejected and His position as leader usurped by man. The results are written in history. The missionary movement halted. The Dark Ages ensued.

Christian Revivals in History
Many of the great Christian revivals in the records of history could be traced back to the influence and ministry of mighty men of God whose lives and teachings continued to affect the movement long after they had passed from the

---

* Known internationally as "Mr. Pentecost," David J. du Plessis is one of the leading emissaries of world pentecostalism. A native of South Africa, du Plessis began his ministry with the Apostolic Faith Mission. His life later touched all world-wide pentecostal churches due to his leadership in the triennial Pentecostal World Conferences. Eventually, he was to become one of the chief bridge-builders between the mainline pentecostals and the historic Protestant and Catholic churches through his involvement in the Charismatic Movement. He speaks, travels, and writes from his home base in Pasadena, California.

scene. In a number of instances it was the new emphasis on one or other doctrine that caused a stir in the hearts of the people and soon a new society was formed to propagate and perpetuate that particular truth. Thus, we have in our Christian society of today those who are called Lutherans, Calvinists, Methodists and others.

The Pentecostal revival of this century is different. In the first place, there is no man who can claim to have been the founder of this great worldwide Christian revival. In the second place, there has been no new emphasis on any special doctrine. Rather the emphasis is upon an experience. All through the ages the Church has taught that the Holy Spirit, who came on the day of Pentecost, was in the world, but there was no emphasis upon the need of receiving Him. Many who claimed to have received Him by faith never showed any supernatural manifestations of His presence in their lives such as the apostles and the saints in the early days of the Christian Church had shown. The experience of a life-changing salvation and of an empowering Baptism of the Spirit was left so completely in the background that the churches began to be packed with members, ministers and teachers who were merely hearers of the Word and not doers. Their profession of faith is based almost universally upon the experience of Christians in apostolic times as recorded in the New Testament, but there is seldom an experimental knowledge that these doctrines are true.

The Pentecostal revival today is merely a restoration of a personal experience of a life-changing salvation followed by the receiving of the Baptism into the Holy Spirit with the evidence or confirmation of the initial manifestation of speaking in unknown tongues, which in turn is usually followed by experiences of power to cast out devils, heal the sick and miracles. There never was a question of educating or training the people to do certain things. All are taught that it is done by the Holy Spirit, who will manifest himself in a supernatural and miraculous way through the lives of all who receive Him, be they laymen or clergy.

The Pentecostal Missionary Movement

In the years 1906, 1907 and 1908 the Pentecostal missionaries began pressing on to the regions beyond. Whole families volunteered for the work, sold their possessions and started for the field. They were possessed with a passion to go to the ends of the earth for their Lord, and no sacrifice seemed too great to them that the Gospel might be proclaimed and the coming of the Lord might be hastened. These Pentecostals had the fiery passion for souls of the early Methodists, followed by Baptists in baptizing by immersion and emulated the Salvation Army in the directness of their methods. It was revivalism, pure and simple.

In the *News Chronicle,* September 15th, 1936, the Reverend Hugh Redwood wrote concerning his investigation of one of the Pentecostal movements.

     I was prepared for what some of my friends called extra-vagances, though it seems to me a strange and sorry business that

Christian people, who profess to accept the story of Pentecost,
should regard as extravagant almost all that tends to corroborate it.
. . . These men who once lamented the lack of power in their life
and ministry are now possessed by a new compassion and courage.
They preach with all boldness the Full Gospel . . . and in a world
like ours, anything short of the Full Gospel is useless

But in the early days of this revival, writers and church leaders were not as
complimentary as Mr. Redwood. Rather, the Pentecostals were denounced as
false prophets and apostles, and almost everything supernatural in their
experience was attributed to the devil. In many Christian countries they were
persecuted with the same zeal evidenced by the religious leaders against the new
Christian Church of apostolic times.

Golden Jubilees

The word "Pentecost" means fifty, and the experience of receiving the Holy
Spirit is referred to as Pentecostal merely because the Holy Spirit came into the
hearts of the apostles on the day of the Pentecostal feast in Jerusalem. After fifty
years of glorious world-wide revivals, through this experience, Pentecostal
movements can truly claim to have come to the Pentecostal year of Pentecostal
experience.

The church that sparked a national revival in the United States was the
Apostlic Faith Mission of Azusa Street, Los Angeles, where, in 1906, there was a
true repetition of the experience of the apostles in Jerusalem. Hundreds came
from every part of the North American continent and received the Holy Spirit
with the confirmation of tongues in these glorious meetings in Azusa Street.
Many thousands attended the Jubilee celebrations in Angelus Temple during
1956.

Sparks, or shall we say "tongues of fire," from the Azusa Street revival were
blown in every direction, from the Pacific to the Atlantic Coast and from the
Gulf of Mexico to the Great Lakes. The majority of the outstanding pastors and
evangelists were simple laymen from the ranks of the working classes, and often
with little education. What they lacked in worldly knowledge seemed to be
supplemented by a double portion of spiritual power. Frequently it was what
they did rather than what they said or how they said it that convinced their
followers that they were being used of God. If they lacked the education to speak
with authority on matters of doctrine, they certainly did not lack the power to
cast out devils and heal the sick. If they could not argue with theologians whose
terminology they could not understand, they were able to speak the language of
the masses and understood their problems. The consequence was that from the
unchurched masses, multiplied thousands were drawn into missions, chapels
and churches. . . .

Indigenous Movements

The very fact that the Pentecostal revival is based upon a personal
experience of receiving the Holy Ghost, who makes every recipient a powerful
witness, has caused the development of indigenous churches and movements

from the very beginning. The number of native ministers and workers operating under the supervision of foreign missionaries would probably come to 30,000 throughout the world. However, apart from these are powerful indigenous Pentecostal movements in Latin America, Africa and Asia, in which ten thousand more of ordained ministers and workers could be found. During the last ten years there has been a very decisive move throughout all Pentecostal missionary operations toward the indigenous principle. . . .

Pentecostal Institutions

In the early days of the revival the burden of every preacher and missionary and convert was to win others for Christ. However, as soon as churches became established, it was found that there was a need for teaching and training in order to maintain sound doctrine. During the last two decades Bible training centers have been opened all over the world. According to the 1957 *Yearbook of American Churches,* with approximately 260 denominations reporting, it is found that the Assemblies of God is first in the number of foreign Bible schools, of which there are 60. This society has ten Bible institutes and colleges in the U.S.A. The Church of God, Cleveland, Tennessee, has 33 Bible schools in foreign fields. The strong move towards indigenous churches has caused the younger churches in foreign fields to clamour for assistance to establish more training centers.

In the matter of health services, Pentecostal societies have concentrated chiefly, though not exclusively, on maternity and baby welfare, the line on which governments, too, are mostly concerned. This does not mean, however, that we have passed over from evangelization to education and hospital work. It has simply enlarged the sphere of operations to include these on a bigger scale in order to maintain and increase opportunities of furthering the spiritual ends for which we have gone out into all the world.

Pentecostal World Conference

The very first suggestion of such a conference came at an international meeting of Pentecostal leaders at Memphis, Tennessee, in 1937. An international European conference was held in Stockholm, Sweden, in 1939. Then came the Second World War and a world conference did not materialize until 1947, when the first world conference was held in Zurich, Switzerland, and the theme was "By one Spirit we are all baptized into one Body." That conference approved the publication of a quarterly review called *Pentecost,* edited ever since by Donald Gee, of Kenley, Surrey, England.

The writer had the privilege of organizing the second world conference in Paris, during 1949. This conference adopted a manifesto declaring that the common purpose and objective of world conferences should be (a) to encourage fellowship and facilitate coordination of effort among Pentecostal believers throughout the world; (b) to demonstrate to the world the essential unity of Spirit-baptized believers, fulfilling the prayer of the Lord Jesus Christ that they all may be one; (c) to cooperate in an endeavour to respond to the unchanging commission of the Lord Jesus to carry His message to all men of all nations;

(d) to promote courtesy and mutual understanding "endeavoring to keep the unity of the Spirit in the bond of peace . . . till we all come in the unity of faith" (Eph. 4:3, 13); (e) to afford prayerful and practical assistance to any Pentecostal party in need of such; (f) to promote and maintain the Scriptural purity of fellowship by Bible study and prayer; (g) to uphold and maintain those Pentecostal truths "most surely believed among us" (Luke 1:1).

The third Pentecostal world conference was held in London in 1952. The number of countries and movements represented increased greatly and the fourth world conference in Stockholm, 1955, surpassed all the previous ones in attendance. We feel certain that the greatest yet will be the fifth, in Toronto, Canada, September 14th to 21st, 1958.

Pentecostal Statistics

As a result of international and world conferences held in the last decade, the curiosity of many had been stirred as to the scope and size of the Pentecostal revival. We began to collect information and statistics and finally, in 1956, published a list of statistics from information which in some cases was almost ten years old. The first list showed that there must be over five million Pentecostal adherents throughout the world. However, many countries are not listed and the figures given for some were completely outdated. During the last twelve months we have obtained more up-to-date statistics and from almost every part of the world. It is now clear that the Pentecostal community in the world must be over eight million and possibly nearer ten million.

We must point out that Pentecostal churches usually record only the names of their adult members who have actually joined the society. They do not give the number of children or the number of regular attendants at their services who might be considered adherents to the Pentecostal faith. Therefore, these figures may yet be far from the actual facts. We also know that there are thousands of independent churches and many indigenous movements from whom we have not yet received a report at all.

Part Two
Theological Motivations

Introduction
Truth on Fire:
Pentecostals and an Urgent Missiology

L. Grant McClung, Jr.

"Truth on Fire" headlined Chapter 21 of David J. du Plessis's autobiography *A Man Called Mr. Pentecost*. In that section, he recalled his 1956 meeting with a number of ecumenical leaders from across America. "Please tell us," asked one of the churchmen of this well-known pentecostal:

> What is the difference between you and us. We quote the same Scriptures you do, and yet when you say those words they sound so different. We say the same things that you do, but there seems to be a deeper implication in what you say. You have said nothing with which we want to differ and yet there seems to be a distinct difference somewhere. (1977:181-182)

The "distinct difference" in the pentecostal theology of missions is found in du Plessis's reply:

> Gentlemen, comparisons are odious, and I do not wish to injure anyone's feelings or hurt your pride. But the truth as I see it is this: You have the truth on ice, and I have it on fire. (1977:181-182)

This "on fire" pentecostal mission theology has tended to be a "theology on the move." Its character has been more experiential than cognitive, more activist than reflective. Pentecostals have often acted now and theologized later. Though pentecostal theologians, apologists, and historians have articulated their faith for some time (see the Annotated Bibliography) only recently have pentecostal missiologists begun to solidify a more formalized "pentecostal missions theology" (Hodges 1972 and 1977; Pomerville 1982).

Yet, since its inception, the Pentecostal Movement has had underlying theological assumptions which have formed the impulse for its missionary expansion. Three of those assumptions are briefly examined in this essay: the centrality of the Word and the Spirit; pentecostal eschatology; and the pentecostal sense of destiny. This survey is not exhaustive but introduces the internal essence of the theological infrastructure of pentecostal missions. It highlights some specific motivational elements in pentecostals' worldview and theology which have propelled them into continuous missionary outreach since the turn of the century.

In Spirit and In Truth

If Francis Schaeffer has characterized God as *The God Who Is There,* pentecostals have traditionally understood Him to be the "God who is there—now." For pentecostals, the declaration of divine omnipotence and omnipresence has been more than an abstract theological formulation; it is an incarnational truth available and experienced by faith. The pentecostal "theology of immediacy" has seen the kingdom that is coming but has also lived in the kingdom that is now. For pentecostals, "God is not an idea but a presence and a power. God saves; He has the power to save, and even more concretely the power to cure, whether it be from the effects of sin or of illness" (Epinay 1969:204).

People of "The Book". The accessibility of God and His power has been understood by pentecostals due to their literal acceptance of "thus saith the Lord." This, said pentecostal missions strategist David A. Womack:

> . . . was one of the major causes for the rise of the Pentecostal Movement; for, as people read their Bibles with renewed interest and better understanding, they found the description of a kind of Christianity very different from that of their own churches. Once the new approach to Bible interpretation was established, it was inevitable that some group would call for a return to the full gospel of the apostles. (1968:84)

Growing out of the fundamentalist and holiness roots of literal biblicism, the pentecostals have taken the literal interpretation of scripture another step further into their missionary practices. For them, the issue of biblical authority determines their basic beginning point for missions theology and strategizing. "They are people of 'The Book,' " said Assemblies of God missiologist Paul A. Pomerville (1982:352):

> While some may question their *use* of The Book, their hermeneutics, nevertheless Pentecostals seek to be led by Scripture as by the Spirit in their missions efforts. Their textbook for missions strategy often boils down to the Book of Acts. (1982:352)

As the result of "going by 'The Book' " in their theology, pentecostals have sought to be as identical to Scripture as possible in their mission practices. If they have seen something in the Bible, they have taken it as applicable for today, whether it be healing (Dollar 1980:197ff), power encounter (De Wet 1981:81ff), speaking in tongues (Harris 1973:120ff) and other spiritual gifts (Gee 1963:81ff; Hodges 1977:31ff; Buntain 1956:63ff), and other apostolic practices.

In his April, 1982 "Global Report," *Evangelical Missions Quarterly* reporter Robert Niklaus chronicled the mushrooming growth of Brazilian pentecostalism. His article, headlined "Pentecostal Invasion," told of 8.5 million pentecostals in 26,000 churches (1,000 of them in Sao Paulo—the largest city in the largest Catholic country in the world) and attributed their growth to a literal interpretation of the Bible. Though nominal churches had been in Brazil for at least 150 years, the pentecostal "invasion" began in 1910. Unlike the denominational clergy, the pentecostals believed in a literal interpretation of the Bible and took a "strong stand on the scriptures" which "found immediate acceptance among the people, if not among the church leaders" (1982:117).

People of the Spirit. But, as Pomerville has said, pentecostals are not only people of the scriptures but people of the Spirit. The Holy Spirit and His ministries are at the center of pentecostal theology. Pentecostal beliefs and practices cannot be understood until one grasps:

> . . . the centrality of the Third Person of the Trinity in their theology and in their lives. To them Pentecost is not a mere historical event that took place almost two thousand years ago, but an always renewed presence of the Spirit in the world. The Holy Spirit is now, as then, the "creator" and the "vivifier" of men. (Damboriena 1969:87)

Though some pentecostals have at times overemphasized the Holy Spirit at the expense of a more holistic view of the Godhead and have tended in some quarters to major on the existential and personal benefits from the Holy Spirit, there have traditionally been at least two main biblical emphases concerning the Holy Spirit among pentecostals. They have been: (1) the necessity of the Baptism of the Holy Spirit as an indispensable enduement of power for service; and (2) the exaltation of Jesus Christ as the Baptizer in the Holy Spirit (Kydd 1983:22; du Plessis in Roebck 1983:6; du Plessis 1977:202; Luke 24:49; Acts 1:8; Matthew 3:11; Mark 1:8; Luke 3:16; John 1:33).

The pentecostals have exploded into phenomenal growth around the world not only because they have reached the masses and the poor, or have concentrated upon the receptive, or have utilized the energies of the common man, or have done whatever else outside observers have marked as good methodology. The primary pentecostal distinctive in their theology has been their insistence upon the outpouring of the Holy Spirit personally into the life of each believer in a "personal pentecost." This, said Donald Gee at the 1952 Pentecostal World Conference, is "The Contribution of The Pentecostal Movement to the Church Universal":

> It is not distinctive (and let us therein rejoice) to possess evangelical zeal; neither is it peculiarly "Pentecostal" to believe in Divine healing. There is nothing whatever Pentecostal in contending for some particular form or idea of church government hoary with age,

and already embodied, if not embalmed in more than one existing denomination. The true Pentecostal Revival offers a testimony to a definite spiritual and personal experience, based on the significance and story of the Day of Pentecost. Hence its name, and its only justification for its name. In that distinctive witness lies its strength, its vindication, and its value. (Greenway 1952:11)

Though some pentecostal theologians may move in other directions, pentecostal *missiologists* will contend that the Baptism of the Holy Spirit is primarily for ministry, especially for evangelism (Robeck 1983:5). One of the oldest living inside interpreters of the movement, David J. du Plessis, made this very clear in a recent interview:

> I have held from the beginning that the Baptism in the Holy Spirit has really no place, no need in the church unless it is to equip the church for ministry, and the tragedy to me is that there are millions today who have received the baptism of the Holy Spirit but were never taught what really is the responsibility they've taken upon themselves by accepting the baptism. I say there is no reason for the baptism but to minister, for the ministry of Christ began after his enduement on the bank of Jordan. (Robeck 1983:6)

This position is characteristic of the teaching of William J. Seymour from Azusa Street. In one of his earlier writings on the subject of the Baptism of the Holy Spirit, Seymour said:

> There is a great difference between a sanctified person and one that is baptized with the Holy Ghost and fire. A sanctified person is cleansed and filled with divine love, but the one that is baptized with the Holy Ghost has the power of God on his soul and has power with God and men, power over all the kingdoms of Satan and over all his emissaries. . . .
> When the Holy Ghost comes and takes us as His instruments, this is the power that convicts men and women and causes them to see that there is a reality in serving Jesus Christ.. . . .
> The Holy Spirit is power with God and man. (Corum 1981, Volume II, No. 13:3)

A strong Christology. Of course, since Seymour and Parham's time the Baptism of the Holy Spirit has become a cardinal pentecostal doctrine. Accompanying this experience has been the phenomenon of speaking in tongues, so much so that critics have been inclined to label pentecostalism as "the tongues movement." It was Seymour, however, who began early to exhort the people, "Now, do not go from this meeting and talk about tongues, but try to get people saved" (Frodsham 1946:38). Seymour, and subsequent pentecostal leaders since him, had a strong Christology which centered more on the Giver than the gift. He constantly exalted "the atoning work of Christ and the Word of God. . . ." (Frodsham 1946:38).

Stanley H. Frodsham, pentecostal historian and biographer, has insisted that speaking with tongues has *not* been the principal feature of the movement:

> By no means. Our Lord and Saviour Jesus Christ has been exalted as the One altogether lovely and as the chiefest among ten thousand, yea, as all in all. The first and foremost thing in the outpouring has been *the magnifying of the person of the Lord Jesus Christ.*
>
> We heard Pastor Jonathan Paul of Berlin, an acknowledged Pentecostal leader in Germany, say, "I have not put the word 'Pentecost' on my banner. I have the word 'Jesus' on it and expect to keep it there." And the rest of us say, "Amen." (1946:272)

Last Days Mission Theology

A second motivational element in the pentecostal theology of mission has been an intense premillennial eschatology. Premillennialism, dispensationalism, and the belief in the imminency of Christ's return forged the evangelistic fervor of the movement in its infancy (Bloch-Hoell 1964; Waldvogel 1977; Hunter 1983).

Pentecostals have interpreted the promises of Joel 2:28-32 as being for our day. They have taken the promises of the former and latter rain (Hosea 6:1-3; Joel 2:23-27; James 5:7-8) to be the last days' spiritual outpouring just prior to Christ's imminent return (Flower in Jones 1978:111).

One wonders whether or not this "eschatological intensity" is as dominant today as it was in the early 1900s. It is this writer's concern that the conviction of Christ's soon return may have waned in some pentecostal quarters. Readings and analyses would need to verify this assumption and look for causes. It is supposed, however, that one element that may have contributed to this change would be what Donald A. McGavran calls "halting due to redemption and lift" (1980:295ff).

This does not obscure the fact that by and large pentecostal theology has continued to have a central eschatological element. Some forty years into the movement, for example, Frodsham cited a 1941 report from China in which the field chairman tells of a six-day convention which was stretched to nearly fifty days due to the outpouring of the Holy Spirit. The summary of the messages, he said, could be summed up as follows:

> The time is short; the coming of the Lord is near; the present opportunities of evangelism will not last long; the Lord longs to work in a new, glorious, and mighty way to show forth His glory and save souls. . . . (1946:275-276)

After recounting the China report, Frodsham concluded:

> And thank God, He is mightily pouring out His Spirit in the last days, at what is surely the end of the church period. . . . Christ is pouring the oil and the fire still blazes, and we all believed it will blaze until that glad day when the Lord Jesus Christ shall descend from heaven and take His church to be with Him forevermore. (1946:278-279)

At the half-century mark of modern pentecostalism, Gloria Kulbeck produced a history of the Pentecostal Assemblies of Canada, *What God Hath Wrought*. In it, the eschatological dimension is present:

> The morning cometh! How glorious is the prospect of the personal return of Christ for His church. It was the prospect of the return of Christ which cheered the hearts of the first Pentecostal believers of this century. It is the hope of Christ's coming which steadies believers bearing the cross on the mission fields. It was to announce the soon return of Christ that the Pentecostal revival was given. (1958:352)

Throughout pentecostal literature yet today, one finds references to a "last-day ministry" (McGavran 1977:43) or that "time is growing short" (Cary 1976:27) or that the second coming of Christ will be "very, very soon" (Wogen 1973:39). Pentecostal missionary practice is still proceeding from an inherent "last days mission theology."

A Divine Destiny

The theological mood and atmosphere set by premillennialism and the "actualization of the kingdom" experienced by the outpouring of the Holy Spirit in their midst has historically caused pentecostals to be filled with an assurance that has overcome persecution and early rejection. That assurance and conviction has been: "God has chosen us! We are a people of divine destiny for this hour!"

This "Mordecai-Esther factor" ("Thou art come to the kingdom for such a time as this" Esther 4:14) has been a powerfully motivating force thrusting the movement around the world into the face of any opposition. It has been central to pentecostal ideology. Of the *Congregacao Crista no Brasil* in Brazil, for example, outside observer William R. Read has reported:

> A certain mentality has grown up around the prophecy of their founder that the Church has a divinely inspired "particular" mission to fulfill. Members think of the Congregacao as an agency of the Lord at a particular time and place in the work of harvesting. . . . This has a psychological effect upon the whole Church. It creates an atmosphere of expectancy. It aids growth and progress. If God is for us, who can be against us? (1965:42)

Pentecostal sermons, articles, and statements are replete with this persuasion that "God has raised us up." Pentecostals have seen themselves at the climax of two thousand years of Church history and feel a kinship to the early church. In them, they feel, God has restored apostolic Christianity (Womack 1968). They have believed that:

> . . . the missionary spirit which moved in the Book of Acts is presently moving among us. May it ever be so! There is no question but what God has raised up a Pentecostal movement as a means of hastening the evangelization of the world. The latter rain is falling,

and the harvest is ripening for the ingathering which very well may be the last gathering before the return of Jesus Christ to earth. (Hodges 1974:31)

Not only is this pentecostal sense of destiny articulated for the movement as a whole, but entire denominations have interpreted themselves to be God's instrument. This is particularly evident at denominational conventions, councils, and convocations. At the Assemblies of God Council on Evangelism in 1968, for example, Pastor James E. Hamill preached on "The Motivation of the Church." He said:

May this be a dynamic church at work in winning the lost to Christ and in ministering to the distressed and the discouraged and offering strength to the weak.
May this dynamic church send out its young men and women to preach Christ at home and abroad.
May this Spirit-filled church lead all other denominations into the fullness and glorious baptism of the Holy Ghost. (Champion 1968:32)

Ten years later at a Church Growth Convocation, "Higher Goals," Assemblies of God Pastor Marvin Gorman proclaimed, "I feel God is calling us to this hour to go forth preaching the Word." He was joined by a colleague, missionary Melvin L. Hodges, who asserted, "I do believe that God has a special plan for the Assemblies of God at this time and that our Movement can make a contribution to God's eternal purpose for this age" (Jones 1978:12, 31).

Upon the observance of their fiftieth anniversary in 1982, Open Bible Standard Churches author Bryant Mitchell received this comment from a general officer of their denomination:

I believe that we have a divine destiny which God has given to us. . . . We are not an accident or the extension of some man's ego. God Almighty moved on our forefathers. Our movement is manmade, but divinely ordained. . . . We have a ministry to perform. . . .I am not afraid of institutionalism. It speaks to me of strength, security, and stability. . . . The enemy would like to fragment us, but we will not allow this. . . . I believe that Open Bible Standard serves a vital function in the body of Christ. (1982:380)

In a recent report, Jim O. McClain, former director of Church of God World Missions, stressed:

Our World Missions ministry is moving ahead in spite of political, social and economic hindrances thrown up by Satan. A great Pentecostal revival is sweeping across the globe, and we praise God that the Church of God is in the forefront. (Moree 1983:5)

In the same issue of *SOW* magazine (Save Our World) McClain is joined by Lambert DeLong, Superintendent of Europe and the Middle East, who declared,

"I believe the Church of God in Europe has 'come to the kingdom for such a time as this.' We are able to give answers to the questions being asked by the spiritually hungry masses" (Moree 1983:9).

The criticism that these convictions have implications of arrogance and triumphalism has not daunted the missionary fervor of pentecostals. Equal to the pentecostals' statements regarding being chosen by God for a divine destiny are the expressions of humility and gratitude that God has blessed them with this privilege and will also hold them accountable for their stewardship of His gifts. Therefore, one catches a sense of stewardship, responsibility, and mandate in pentecostal literature (Jones 1978:19; Greenway 1952:10ff; Champion 1968:16ff; Walker 1981:173ff).

There is a sense of contribution, of service, in pentecostals' statements regarding their purpose. This is reflected in a somewhat lengthy statement from L.F.W. Woodford, who at the time of this address to the 1952 Pentecostal World Conference was Missionary Secretary for the British Assemblies of God:

> It is the abiding conviction of all who share in this great work for God that He has in His gracious purpose raised up a people in these latter days through whom He may manifest His grace and glory in the pristine power of Pentecost. If there is a unique contribution being made by Pentecostal Foreign Missions to the sum total of World Missions as a whole, it is found in the primacy it gives to direct evangelism—the ceaseless proclamation of the Gospel of the grace of God for the whole man—in the essential equipment of 'power from on High' for all His ambassadors in the Gospel without exception, in the due recognition that in all missionary work it remains as true today as ever, that His Kingdom is established and enlarged, not by might, nor by power, but by His Spirit, and that His people have the right to expect that the supernatural signs promised in His Word shall still accompany the ministry of His servants who go forth in His Name. The stress everywhere laid by pentecostal missionaries upon the near return of the Lord Jesus serves to maintain the work on all fields in separation from the world, in purity and in zeal for the salvation of the lost "whilst it is day." (Greenway 1952:50)

Such are some of the fundamental elements of pentecostal "truth on fire." The primacy of the Word and the Spirit, the "urgent missiology" formed by a premillennial eschatology, and the sense of divine destiny have provided dynamic motivational components in the overall pentecostal theology of mission.

Most researchers and outside observers of the Pentecostal Movement have attributed its success to many sociological, psychological, and historical factors. Thomas Zimmerman, a prominent insider, discounts those theories, and discusses five features of the movement from the perspective of an active participant. His article is taken from *Aspects of Pentecostal-Charismatic Origins,* Vinson Synan, Editor (Logos 1975).

5

The Reason for the Rise
of the Pentecostal Movement

Thomas F. Zimmerman*

Late in 1969, Jessyca Russell Gaver received a clipping from the September 6, 1969, edition of the *New York Times* sent by her publisher, Arnold Abramson. The headline read, "Pentecostal Movement Finding New Adherents."

Abramson wanted Mrs. Gaver to write a book about this phenomenon, and to encourage her to accept the assignment, he included the story of the growth of pentecostals. She accepted, and the result was an almost 300-page paperback entitled *Pentecostalism*.

While there were certainly other considerations which caused Mrs. Gaver to take the assignment, a prominent motivating factor was one sentence in the newspaper article:

> Pentecostalism has developed into the world's fastest-growing denomination at a time when membership in most other churches is declining as a proportion of the population.

Like the initial outpouring of the Holy Spirit on the day of Pentecost, the pentecostal movement today has received widespread attention. It has been referred to by various designations—both kind and unkind. Possibly one of the most appropriate descriptions from a biblical point of view is the term "revival." The rise of the pentecostal movement came under conditions which existed prior to revivals both in Bible times and in later Church history. The rise of the present-day move of the Spirit is directly attributable to believers who fulfill God's conditions for revival.

---

* A foremost leader in world pentecostalism, Thomas F. Zimmerman is the former General Superintendent of the Assemblies of God (1960-1985). Since 1964 he has served as the Chairman of the Advisory Committee for the World Pentecostal Conference.

Great revivals have often begun in times of spiritual and moral darkness. Conditions of gross darkness prevailed before revivals under such leaders as Asa (2 Chronicles 15:1-15), Joash (2 Kings 11, 12), Hezekiah (2 Chronicles 29-31), Josiah (2 Kings 22, 23), Zerubbabel (Ezra 5, 6), and Nehemiah (Nehemiah 8:9; 12:44-47). The people and leaders were guilty of idolatry, neglect of and in some cases contempt for the house of God, unjust and sometimes cruel treatment of fellow Israelites, entangling alliances and associations with heathen nations, and the practice of spiritism and other forms of the occult.

Against this backdrop of ungodliness, there were always those who were earnestly looking to the Lord for His intervention. These people were never disappointed, for when God's people sought the Lord with the whole heart, a spiritual and moral revival always followed.

A quick perusal of history books makes it very evident that conditions prior to the present pentecostal revival were deplorable. Post-Civil War America was fraught with sectional hostility and financial turmoil. Increasing population movements into the cities were accompanied by the usual moral decay—crime, gambling, alcoholism, and prostitution grew rampant. Corruption reached high levels of federal and state governments, and many became rich quickly at the expense of the taxpayers. In the business world, those who became wealthy through stock manipulations, oil speculations, and other fraudulent means often outnumbered those who succeeded through honesty.

Nor was the church exempt from the spirit of the times. American seminaries exchanged professors with the German universities where liberal theology and higher criticism of the Bible were in vogue. It wasn't long until pulpits were being populated by literal apostles of unbelief. They ridiculed the deity of Christ, the virgin birth, and the substitutionary atonement. The social gospel was supplanting the supernatural Gospel, and the theory of Christian nurture preempted the necessity of repentance.

But still there were many devout believers in every denomination who continued to "contend for the faith which was once delivered unto the saints." As these people began to pray more earnestly because of deteriorating world conditions, it was not long until God began to pour out His Spirit and to restore to the remnant Church the gifts of His Spirit, notably speaking in tongues.

Not all these people upon whom the Spirit fell realized, at first, the biblical precedent for the experiences they were having. But soon, from many different places, they began to declare that the Holy Spirit was being outpoured as during the first days of the Church age. Once again God had honored His ancient promise in a time of deep darkness.

This, then, is the explanation for the remarkable growth of the pentecostal movement. Men have tried to adduce all kinds of reasons for it in terms of sociology, psychology, ecology, and economics. But nothing short of the almighty power of God responding to the contrition of His faithful remnant could have produced such results.

Let us then review the essential elements in the lives of these people on whom the Spirit fell.

1. First, *they revered the Word of God, the Bible.* And so it always was.

The revivals under Asa (2 Chronicles 15:8-19), Joash (2 Chronicles 24:6), and Hezekiah (2 Kings 18:6), as well as those under Josiah, Zerubbabel, and Nehemiah, were attributable largely to the fact that these Old Testament leaders insisted on a renewed commitment to the Mosaic documents, especially to Deuteronomy.

Evan Roberts, leader of the famous Welsh revival at the turn of this century, exemplified this same dedication to the priority of Scripture. A contemporary observer said of him, "He is no orator, he is not widely read. The only book he knows from cover to cover is the Bible." George T.B. Davis, in his book, *When the Fire Fell,* reported that a religious paper in Chicago made this observation of Evan Roberts: "First he worked in a coal mine, then became an apprentice in a forge, then a student for the ministry. But all his life he has yearned to preach."

The Bible was given priority in Bethel College, Topeka, Kansas, where about forty students came together primarily to study the Word of God. It was after exhaustive study of the Bible that the students unanimously agreed that speaking in tongues is the initial evidence of the Baptism in the Spirit. What they believed the Word of God taught, they soon began to experience, and so the modern pentecostal movement was launched.

2. Secondly, these people on whom the Spirit fell *lived holy lives.* They studied to avoid sin and to shun the very appearance of evil.

Since the pentecostal movement is strongly biblical, emphasis on holiness is not surprising. It might have seemed that such an emphasis would inhibit its growth, but the opposite has been true. The committed life with all its attendant blessings came to be appreciated by people who recognized the greater price which had to be paid for selfish and sinful living. Holiness was not to them a cross to be borne, but a cherished delight.

While there have been different doctrinal positions on the matter of sanctification, all pentecostal fellowships have emphasized holiness. A careful study of the past seventy years would show that this has certainly been a factor in the growth of these bodies.

3. A third prominent feature of all revivals of Bible and church history has been *a strong emphasis on the truth of substitutionary atonement.* Sin is a reality which can only be taken care of through the transfer of the offender's guilt to Christ, and the transfer of Christ's righteousness to the believer.

The work of the Holy Spirit is to glorify Christ (John 16:14). This is why, when pentecostal believers have emphasized the atoning work of Christ, lost souls have responded with joy. Persuasive human eloquence did not produce these many conversions, but the convicting power of the Holy Spirit who honored the cross-centered preaching of the pentecostals.

4. Perhaps one of the most significant and widely observed phenomena of the pentecostal revival is its *emphasis upon free and exuberant worship.* Man is a worshiping creature. He will worship something. If he doesn't worship God, he is surely an idolater.

When people are filled with the Holy Spirit, they are indwelt by the one who glorified Christ and who also empowers authentic worship. This Spirit of worship which has attracted so many in the past will certainly continue to do so.

Dr. Leland R. Keys, a retired minister who has served many years with distinction both as a pastor and educator, was introduced to pentecost in a mission in an eastern city in the early years of this century. He said there was one custom of that mission which attracted his attention most: a lady would play the pump organ before the service and sometimes would sing familiar choruses and hymns. Without waiting for the service to commence formally, the people as they gathered would join in, and God's presence would become wonderfully real.

Dr. Keys continued, "A Spirit-baptized body of believers, loving the Lord with all their hearts, singing and making melody to the Lord, expressing their joy in the public assembly, prepared the way for what was called a 'Holy Ghost meeting.' The gifts of the Spirit were manifested, and the Word of God was proclaimed with power. The result was that the altars were filled with those who were hungry for God."

Much more could be said about the numerous features which attracted people into the pentecostal ranks from every walk of life. The joy of salvation, their irrepressible happiness, miraculous healings and deliverances, transformed homes—all had great appeal.

Less appealing was the persecution. It happened in the home, in the community, in the schoolhouse. Wary onlookers quickly coined epithets to describe these people whose behavior they considered bizarre. As in the early church, however, persecution didn't hinder the work of God—it helped.

5. The final characteristic of the early pentecostals which accounts for much of their success was their *consuming evangelistic zeal.* In spite of charges to the contrary, pentecostals do not spend all their time talking in or about tongues. They have instead consistently sought to bring people to Christ. Like the people described in the Book of Acts, they have gone everywhere, earnestly proclaiming the message of salvation.

A.W. Orwig, who attended some of the Azusa Street meetings in Los Angeles, later wrote:

> One thing that somewhat surprised me was the presence of so many from different churches. Some were pastors, evangelists, or foreign missionaries. Persons of many nationalities were present. Sometimes these, many of them unsaved, would be seized with deep conviction of sin under the burning testimony of one of their own nationality, and at once heartily turn to the Lord. Occasionally some foreigner would hear a testimony or earnest exhortation in his native tongue from a person not at all acquainted with that language, and thereby be pungently convicted that it was a call from God to repent of sin.

W.J. Seymour, a leader in the Azusa Street mission, was often heard to say, "Now, do not go from this meeting and talk about tongues, but try to get people saved."

In conclusion, we must not overlook the prophetic and eschatological implication of the pentecostal movement. When the multitude gathered at the first pentecostal outpouring, some were angered, some were in doubt, and some mocked. It was then Peter who offered an explanation in terms of the prophecy of Joel:

> And it shall come to pass in the last days, saith God, I will pour out of my Spirit upon all flesh: and your sons and your daughters shall prophesy, and your young men shall see visions, and your old men shall dream dreams: and on my servants and on my handmaidens I will pour out in those days of my Spirit; and they shall prophesy: and I will show wonders in heaven above, and signs in the earth beneath; blood, and fire, and vapour of smoke: the sun shall be turned into darkness, and the moon into blood, before that great and notable day of the Lord come: and it shall come to pass, that whosoever shall call on the name of the Lord shall be saved. (Acts 2:17-21)

The pentecostal revival is a fulfillment of prophecy—a sign of the last days.

Paul made a less buoyant forecast about those days: "This know also, that in the last days perilous times shall come" (2 Timothy 3:1). He followed that with a dreary catalog of evils which would characterize the last days—a list that convinces believers more than ever of the imminence of the end of the age. But pentecostals know that where sin abounds, grace is even more plentiful, and they are optimistic. They expect an outpouring of the Spirit greater than ever.

Thank God for what happened on the day of Pentecost! Thank God for the rise of the twentiety-century pentecostal movement. But let us especially thank God that the best days are not in the past. They are in the future.

Convinced of this, we will continue to sensitively follow the leadership of the Holy Spirit; we will continue in dedicated service to Christ; and we shall continue to pray, "Even so, come Lord Jesus! Maranatha!"

Prophecy, tongues and interpretation, and other supernatural manifestations of the Holy Spirit are known to be a central part of the Pentecostal Movement. That they, and the other spiritual gifts, are central to the process of world evangelization is the thesis of pentecostal spokesman Donald Gee. Gee formulates their relationship to the evangelistic process and offers guidelines toward avoiding their misuse and abuse. Excerpted from *Spiritual Gifts in the Work of the Ministry Today* (Gospel Publishing House 1963).

6
Spiritual Gifts and World Evangelization

Donald Gee*

Wherever the Pentecostal Movement has placed evangelization in the forefront of its activities, whether at home or overseas, it has prospered. From the very outset it has engendered a remarkable zeal for sending forth missionaries. If that zeal has sometimes lacked wisdom and knowledge to direct it, with consequent waste of precious lives and money, we can still point with pardonable pride and joy to the solid achievement of Pentecostal missions throughout the world. They are foremost in promoting Bible schools in many lands. They aim at planting indigenous churches. They now seek intelligent orientation to rapidly changing world conditions. The future is bright for them while the providence of God permits them opportunity to continue.

But world evangelization should involve a demonstration of spiritual gifts in action, and should not be engaged in as a substitute for them. The possibility may be startling, but it must be faced. In a worthy desire to maintain spiritual life and activity of a healthy nature to the churches, if the manifestation of the Spirit by means of His supernatural gifts declines, there can be a turning to absorption in evangelism as a compensation for spiritual gifts rather than an expression of them. This involves a subtle temptation to miss the fullest purposes of God through the Pentecostal Revival, and the supreme importance of evangelization as an end in itself can obscure the issue. There is no need to choose between a passion for souls and a desire for spiritual gifts. They are mutually inclusive, not exclusive. . . .

---

* Donald Gee, from Scotland, is considered one of the most outstanding leaders ever produced by the Pentecostal Movement. He was the first editor of *Pentecost*, a quarterly review emanating from the World Pentecostal Conference. Before his untimely death in 1966, Gee produced a number of outstanding articles and books including *The Pentecostal Movement, Toward Pentecostal Unity*, and *Wind and Flame*.

Therefore we must hold fast to rightly understanding the gifts of the Spirit as a divine equipment for the work of world evangelization. To regard them in any other way is to turn them into a speciality for groups of people that become little more than religious clubs. Particularly is this so when there is an overemphasis upon "messages" through prophetical gifts, and still more if it is by means of tongues and interpretation of tongues. They possess a strange fascination when first encountered that tends to sweep novices off their feet. There is *no* future for gifts of the Spirit on that line, except in the stagnant backwaters of an esoteric sect. When the elements of novelty wears off, which is inevitable, it leaves the devotees isolated from the main stream of healthy evangelical Christianity. This has happened, is happening, and will happen again if we do not keep balanced and sane in our appreciation of spiritual gifts. They are not a hobby to play with; they are tools to work with and weapons to fight with.

But for all that, we must retain a proper place for the prophetical gifts of the Spirit in world evangelization. It is speaking with tongues that has made the Pentecostal Movement a distinct and recognizable entity in the twentieth century. If its critics have dubbed it the "Tongues Movement," we must accept the implied opprobrium. There is nothing to be ashamed of in a right use of a perfectly scriptural gift of the Holy Spirit. It is love that governs such a right use, and when directed by love the gift will be neither unseemly nor disorderly. The shame rests upon those who, in flat defiance of the Scriptures, forbid to speak with tongues.[1] The distinctive mark of the Pentecostal Movement is speaking with tongues, whether we like it or not; and to disavow it is to leave us perhaps "evangelical" and perhaps "fundamental" but not "Pentecostal" in any distinctive sense. And we believe there is a very high value in being expressly Pentecostal in our testimony. If the tongues attract thirsty souls to where there are living waters of the Spirit we can do nothing but rejoice. Balanced teaching and healthy example will soon let them see that the novelty of speaking with tongues is only an introduction to far greater and deeper manifestations and experiences of the eternal Spirit of the living God. And many may never make this life-changing discovery if they are not first attracted by the strange sign of a supernatural power at work in the Church. . . .

It is for the restoration of those gifts that revival movements have prayed.[2] It was a great part of the spiritual hunger in the hearts of the pioneers of the present Pentecostal Revival. They believed that they did not pray in vain. The present charismatic revival among the Episcopalians, and others, is a continuance of the same abiding hunger. At heart it is a hunger and thirst for the living God, but it is none the less that when it longs to taste the manifestation of His Presence and Power. We must not minimize the important part that the speaking with tongues has played in causing the worldwide spread of the Pentecostal Movement, and hence its world evangelization. It thrills participants with hope that more and other restored gifts of the Spirit will follow. That hope must be wisely directed in the truth and not allowed to drift into fanaticism. . . .

The present Pentecostal Movement has girdled the earth. It still is growing. Its health has largely been due to its world evangelization. The divine impetus for that has been the baptism in the Holy Spirit accompanied by spiritual gifts. What is the future for such a movement? That will depend, under God, on its spiritual leadership; and, if it is to remain loyal to its heavenly vision, that leadership will manifest spiritual gifts. In the Early Church the gifts of the Spirit resulted in recognized ministries described in such passages as 1 Corinthians 12:28 and Ephesians 4:11. They were fundamental to its great task of world evangelization. To imitate them without the inspiring power of the Spirit of God would be futile, but to see them as indicating the divine grace should be our delight.

We have become afraid of the designation "apostle" today. . . . But it is worth remembering that "missionary" is only the Latin form of the same word "apostolos"—"one sent forth." A Christ-sent missionary need not be a Peter nor a Paul to humbly qualify for some such designation. All missionaries are not apostles, for their work has many facets. But in our God-appointed task of world evangelization we need, almost more than ought else, men who can pioneer the work of the gospel and plant indigenous churches. It is to be remembered that great and successful evangelists are not necessarily apostles in the scriptural sense. Many Pentecostal evangelists seem strangely deficient of any sense of the importance of planting churches, or of the value of those already planted by others. They live and move and have their being in a whirl of continuous "campaigns." But a true apostle endued with spiritual gifts, coupled with an appreciation of the differing members of the body of Christ with whom he must work if he is to fulfill the purpose of God, will beget spiritual children for whom he will live or die. We have such illustrious names on our missionary roll.

For such leadership in evangelization, whether at home or overseas or both; we desire a scriptural vision of men manifesting a wide variety of spiritual gifts. They will exercise word of wisdom and knowledge in prophetic grace and power, and not come behind in gifts of action or ability to organize. This need not be an impossible idealistic claim if we are prepared to recognize spiritual gifts producing ministries in part. The Lord's plan appears to be a multitude of gifted men and women exercising their varied gifts in harmony for His glory. None will have all the gifts, though some will have more than others. The truly supernatural will remain securely anchored in consecrated natural ability, for all good and great missionary-evangelists are eminently practical. This is what we mean by Spiritual Gifts in the Work of the Ministry Today. . . .

When gifts of the Spirit are lacking there are produced churches that are run by natural gifts just like efficient business concerns in the world. There is nothing wrong in the organization; the failure is in the motive power. In the end such churches produce spiritual starvation, and in the older denominations we see today a hunger and thirst for a new outpouring of the Spirit of God. It is not without cause that the next general council of the World Presbyterian Alliance has deliberately chosen as its theme "Come, Creator Spirit." In its official organ, James McCord has said that "a vacuum exists in the life of the church, and the church's renewal through a fresh outpouring of the Spirit is necessary. It is a question that can no longer be postponed."[3] For our own Pentecostal task of world evangelization we shall, by the grace of God, provide more than the necessary machinery of world missions and evangelism. The all-important dynamic of Holy Ghost power is manifested through spiritual gifts. . . .

We accept without reserve world evangelization as the supreme purpose in the will of God for the Pentecostal Revival. On the cornerstone of the new Administrations Building of Assemblies of God in Springfield, Missouri, are the words, "INTO ALL THE WORLD." Nothing could be more fitting, not only for our friends of the Assemblies of God, but for the whole world Pentecostal Movement. When our Lord gave his final charge to the apostles just before He ascended to the Father He coupled with it the promise of the gift of the Holy Ghost for power to fulfill a commission that extended to the "uttermost part of the earth."[4] It is recorded that they obeyed and preached everywhere, the Lord working with them, "confirming the word with signs following."[5] The continuance in spiritual prosperity of the Pentecostal Revival depends upon continual consecration to worldwide missions. If our spiritual gifts cannot flourish in the wide arena of universal witness there is something wrong. Their use in evangelism is a healthy test for their validity and our use of them. . . .

The divinely appointed instrument for all this is preaching and teaching and all that should accompany the ministry of the Word in the power of the Holy Spirit. Our Great Commission is quite specific: it is to go and *teach* all nations . . . to observe all things that our Lord commanded. They went forth and preached everywhere, and the signs that followed confirmed the Word. Repentance and remission of sins was to be preached in His Name among all nations. Simon Peter's final charge was to *feed* My sheep, which he later interpreted himself as giving the sincere milk of the Word.[6] All this brings us back to the declared first purpose of the present work: "To promote and perpetuate the Spirit-filled preaching of the full-gospel message; and, secondly, To propagate the distinctive and characteristic qualities of the Spirit-filled preaching of the full-gospel message. . . ."

We believe that the distinctive testimony of the Pentecostal Revival is that we may "full often" experience this divine energy in our preaching through the supernatural gifts which are manifestations of the Spirit of God. Christ promised the power of the Spirit coming upon His witnesses. . . .

The Pentecostal Revival has caught the vision of the possibilities of the gifts of healing and working of miracles as ancillary to the preaching of the Word as they draw attention to its proclamation, and confirm its power. The Movement has also made much, some would say too much, of the gifts of diversities of tongues as a Pentecostal evidence of the presence and power of the Holy Spirit in the individual and the Church. There have been instances of a miraculous speaking of recognized languages as a sign to them that believe not. There have very often been utterances of a prophetic nature with a sincere desire to give it a proper place for speaking by the Spirit of God to exhortation, edification, and comfort. We are happy that these persist in spite of the fanatical twists that have been given the gift of prophecy in some quarters.

But we still seem to need the full appreciation and understanding of the supernatural gifts of the Spirit as they apply to this supreme task of preaching and teaching the Word of God. It is my hope that some ideas suggested in these studies may help toward that end. For myself I cannot be satisfied with a conception of gifts of the Spirit that keeps them separate from the preaching of the Word. Nor can I be satisfied with a conception of the ministry of the Word that excludes spiritual gifts as a vital part in it. Indeed, I believe that we should covet earnestly the best gifts for that very purpose.

And yet there remains the "more excellent way."[7] It is a breath-taking affirmation of the apostle that if we have not love our very best preaching, whether by consecrated natural ability or by supernatural gifts of the Spirit, even by tongues of men and of angels, can in the final analysis amount to nothing. Can this, to use the phraseology of the purpose of this work, be "Spirit-filled preaching" at all? I hesitate to reply. Can our preaching, and our use of all the gifts of the Spirit for that matter, be supernaturally inspired and yet fail at the last? The thought is staggering. Yet the Bible says so. I am reminded of Conybeare's penetrating observation that inspiration is not sanctification. To recognize this may help us in face of some cutting problems where apparently supernatural and evangelistic success has accompanied the unsanctified. As Spirit-filled preachers our commandment is plain: we are to follow after love and desire spiritual gifts. As for these others—the Day shall declare the secrets of every heart, and the Bible declares that for some the Judgment-Seat of Christ will have some startling and terrible verdicts.

I must close, and I can do so in no more appropriate way than by magnifying love as the supreme priority where any study on the gifts of the Spirit is concerned. Love itself is not a gift of the Spirit in the same way that we have been considering those gifts as the base of our varied ministries in the Body of Christ. Love is a *fruit* of the Spirit[8] and grows in the believers by abiding in Christ, the True Vine. It is a quality of character. I am persuaded that certain gifts of the Spirit, and not least the gift of tongues, fulfill a real function in the spiritual life by enlarging and liberating the soul in communion with God. Paul testified that in this way he edified himself. Therefore, they can aid character. For our present studies it is sufficient to insist that the final measure of truly Pentecostal power in any witness for Christ is not what the Spirit-filled believer can say, nor yet what he can do, nor even what he can see; it consists in the final anaylsis of what he *is*.

All comes to us through the grace of our Lord Jesus Christ. The ultimate purpose of spiritual gifts in the work of the ministry, and the ultimate purpose of world evangelization is the glory of God, the giver of all grace. Therefore of Him, and through Him, and to Him are all things: to whom be glory for ever.

Footnotes

1   1 Corinthians 14:39.
2   Carl Brumback, *What Meaneth This?* p. 85.
3   *Pentecost,* June, 1962.
4   Acts 1:8.
5   Mark 16:20.
6   Matthew 28:19, 20; Mark 16:20; Luke 24:47; John 21:17; 1 Peter 2:2.
7   1 Corinthians, chapters 12, 13, 14.
8   Galatians 5:22.

Part Three
Strategic/Practical Issues

Introduction

Spontaneous Strategy of the Spirit
Pentecostal Missionary Practices

L. Grant McClung, Jr.

Since pentecostals have done theology on the move and have tended to be more activist than reflective, they characteristically have been known as "doers." Indeed, missiologists, researchers, and other outside observers from the Church Growth Movement have not majored on pentecostal origins (history) or on what they believe (theology). That has been left to the historians, apologists, and theologians. Outside inquirers into the dynamics of the movement have been more interested in what pentecostals do (practice) and how they do it (methods).

Church Growth proponents such as Donald A. McGavran, C. Peter Wagner, Read, Monterroso, and Johnson, and Jim Montgomery have studied the Pentecostal Movement and have theorized reasons for its missionary success. Read, Monterroso, and Johnson's *Latin American Church Growth,* for example, highlighted such elements as worship, incorporation, and ministerial training (1969:313ff). C. Peter Wagner's celebrated *What Are We Missing?* (formerly titled *Look Out! The Pentecostals Are Coming)* added other dimensions of pentecostal growth such as aggressive evangelism, church multiplication, and faith healing (1973).

Pentecostal insiders have also set out to interpret their growth dynamics. Carl Brumback, for example, has isolated seven major reasons for the success of the Assemblies of God foreign missions program in his *Suddenly . . . From Heaven* (Gospel Publishing House). Among them are such factors as the Baptism in the Holy Spirit, Bible schools, literature, and indigenous leadership. Pentecostal missions are not without an adequate number of spokespersons who have proposed reasons for their amazing growth (Douglas 1975:242ff; McGavran 1972:142ff; De Wet 1981; Hughes 1981; Cho 1984:559ff).

71

A potpourri of growth factors could be cited. For the purposes of this overview, four broad characteristics of pentecostal missionary practices will be discussed: supernatural power; biblical pragmatism; committed personnel; and systematic propagation.

Supernatural Power

Holy Spirit emphasis. A point of disagreement between pentecostals and outside observers has been over the outsiders' tendency to find factors other than the direct and personal ministry of the Holy Spirit in the growth and success of pentecostal missions (Hodges 1977:35-36; Kane 1981:212).

Outside observers have said that pentecostals were too simplistic in attributing everything to the Holy Spirit. Pentecostals have said that the observers have placed too much emphasis on other factors. This tension has been discussed in another essay which describes the relationship of pentecostals to the Church Growth Movement (Part Four: Pentecostals and the Church Growth Movement).

It should be noted from the outset, however, that the very heartbeat of pentecostal missions is their experience with the power and Person of the Holy Spirit. This is the beginning point in understanding the "Pentecostal methodology for church growth" (McGavran 1972:144). "Pentecostal Christianity," says Larry Christenson, "does not merely assume the presence and activity of the Holy Spirit in the Church. It expects it, plans for it, and depends upon it" (Synan 1975:31).

Thomas F. Zimmerman has noted the dynamic of the Holy Spirit as foremost among reasons for the rise of the Pentecostal Movement (Synan 1975:5ff). Zimmerman, former General Superintendent of the Assemblies of God and the single most influential pentecostal leader on the world scene in the last two decades, sounded a warning to his colleagues at a 1978 National Church Growth Convention:

> Though we have grown in number, it would be foolish for us to assume that "having begun in the Spirit," we could ever substitute mass strength for the power and presence of God in our lives. Our strength is "not by might, nor by power, but by my Spirit, saith the Lord of hosts." (Jones 1978:v)

Following the steps of Andrew Murray, A.J. Gordon, A.B. Simpson, and others, pentecostals have emphasized the need for "enduement with power" but have understood the pentecostal Baptism of the Holy Spirit with the initial evidence of speaking in tongues to be that "gateway through which have poured thousands to the farthest reaches of the earth" (Brumback 1961:341).

The Holy Spirit is central to pentecostal missionary recruitment. Pentecostal literature is full of instances in which a person was recruited into cross-cultural ministry through supernatural means such as dreams, visions, prophecies, tongues and interpretation, and the like (see "Supernatural Recruitment" in the first essay under "Historical Perspectives").

Pentecostal worship. Another point that illustrates the element of supernatural power in pentecostal missionary practices is pentecostal worship. That pentecostal worship is a key growth factor is agreed upon by both inside and outside observers of the movement (Gee 1963:81ff; Wagner 1973:78). Pentecostal worship allows the participant to be involved in a personal and direct way with the manifestation of God among His people in the congregation (Epinay 1969:53-54; Walker 1981:91ff).

One of the central elements of pentecostal worship is the anointed preaching, which is more than an intellectual exercise. In the fashion of a dialogue, the pentecostal preacher challenges his followers and, in turn, receives back their approval of the message with a barrage of "Amens," or "Alleluias." Outside commentators of pentecostal worship have noted a distinct quality in pentecostal preaching. "A good Pentecostal preacher is well worth hearing," says researcher Christian Lalive d'Epinay, "for he has a genius for communication . . ." (1969:53).

Pentecostal preaching is "a Spirit-endowed preaching which is pungent and penetrating," says pentecostal leader Ray H. Hughes (1968:71). Hughes, who is well known for his effective communication in preaching, says that there is a "miracle element" present in pentecostal preaching which makes it a powerful evangelistic force (1981:149).

This is illustrated in an anecdote from T.B. Barratt, the pentecostal pioneer to Europe. In a letter to Barratt from Mrs. Anna Larssen Bjorner, she related the remarks of a Professor Amundsen, one of the most learned theologians in Denmark at the time. Amundsen told of a meeting held against the Mormons:

> None of the speeches seemed to have had any influence on the people. Suddenly, pastor Morten Larsen fell down from his seat on the floor with a great bang, and remained lying there. He was as heavy as lead, but suddenly he rose up and went direct to the pulpit, and held a sermon with such power and authority, that it cut the people to the marrow and bones, and one unbelieving journalist present said that he saw a bright light encircle the preacher's whole being. Mr. M. Larsen said, when relating the circumstance later on, that he had never experienced the like of it. He came to the meeting to listen, and had nothing to say; then God gave him words to speak, and this marvelous power and authority. (1927:184-185)

The dynamic power of pentecostal preaching and its relationship to church growth will need to be further researched and examined as a church growth factor. Dr. Paul Yonggi Cho, pastor of the 500,000 member Full Gospel Central Church in Seoul, Korea, has said that preaching is one of the key elements in the growth of his church. "To a pastor," he says:

> . . . the message being preached is like life. The right interpretation of the Word of God is the most important part of the message. How to interpret the Bible determines what to preach. What to preach determines the growth of the church. (1984:360)

Power to the people. Pentecostals have grown and are growing because they have taken their own personal experiences of God's power to their friends, neighbors, and family members. Their "theology of power" has led to what Hughes calls "supernatural evangelism" (1968:63). It is no secret among pentecostal missionaries that divine healing is an "evangelistic door-opener." Numerous accounts are typical of the story of a Chilean pentecostal pastor:

> One night—at that time I still had a little workshop and a lorry—a family came looking for me. The mother was quite paralysed in one leg, and they asked me to take her at once to the hospital. My lorry had broken down, and it would have taken me several hours to mend it. I said to them, "Listen, I will gladly take you to the hospital, but it will take time to mend the lorry. But I also know that we, the Pentecostalists, can cure your mother." They would not hear of it, so then I made a bargain with them: "We will mend the lorry, but while we are doing it, the brothers will come and pray. If by the time we are ready to go your mother is cured, will you all agree to be converted to the Lord?" They agreed . . . when the lorry was ready and we picked up the mother in our arms, she gave a cry and moved her leg. She was cured. Since then that family always comes to our services. (Epinay 1969:204-205)

Frodsham documents the ministry of missionary Douglas Scott who went from England to Le Havre in 1930. Scott reported, after nine years of ministry in healings and miracles, "Every new work is opened on the ministry of Divine Healing, for without the supernatural it would be impossible to get any interest created in the gospel message . . ." (1946:91-92).

For pentecostals, every healing and miracle, every spiritual manifestation, is a witness and testimony to the power of God (Damboriena 1969:121). Healing leads value to conversion and becomes in a sense, ". . . an earnest of the heavenly kingdom . . ." (Epinay 1969:207). Signs and wonders become evangelistic means whereby the message of the kingdom is actualized in "person-centered" deliverance (Glasser and McGavran 1983:119).

"Besides this," says Arthur F. Glasser, "Pentecostals were willing to tackle 'the dark side of the soul' and challenge the growing phenomenon of occultism, Satan worship, and demon possession" (1983:119-120). This head-on tackling of the enemy's power has become known in missiological circles as the "power encounter," "a dynamic confrontation between two different and opposite religions in which the two are pitted against each other in open confrontation of power" (De Wet 1981:81). Power encounters are found quite frequently in pentecostal missionary literature and form a central part of pentecostal missions strategy (De Wet 1981; Janes 1982:110ff; Humphrey 1967:44ff, 1968:69ff; Garlock 1974:51ff; Daniel 1978: Chapter 7).

Biblical Pragmatism

Evangelistic zeal. Evangelism and pentecostalism could be said to be synonymous terms. It is expected, especially in the Third World, that to be a pentecostal Christian one is to be a witness (Wagner 1973; Palmer 1974). Pentecostals feel an obligation to reach all men with the gospel and have traditionally felt, "One of the chief reasons for the existence of the Pentecostal movement is evangelism" (Conn 1956:28). Pentecostals see aggressive evangelism in the pages of the New Testament and feel that they must respond accordingly. It is the result of their literal interpretation of scripture and task-oriented approach to world missions. This leads them to:

> . . . examine Paul's strategy and observe him planting churches, training leaders, and trusting the Holy Spirit to equip and develop the church in its native setting. Therefore, it is this "biblical pragmatism" which characterizes Pentecostal missions strategy and leads Pentecostals to emphasize that which they find in Scripture in their missions approach. (Pomerville 1982:353)

Pentecostals have tended to be very practical and literal in their missions strategy. "If it is working, fine. If not, let's try something else." In Latin America, for example, leaders are chosen not on the basis of what they idealistically *intend* to produce someday but what they are *already* doing presently (Read, Monterroso, Johnson 1969:313ff; Enns 1967:117ff; Wagner 1973:89ff).

The pragmatic attitude of pentecostal leaders and mission executives is summed up in the incisive remarks of Church of God leader Cecil B. Knight as he addressed a group of missionaries and mission executives:

> It is time for us to take a hard look at where we are in our field endeavours. Research could reveal that the interest of the church and the kingdom of God would be better served by directing our attention and finances into other areas. Possibly, some nonproductive schools need either to be reorganized on a different premise or disbanded altogether. Some countries might need to assume greater responsibility of operation through a planned reduction of funds sent to that country. In some cases non-reproductive missionaries need to be informed of our expectations; and if decided improvement does not ensue, their termination might be advisable. This painful process of evaluation is essential if the·church is to keep pace with the need. (White 1978:4)

This calculated forethought, coupled with "a reckless penetration into unconverted lands and areas" (Warner 1978:141), has welded together a pragmatic approach which has resulted in a "world-embracing movement" (Damboriena 1969:viii).

Reaching the receptive. It is also a biblical pragmatism which has caused pentecostals to concentrate on the winnable, going where the harvest is ripe. Following Jesus' example, pentecostals have "looked on the fields" and have responded where there has been "the immediate possibility of a harvest" (McGavran 1977:42). Pentecostals have located where growth is happening, either by the leading of the Holy Spirit or by observing social and demographic trends. In Latin America, for example, Arno Enns found,

"They are alert to responsiveness and deploy their forces accordingly" (1971:237).

Most the the responsiveness, at least during the first fifty years of the movement, has been among the lower classes—masses of suffering, deprived, and oppressed humanity. This was apparent to pentecostal analysts themselves before it became a Church Growth dictum. Church of God historian Charles W. Conn commented at the movement's fifty-year mark that:

> The Pentecostal movement is comparatively young, but it is vital to the Christian faith of today. Its "grassroots" approach to the needs of man is reaching multitudes who have long been neglected by the larger and older church groups. Its simple form of worship answers the spiritual longing of masses of hungry souls. . . . (1956:37)

William R. Read has pointed out that when the Assemblies of God in Brazil have been criticized for being a church of the lower classes, "they take it as a compliment rather than a criticism. The majority of the people are close to the bottom of the social structure. The majority provides a tremendous field in which to work" (1965:141).

Committed Personnel

Leadership training. Coming as they have from mostly the lower strata of society, pentecostal leaders have tended to be loyal to the movement which has made them. They have responded faithfully to apprentice-style training because they were not accustomed to the elite practice of seminary level education. In many instances they have shunned the opportunity for higher level study because of the implications of worldly respectability and irrelevance to the grassroots (Wagner 1973:89ff). In most cases they have had no choice. In Brazil, for example:

> . . . only 10 percent of the fifty-five thousand pastors in the Assemblies of God have had even Bible-school training. Indeed, many of them are either illiterate or only semiliterate. They learned to read only after they became Christians. The only books they possess are a Bible and a hymnbook. (Kane 1981:105)

It should not be supposed, however, that leadership training is limited to a Sunday school level oral instruction (Epinay 1969:55). One of the earliest items on the pentecostal missions agenda was the establishment of Bible schools around the world. In many areas, pentecostals are actually the leaders in the number of Bible schools and even higher level training institutes. They have also established innovative decentralized training models such as TEE (Theological Education by Extension) (Brumback 1961:343; McGavran 1977:235; McGavran 1977:236-237; Calderon 1980:12ff). Pentecostals have effectively used imitation modeling training and other informal styles (Epinay 1969:55).

Your daughters shall prophesy. A large part of the dynamic growth of the Pentecostal Movement is due to its ability since its inception to mobilize and effectively deploy women into missionary service. Many pentecostal organizations have provisions for "Lady Ministers" or "Lady Evangelists" and will allow for their licensing. Interestingly, seven of the twelve members of the Azusa Street Credential Committee were women. These included Rachel Sizelove, Sister Evans, Sister Lum, Sister Jennie Moore (mistakenly called "Moon" by later writers), Sister Florence Louise Crawford, Sister Prince, and Phoebe Sargent. This committee selected and proved candidates for licensing (Corum 1981:6).

The pentecostal experience on the day of Pentecost broke the last barrier of separation between humanity, according to David J. du Plessis. On the day of Pentecost, he notes, Jesus "baptized the women exactly like the men, and I say for the exact same purpose as the men are baptized so the women are baptized" (Robeck 1983:6).

This was a great source of encouragement to Agnes LaBerge nee Ozman, the first recipient of the Baptism of the Holy Spirit in this century (Synan 1971:101). Within the backdrop of Scripture, she recalled that egalitarian experience some years later:

> As first former outpouring of the Spirit, the Word says: "Then returned they unto Jerusalem" the eleven are named, and it reads: "These all continued with one accord in supplication with the women and Mary the mother of Jesus" was present and among those who tarried for the promise of the Father, and received the Holy Spirit. That is a great encouragement to us women today. We know God who gave the woman the langauges spoken in them also is giving today. (n.d.:31)

Systematic Propagation

It was in 1974 at the International Congress on World Evangelization at Lausanne, Switzerland, when Dr. Ralph Winter delivered his seminal address depicting the cross-cultural dimensions in completing the task of world evangelization. In responding to Winter's paper, Philip Hogan, the Executive Director for Foreign Missions of the Assemblies of God stressed the utmost importance of the spontaneous working of the Holy Spirit in mission. Lest he be misunderstood, Hogan said, "Please understand me, I am not pleading for a kind of 'sitting where they sit and letting God happen' kind of attitude" (Douglas 1975:244). That they are simply "letting God happen" is often the estimation of pentecostal missions practices by outside observers.

Even though pentecostals are characterized by a "spontaneous strategy of the Spirit," they have not been without a plan. Their master plan has included numerous elements, methods and strategies for the systematic propagation of the movement. Among them are: indigenous churches, church planting, urban strategies, literature distribution, and missions stewardship.

Indigenous churches. Pentecostal missions have sought from the outset to develop indigenous churches. One of the leaders in this effort has been the Assemblies of God (Brumback 1961:341). Enns has observed that in Brazil the national church expanded so rapidly that it absorbed and controlled the parent organization. "The mission still makes its contributions," he found, "but the main thrust of the movement is unmistakably Brazilian, not only in leadership, but even more important, in forms" (1971:236).

One of the persons most responsible for this emphasis in the last forty years has been Assemblies of God missiologist Melvin L. Hodges whose book *The Indigenous Church* (Gospel Publishing House 1953) has become accepted as a standard work on the subject. A sequel, *The Indigenous Church and the Missionary,* was published by William Carey Library in 1978.

Church planting. After he returned from researching pentecostals in Brazil, William R. Read wrote, "This is not merely rapid growth, but a new kind of growth. The Pentecostals are engaged almost wholly in church planting" (1965:12). Pentecostals have believed that church planting is the "abiding fruit of world evangelism" and have measured their progress "by the development of mature congregations and the buildings which they erect" (Mitchell 1982:371). Evangelistic priority has been directed toward church planting (Wagner 1973:53-63). Evangelism has been understood not only as proclamation but in "persuading men and women to commit their lives to Christ and become members of a local church" and that these churches should multiply (Pomerville 1982:357: Champion 1968:118). This is "The Imperative of Church Planting" which Hodges sees as the fulfillment of the primary mission of the church:

> . . . to witness to men everywhere of the gospel of the grace of God
> and to plant churches which will multiply themselves and extend
> the witness of their living Lord. (1973:18)

Urban strategies. As the pentecostal message spread around the world, it was true to its "urban heritage" inherited from cosmopolitan Los Angeles in 1906 (Synan 1971:96). The movement had begun in a city and continued to be at home in urban areas. In many places of the Third World in particular, pentecostal growth and urbanization have seemed to develop side by side. This was Read's estimation, who found an urban predominance among pentecostals and concluded, "Their strength is in the city" (1965:219-221).

After a field visit, McGavran wrote of general "Impressions of The Christian Cause in India: 1978" and found that pentecostals were taking advantage of the migration from villages to cities. His *Church Growth Bulletin* report concluded that pentecostals were "buying up urban opportunities" (1979 January:247).

Prophets with a pen. Among some fifteen "Causes for the Initial Success of Pentecostalism" John Thomas Nichol has given strong emphasis to tabloid-sized newspapers and other early publications which became the "means of disseminating the message of Pentecostalism to the far-flung corners of the globe" (1966:60). Nichol has documented no less than thirty-four pentecostal periodicals which came into existence between 1900 and 1908:

> The pioneering effort in American Pentecostal journalism
> was Charles Fox Parham's *The Apostolic Faith,* which appeared
> just before the turn of the century. It was published twice a month
> and distributed freely. In the next few years other papers with

the same masthead appeared, originating from such places as Los Angeles, and Portland, Oregon. (1966:61)

Of the issues which came from Los Angeles, there were 5,000 copies of Volume 1, Number 1 which was dated September, 1906. The last issue, Volume II, Number 13 was dated May, 1908, less than two years following (Corum 1981:4). Though its circulation time was short, the impact of *The Apostolic Faith* (Los Angeles) was far-reaching. One of its columns, for example, reported, "A brother received the Pentecost by hearing of God's work through the paper" (Corum 1981 Volume 1, No. 6:1).

Rachel A. (Harper) Sizelove was one of the original Azusa Street alumni. She kept a complete collection of the Azusa Street papers, *The Apostolic Faith,* and later sent them to her nephew Fred Corum for compiling (Corum was the editor of another pentecostal paper called *Word and Work*). In her letter of March 15, 1934 (with which she sent the original thirteen copies of *The Apostolic Faith*) she noted the power of the pentecostal message in print. Referring to the letterhead from the Azusa Street Mission she said:

> I think it would be nice to have a picture of the letterhead they used in the beginning of Pentecost, to be printed just above the picture of the Azusa Street Mission, for God did get glory out of those letters. For, when so many just saw the top of the letter, conviction would seize them for their baptism, and the power of God would fall upon them, Hallelujah! (Corum 1981:1-2)

Numerous testimonies could match that of J.H. Ingram who was recruited into the Pentecostal Movement by a pentecostal magazine. He recalls:

> Someone . . . came our way giving out copies of a little paper called "The Church of God Evangel." I got one and began to read, and saw where they had the same blessings we enjoyed, only in a fuller measure. So I subscribed for the paper, which has been coming to my home ever since. This was in 1919, a year before I received the Holy Ghost. (1938:11-12)

Ingram subsequently became one of the leading spokesmen for world missions in the Church of God and made numerous around-the-world trips in order to bring independent movements into his denomination (Conn 1959:28-29).

Frodsham recounts a related incident, told by a reporter from West Africa:

> A most gracious outpouring of the Spirit has come to Nigeria, on the West Coast of Africa. It came through the sending of copies of the *Pentecostal Evangel* to some Christian workers in Nigeria. They sought and received the Baptism in the Spirit. . . . Pentecostal churches sprang up everywhere as a result of the manifestations of the power of God. (1946:171)

In more recent times, Read has attributed a massive literature program as one of the elements in the phenomenal growth of the Assemblies of God in Brazil.

He notes that "tons" of evangelical literature and 100,000 copies of the Assemblies of God hymnbook are sold every year. In the hymnbooks, for example, "some of the most important forms of indigenous music can be seen . . ." (1965:167-168).

Such has been the power and influence of pentecostal literature. Though not publishing analytical and systematized theologies and not producing formal theological works, the pentecostals have not been silent when it came to popular literature read by the common man. On the other hand, much more scholarly literature has been produced than what might normally be supposed (see the Annotated Bibliography).

Missions stewardship. Finally, among numerous other elements contributing to the systematic propagation of the movement, pentecostals have given generously to the cause of foreign missions. Though not generally people of means, pentecostals have given sacrificially because there was a cause. In the very first issue of *The Apostolic Faith* from Azusa Street, for example, the following account of sacrificial giving was recorded:

> When Pentecostal lines are struck, Pentecostal giving commences. Hundreds of dollars have been laid down for the sending of missionaries and thousands will be laid down. No collections are taken for rent, no begging for money. (Corum 1981, Volume 1, No. 1:1)

By the 1980s those hundreds and thousands have turned into multiplied millions. The January 1984 issue of *Mountain Movers* (from the Assemblies of God Divisions of Foreign Missions) was devoted to an explanation of "How Your Dollars Affect the World." The periodical explained how Assemblies of God foreign missions giving had increased from an annual amount of $389,111 in 1939 to more than $48,000,000 in 1982 (just 43 years later)! Their formula was:

Prayer
+ Missionary work
+ *Support dollars*
= Souls saved

They noted that twenty-five local churches gave more than $100,000 each to foreign missions in 1982 and closed with the following challenge:

> If each of the 1,879,182 persons in the U.S. Assemblies of God gave $1 more per month than they are presently giving to foreign missions, it would increase the 1982 total ($48.5 million) by $22.6 million or 46 percent.
>
> All of the above illustrates a simple truth: when all of us do a little, it amounts to a lot. Your dollars do affect the world.

Pentecostals have been doing the job because they have put their money where their heart is and God has blessed their missions stewardship.

Numerous elements have accounted for the unprecedented spread of the pentecostals into all the world—above all the sovereign working and blessing of God. Pentecostals have followed and used a "spontaneous strategy of the Spirit" with supernatural power, biblical pragmatism, committed personnel, and systematic propagation.

Having done theology "on the move," pentecostals have become known as "doers." Consequently, outside observers, particularly from the Church Growth Movement, have wanted to know what pentecostal missionaries do and how they do it. To provide biblical foundations to that answer, Melvin Hodges formulated this response which beame part of a literary forum called *Eye of The Storm,* Donald A. McGavran, Editor (Word Books 1972).

7
A Pentecostal's View of Mission Strategy

Melvin L. Hodges*

Pentecostals have their roots imbedded in *The Book*. They strive constantly to follow the New Testament in every aspect of faith and practice. It follows that Pentecostal missiology should be based on biblical doctrine, experience and methodology.

The Role of the Holy Spirit in Mission Strategy

Pentecostals are so called because they believe that the Holy Spirit will come to believers today as He came to the waiting disciples on the day of Pentecost. They recognize the Holy Spirit as the divine Agent of the Deity in the earth, without whom God's work of redemption through Jesus Christ cannot be realized. Since there can be no effective mission to reconcile men to God without the Holy Spirit, it follows that His leadership must be sought and His empowering presence just be in evident manifestation if there is to be any success in carrying out the Church's mission. Beyond His work in regenerating the believer, the Holy Spirit comes as a baptism to empower the believer for his role as a witness (Acts 1:5, 8); his body becomes a temple of the Holy Spirit (1 Corinthians 6:19); and joined with other believers, he forms part of the Church, which is the temple of God for the habitation of God by the Spirit (Ephesians 2:21, 22). This marvelous privilege is not reserved for the spiritual elite but is the heritage of every believer, regardless of age, sex, or social station. Even the servants (slaves) shall prophesy (Acts 2:17, 18). The Holy Spirit is poured out on the common man, and he finds an important place

---

* Melvin L. Hodges began his missionary career with the Assemblies of God in 1936 in El Salvador. Later, he supervised their missionary efforts in twenty-six countries of Latin America and the West Indies from 1954 to 1974. A prolific writer, Hodges has authored scores of missions articles and a number of books including *The Indigenous Church,* and *A Theology of The Church and Its Mission: A Pentecostal Perspective.*

in the body of Christ according as the Holy Spirit grants His gifts and enablements (1 Corinthians 12:4-13).

According to these concepts, the spiritual life of the believer and the activities of the Church are to be realized on a supernatural plane. The Church is to be directed by the Spirit; believers are to be led by the Spirit. The supernatural Presence should be manifested in healings, miracles, and answers to prayer. Is not Jesus the same today? Inspirational utterance will be given by the Spirit for the encouragement of the Church. Divine direction will be received through a Spirit-guided administration. The Holy Spirit is the Chief Strategist of the Church in evangelism and mission. Human planning is valid only as it reflects the Divine Mind. The Holy Spirit has a strategy for each age and place. It is the Church's responsibility to discern this and to put the strategy into effect. The apostle Peter probably was not planning to evangelize the Gentiles, but in prayer the Holy Spirit showed him the next move and commanded him to go. He found himself shortly after in the house of Cornelius with the Gentiles turning to Christ and receiving the gift of the Spirit (Acts 10:19, 44-48). The church at Antioch would doubtless have desired to retain Paul and Barnabas as their chief ministers, but the Holy Spirit said: "Separate me Barnabas and Saul for the work whereunto I have called them" (Acts 13:2).

This prominence given to the role of the Holy Spirit should not lead us to believe that the human role is one of complete passivity. There is need for the engaging of all our mental, physical, material and spiritual powers in the planning and execution of God's work. Once the will of God is determined, we should set forth as did the apostles in an active effort to fulfill the divine commission. As the Holy Spirit corrected details in their planning as they went along, so we may also expect His continued guidance as we launch forth (Acts 16:6-10). As the Holy Spirit directs the strategy, and we respond, converts will be won and churches planted, as occurred in the apostles' ministry.

The Role of the Church in Mission Strategy

Since the Scriptures teach that the Church is the Body of Christ and the temple of the Holy Spirit—the Body that Christ directs and the temple through which the Holy Spirit manifests himself—Pentecostals see the missionary task as that of winning non-Christian men and women, whether they be civilized or pagan, to Christ, so that they can experience regeneration and become vital members in the living Body of Christ. Each local church (where two or three are gathered together in His name) becomes a living cell of the Body of Christ, and God's agent for the bringing of the message of reconciliation to its community. Therefore church-planting and church growth (cell multiplication) are of supreme importance in the Christian mission. Whatever other good things the Church may do, its success in promoting the Kingdom of God must be measured by the number of people it can bring into vital relationship with Christ and the number of local units of the Body of Christ that it can produce.

Strategy for Evangelism and Church Growth

Pentecostal methodology for church growth emphasizes the importance of the individual believer's response to the Holy Spirit. Every Christian is called to be a witness and, upon receiving the gift of the Spirit, is empowered for this service (Acts 1:8). True converts do not have to be urged to witness, but overflow with zeal to share their experience with others. They do need to be taught and guided in order that their witness may be effective. Believers understand intuitively that as the "good seed of the Kingdom" they should multiply themselves by bringing others to a knowledge of Christ. This witness assumes many forms:

Local churches start new churches. In general practice, local churches make a systematic effort to reach their community. Lay workers are sent to open outstations with the expectation that they will develop into churches. When this is accomplished the new church in turn sends out its own local workers to open still other outstations. So the church grows by cell multiplication.

Laymen develop into pastors and evangelists. Most pastors begin their ministry as laymen in a local congregation, often by taking the responsibility for opening an outstation. Thus they receive practical "on-the-job" training under the supervision of a pastor and the local church board. As the outstation develops into a church, the lay worker may become a full-time pastor. Many attend a Bible school for a period of basic training in Christian doctrine and church administration, etc., but they would doubtless still be considered as laymen by some who insist on a highly trained clergy as the only qualified church leaders. Nevertheless, many of these men have been outstandingly endowed by the Spirit with gifts for ministry. They have the advantage of being close to their people and identified with the local culture. Without question they are as qualified as were many of the "elders" of the Primitive church.

This work of developing outstations is supplemented by the forming of *branch Sunday schools* in the outstations. Also there are often organized efforts of *house-to-house visitation* by the members, both for the purpose of personal witness and for the *distribution of appropriate literature.* The object is to win men and women to Christ and bring them into the local church. *Street meetings,* where permitted, are a common and fruitful practice, and attract new people to the churches.

Emphasis on indigenous principles of self-propagation, self-government and self-support. In those cases where the Church has made notable advances in Latin America, it will be noted that without exception the Church has assumed the responsibility for its own decisions and has found within itself the resources necessary to maintain its operation and advance without dependence on foreign personnel or funds. There is a keen sense of responsibility among the national Christians for evangelizing their own people. There is an absence of "foreignness" in the atmosphere, the Church being rooted in the nation itself and prospering in its climate.

Mass evangelism. Pentecostals are interested in reaching the masses. Great evangelistic campaigns have been held in the large cities of Latin America, sometimes with scores of thousands in attendance. Emphasis is on the good news of salvation and healing. Such a campaign was held in San Salvador (El Salvador) in 1956. Thousands attended the open-air worship, standing during the entire service. At the end of four months, 375 new converts were selected for baptism. These all had attended a series of classes for new converts. At the beginning of the campaign, the Assemblies of God had one small organized church in the city. At the end of the year there were twelve congregations, either launched or already organized as churches. Within five years the numbers attending the churches or the branch Sunday schools had reached seven or eight; and now, ten years after the campaign, the number of churches in the city has increased to about forty. The campaign gave this church growth its initial impetus; and the faithful, sacrificial work of pastors and laymen produced the multiplication of churches experienced after the initial campaign had terminated.

Literature, radio, and television evangelism. Literature has become an increasingly important instrument of evangelism. The use of radio is widespread, and television is gaining recognition as an effective medium.

Pentecostals believe that the gospel is for the masses and that it is God's will today, as in New Testament times, that multitudes should believe on the Lord, that the Word of God should increase and the number of disciples multiply (Acts 5:14; 6:7).

Flexibility of strategy. Pentecostals would agree with Dr. McGavran that the strategy for missions must be kept flexible. Even so, certain principles are inviolable. The message we preach, the spiritual new birth of individuals, the control of the Holy Spirit in the believer's life and in the activities of the Church, the responsibility of Christians to form themselves into churches and to multiply themselves—all of these things are basic and must not be modified. The approach, however, must vary with the widely differing opportunities. If a particular tribe or section of society is "ripe for the harvest," the Church must be sufficiently flexible to find the means for taking advantage of the occasion. The Pentecostal's deep conviction that the guidance of the Holy Spirit must be sought for each situation makes for flexibility and ensures variety in method.

In one place an evangelistic campaign may be the means for opening the area to the gospel. Elsewhere the beginning will be made by opening a small outstation in a home, following up with literature saturation. Again the healing of a paralytic, or the restoring of sight to a blind person through the prayer of faith may be the means of stirring interest and founding the church. Pentecostal believers pray for their sick neighbors and lead them to Christ. The deliverance of an alcoholic or a narcotic addict may open the door in a community. Admittedly, all this may seem foreign to those who are accustomed to an institutional approach to the mission of the Church, but to Pentecostals such happenings are to be expected and are entirely in accord with the New Testament concept of the Church's mission.

Pentecostal Strategy Results in Church Growth

The Pentecostal movement has made rapid strides in its world-wide outreach since its humble beginnings at the turn of the century. Although pentecostals have been labeled the *third force* in modern Christianity, they see themselves not as a "third force" or a "fringe movement" but as New Testament Christians returning to the simplicity, central truths, and vitality of the Apostolic Era. Pentecostals form a vital part of evangelical Christianity round the world. Without dispute, the Pentecostals stand at the front of the Evangelical[1] advance in Latin America.

One of the outstanding examples may be observed in Brazil. The Assemblies of God of Brazil began when two Swedish missionaries went to that country in 1910 in response to a definite guidance of the Holy Spirit. Beginning their work in Belem, a city at the mouth of the Amazon, they established a church which spread rapidly throughout the country until every city, town, and most hamlets had an Assemblies of God congregation or at least a sign of their foothold in the community. Today, estimates of membership in the Assemblies of God churches in Brazil is placed at one million or more. Probably there is an equal number to be found in the churches of sister Pentecostal organizations throughout the country. William Read, a United Presbyterian missionary, estimates that the Assemblies of God membership in Brazil is increasing at the rate of 250 percent every ten years.[2]

In Chile, the indigenous Pentecostal churches, represented by the Methodist Pentecostal Church and sister groups which grew out of a pentecostal revival in the Methodist Church early in this century, have now grown until they dwarf in size the church from which they emerged. It is estimated that somewhere between 80 percent and 90 percent of all Evangelicals in Chile are Pentecostal, with a combined constituency of all pentecostal groups in the country reaching a million or more. This has been accomplished without the help of missionary personnel or foreign funds, except for the guidance that Doctor Hoover, the Methodist missionary, gave in the beginning. Representatives of these groups are to be found everywhere in Chile; and like the Assemblies of God of Brazil, they have gone beyond their own borders in missionary effort, so that churches affiliated with them are now found in neighboring countries.

In passing it should be mentioned that Pentecostals also take the lead in several other Latin American countries, such as Peru, El Salvador, Guatemala, and the Dominican Republic.

Pentecostal Strategy and Social Concern

There are those who contend that the Pentecostals' view of Christian mission is too narrow, and that emphasis on evangelism and personal conversion leaves much to be desired in the area of men's physical and economic needs. To this, Pentecostals answer: Let us put first things first!

There is nothing as important as getting men's hearts right with God. The center must be put right before the periphery can be corrected. To try to remedy peripheral conditions leaving the heart unchanged is useless and deceiving. When a man is truly converted, he seeks a better life for himself and for his family. One has only to observe the families of Evangelical Christians over a period of a few years to note that spiritual conversion leads to improvement in every aspect of a convert's life.

When the Evangelical community gathers strength, the Christians themselves show concern for the betterment of their own people. For example, many of the larger Pentecostal churches establish day schools. In San Salvador, an Assemblies of God church has established a large school which now includes a junior college. This is entirely a local effort. In Brazil the churches have established orphanages and homes for elderly people. The larger churches have commissaries to aid the poor. All is carried on in an unassuming way, without fanfare, and with a minimum of outside help. The image of the Christian witness is not distorted by the political and cultural implications involved in a "rich America helping an underprivileged people."

It is interesting here to note the observations of William Read:

> Ceaseless migrations from rural to urban areas are occurring in Brazil. . . . Continuous uprooting and transplanting of a restless people driven by cultural changes of all types—inflation, drought, industrialization, illness, illiteracy, and idolatry—have created a great sociological void. . . . Of all the Evangelical Churches in Brazil, only the Assemblies and their sister Pentecostal Churches are in a position to take full advantage of the sociological receptivity of a people in revolution.[3]

And again:

> The Assemblies of God is a Church of and for the masses, and as long as it continues to minister to their needs it will grow. . . . There is a social revolution in Brazil today, and all governments are certain to make better and better provision for the common man. . . . The Assemblies under God are becoming the greatest upward movement of lower-class people in all Latin America. They are rising everywhere into new levels of character and godliness. God is blessing them with income, education and status.[4]

Pentecostal Strategy and Eschatology

It should be observed that Pentecostals do not expect all the world to become Christian through the efforts of evangelism. Rather, they see that the remedy of many of earth's ills must await the Second Advent of the King of kings, for which they earnestly pray and wait. His coming will solve the problems of the social order. Until then, Christians must faithfully witness by life and word, and prepare that body of transformed men which is the very salt of the earth in this present age and which will form the nucleus of the redeemed race in the coming Kingdom. Converts must be won, churches planted and multiplied; Christian leaders called, prepared and sent forth until every soul on earth shall have had an opportunity to hear God's message of love and redemption in Christ Jesus.

Footnotes

1 Latin American Christians dislike the term "Protestant," preferring to be known as "Evangelicals" without making a distinction between liberal and conservative theologies as in the case in North America.

2 William R. Read, *New Patterns of Church Growth in Brazil* (Grand Rapids: William R. Eerdmans. 1965), p. 142.

3 Read, 1965:130.

4 Read, 1965:143.

"Spontaneous, free-flowing" worship will often surface as one of the chief reasons for the phenomenal growth of pentecostalism. Forceful and dynamic preaching is an integral factor both in the pentecostal worship service and outside the four walls of church buildings. Whether on the street, in parks, in large stadiums, or within church facilities, pentecostal preaching has been a key element in pentecostal growth. The author of this contribution, Ray H. Hughes, is known as a master pulpiteer and skillful preacher of the Word. His article is taken from his book, *Pentecostal Preaching* (Pathway Press, 1981).

8
The Uniqueness of Pentecostal Preaching

Ray H. Hughes*

Introduction

Pentecostal preaching is so unique in its nature and so encompassing in its power that no word other than "supernatural" seems adequate to describe it. . . .

Thus, the word "supernatural" is used herein to refer to signs, wonders, healings, and miracles such as happened during New Testament times.

Not only will pentecostal preaching produce the same miraculous results as those recorded in the New Testament, it will always produce them in keeping with the spirit and the tone of the New Testament. It is precisely for this reason that pentecostals emphasize so strongly a belief in the "whole Bible, rightly divided."

Three points should be reiterated here: (1) True pentecostal preaching always centers in the Word; (2) Pentecostal preaching always exalts Jesus Christ; and (3) Pentecostal preaching is always directed and empowered by the Holy Spirit. So long as these three basic guidelines are kept in perspective, one need have little fear of fanaticism or heresy. . . .

Pentecostal Preaching Convicts of Sin and Produces Revival

Pentecostal preaching is not predicated upon human assumptions. Rather, it builds upon the Word, according to the leading of the Holy Spirit, and depends upon the Spirit to convict and bring miraculous results.

---

* Ray H. Hughes has been one of the leading pentecostal world leaders since the movement's half-century mark. He has been twice elected as General Overseer of the Church of God (Cleveland, Tennessee) and has served on the Advisory Committee of the World Pentecostal Conference for many years. Currently, he is the president of the Church of God School of Theology in Cleveland, Tennessee, and the president of the National Association of Evangelicals (NAE).

Such has happened over and again in this author's personal ministry. Even while the message was in progress, men or women have been known to cry out, to stand, and to run forward to an altar of prayer, conviction too heavy for them to wait. Many times these individuals—so the author learned subsequently— were people thought to be either in fellowship with God or totally immune to the invitation. A pastor or some friend would say afterwards, "I never would have suspected he or she was struggling with such a burden."

These matters are not humanly known; they are discerned of the Holy Spirit. They illustrate the miracle element in Pentecostal preaching. They remind us that wherever and whenever there is pentecostal preaching, revival is possible.

Pentecostal Preaching Moves Men and Women to
Be Baptized With the Holy Ghost

Throughout our world there is renewed interest in the person and work of the Holy Spirit. While some men propose to instruct seekers in receiving the baptism of the Holy Ghost, and others emphasize the human elements of submission and obedience, let it be noted that the New Testament gives preaching a prominent role in pentecostal outpourings.

At the conclusion of his pentecostal sermon, when Peter was asked what his hearers should do, he answered: "Repent, and be baptized every one of you in the name of Jesus Christ for the remission of sins, and ye shall receive the gift of the Holy Ghost. For the promise is unto you, and to your children, and to all that are afar off, even as many as the Lord our God shall call" (Acts 2:38, 39).

At the home of Cornelius, what is often referred to as the Gentile Pentecost took place. While Peter was in the middle of a pentecostal sermon, "the Holy Ghost fell on all them which heard the word" (Acts 10:44).

While one would not wish to imply that it is only during preaching that men and women receive the Baptism—both Scripture and experience confirm that people receive the Baptism of Holy Spirit under varying circumstances—neither should one forget that such is a New Testament pattern. A powerful, anointed sermon centers the listener's heart and soul on things eternal; it points one heavenward; it stirs hope and faith; and, quite often, it inspires one to believe and accept the promised gift of the Holy Spirit.

Time and again this author has seen the Holy Ghost fall upon believers during the message, just as He fell upon believers while Peter spoke at the home of Cornelius. A case in point was during a message delivered at a camp meeting in Doraville, Georgia. Spontaneously the Spirit swept over the audience and some believers received the Baptism of the Holy Ghost while they were in their seats; some stood with upraised hands and received the gift; while others received the Spirit en route to the altar. Forty souls received the Baptism of the Holy Ghost in that service. The experience of Pentecost was repeated. The Holy Ghost fell on them as on believers at the beginning (Acts 11:15).

Another divine interruption was experienced as this author spoke at the Roberto Clemente Coliseum in San Juan, Puerto Rico. More than two hundred received the gift of the Holy Ghost in a single service! Pentecost indeed!

Pentecostal Preaching Produces Faith

Christian faith, saving faith, is of divine origin. Not only is this truth set forth explicitly in the Scriptures—"For by grace are ye saved through faith; and that not of yourselves: it is the gift of God" (Ephesians 2:8)—but it is likewise verified through human experience. . . .

It was the Word which sparked our faith. We may not have been converted during the preaching of a sermon, or even in a church building, but it was the Word—what Paul referred to as "the power of God unto salvation" (Romans 1:16)—which planted the seed of faith; and it was the Holy Spirt who inseminated that seed and brought forth a new creation in Christ Jesus.

So it is with other manifestations of faith. The Word produces faith, and there are few moments when, or few places where, the Word is more piercingly sent forth than during an anointed, pentecostal sermon.

During one of this author's messages in Pacific Palisades, California, the Spirit hovered over the audience. It was evident that God was present to do some miraculous things among us. As the people lifted their hands toward heaven, they were urged to receive healing. A woman in the rear portion of the tabernacle shouted in excitement. After a time of rejoicing in the Lord, the service continued. After the service a young lady made her way to the pulpit and asked if I had heard someone scream in the back of the tabernacle.

"I certainly did."

"That was my mother," she said. "Mother had a growth on her side the size of your fist. She lifted her hands to worship and then felt for the growth and it was gone."

God confirmed His Word with a miracle of healing. The woman believed and it happened. Faith was created by the Word. God "sent His word, and healed" (Psalm 107:20).

Pentecostal preaching has always produced miraculous results.

A beautiful example of the power of preaching to evoke faith is seen during the first missionary journey of Paul and Barnabas to Lystra.

"And there sat a certain man at Lystra, impotent in his feet, being a cripple from his mother's womb, who never had walked: the same heard Paul speak: who steadfastly beholding him, and perceiving that he had faith to be healed, said with a loud voice, stand upright on thy feet. And he leaped and walked" (Acts 14:8-10).

When one reads this passage carefully, at least two miraculous things are seen to be taking place. While Paul is preaching, the man's faith builds to a peak: "the same heard Paul speak" (verse 9). This was faith of an unusual nature. It was divine faith, immediate faith, miracle faith produced by the Word. At the same time, Paul perceived the man had faith to believe. Paul discerned this supernaturally, through the Holy Spirit—not with human ingenuity, not with human understanding, but through and by the power of the Holy Ghost. The two miracles coalesced. They merged into a triumphant moment that brought immediate results. Though he had never walked before, the man leaped to his feet and walked.

Pentecostal preaching produces just such faith today.

It is a rewarding experience to see faces light up with expectation as faith is created by the preached Word. One can sense that listeners believe the Word and are willing to act upon it.

It has been this author's pleasure to see faith come alive in many hearts during the preaching of God's Word. One such occasion was while ministering during a camp meeting at Beckley, West Virginia, on the "Gifts of the Spirit." I perceived that a woman in the audience had faith to receive the Baptism. When I paused to recognize her desire, the Spirit fell upon her as she sat in the pew.

It is through faith produced by the Word that signs and miracles follow pentecostal preaching. These signs, in turn, confirm the Word just as Jesus insisted they would in the Gospel of Mark. Miracles, signs, wonders, mighty works—these are not in themselves the objectives of pentecostal preaching; but they are evidences, proofs, witnesses to the power and authenticity of the eternal Word.

Pentecostal Preaching Confronts Demonic Powers

This world is in rebellion against God. There can be no compromise between righteousness and wickedness. While one sees evidence of this conflict on many levels, none is more clearly exposed than when the anointed preacher speaks as God's voice. For this reason the pentecostal minister may as well recognize that true preaching will inevitably conflict with entrenched powers and interests of this world.

Anointed pentecostal preaching places the man of God in an unusual position. He feels the message burning in his heart, he knows what the Spirit bids him say, he may even realize that his words are being opposed by some outside power or being; nevertheless, the man of God preaches. He speaks forth the commandments and the directives of God and leaves the spiritual confrontation to the Holy Spirit. This explains why the preacher sometimes finds himself in a conflict he did not realize was coming, or why emergencies are both created and taken care of without his conscious knowledge.

One familiar example of this is found in the seventh chapter of Acts, occasioned by the preaching of Stephen. This original deacon of the Church was powerfully anointed of the Holy Spirit. Stephen applied God's message white-hot to those who heard him, and it was the cutting sharpness of what he said that disturbed their evil hearts. Note the mob's reaction: "When they heard these things, they were cut to the heart, and they gnashed on him with their teeth. . . . Then they cried out with a loud voice, and stopped their ears, and ran upon him with one accord, And cast him out of the city, and stoned him" (Acts 7:54, 57, 58).

Yet another example concerns Paul's preaching at Ephesus and the resulting conflict between the gospel and the silversmiths (Acts 19:23-41). Paul's preaching impacted the city so dramatically that the silversmiths were hurt financially. Demetrius, apparently the leader of the silversmiths, called together other members of the guild, saying, "Not only this our craft is in danger to be set at nought; but also that the temple of the great goddess Diana should be despised, and her magnificence should be destroyed, whom all Asia and the world worshipeth. And when they heard these sayings, they were full of wrath" (Acts 19:27, 28).

We understand that there is but one God and that the goddess Diana was, as are all idols, but the work of men's hands. At the same time, we know demonic powers become involved in idol worship and that Satan stirs up this type of opposition because he opposes any worship of the true God. "We wrestle not against flesh and blood, but against principalities, against powers, against the rulers of the darkness of this world, against spiritual wickedness in high places" (Ephesians 6:12).

Pentecostal preaching—anointed preaching which is empowered by the Holy Spirit—will stir up opposition. It will upset economic and social orders. It will conflict with established patterns and habits. Such is to be expected. However, the pentecostal preacher must not cease preaching. This is what the hireling would do. God's man must continue to proclaim the Word, and this preaching will bring victory of a miraculous nature.

Pentecostal Preaching Produces Godly Fear and Respect for the Church

The Bible makes it clear, following the death of Ananias and Sapphira, that "great fear came upon all the church, and upon as many as heard these things. And by the hands of the apostles were many signs and wonders wrought among the people" (Acts 5:11, 12).

While it is not our purpose here to give a rationale for signs and miracles, it does seem obvious that God uses them as one method by which to enter human lives. Such marvelous things have taken place in the wake of pentecostal preaching that an entire town has become stirred.

The effectiveness of such preaching is not in words alone, but rather in the listener's perception of what God is saying and doing at the moment. When the Word is preached uncompromisingly, when the Word goes forth with power and under the anointing of the Holy Spirit, people will develop an awesome respect for things spiritual. This is the soil from which comes miracles and transformed lives.

Pentecostal Preaching Is Confirmed by Operation of Spiritual Gifts

In writing to the church at Corinth, Paul instructed believers to "covet earnestly the best gifts" (1 Corinthians 12:31). When one places this statement alongside what follows in chapter thirteen—Paul's "more excellent way"—and when these two passages are viewed within the context of the first part of chapter twelve and with chapter fourteen, balance is achieved. Paul did not wish the church to ignore or forget spiritual gifts, as some tend to do today, nor did he wish spiritual gifts to become an end in themselves—in fact, Paul clearly profiles the error of the latter choice. Instead, Paul wished the church to realize that the operation of spiritual gifts goes hand in hand with the preaching and teaching of God's Word.

As noted earlier, a key ingredient in pentecostal preaching is prophecy. Under the anointing of the Holy Spirit, God's men *prophesy*—they "speak forth"—the things which are of God. Prophecy is a key operation of the Holy Spirit, one of the nine spiritual gifts (1 Corinthians 12:8-10). Prophecy is a gift which may be further confirmed by the operation of other gifts, all of which should be accepted as the natural result of pentecostal preaching. . . .

Summary

Since it is the gospel which is "the power of God unto salvation" (Romans 1:16), and since God has chosen through "the foolishness of preaching" (1 Corinthians 1:21) to bring men and women to a knowledge of the truth, it follows that those who are called of God should give top priority to preaching.

It is this emphasis which *Pentecostal Preaching* has tried to make. Preaching the Gospel of Jesus Christ is not merely a task, not just something which one may or may not do: It is a divine commission, with heavy responsibility and with eternal rewards.

Equally important is our emphasis that a man preaches as he ought—a man preaches with power and authority, with honor and success—only when he follows the New Testament pattern. This means pentecostal preaching as demonstrated on the Day of Pentecost and throughout the Book of Acts. The New Testament pattern of preaching means pentecostal preaching which is precise, productive, and prophetic; it is unique preaching which produces the same signs and wonders, the same miracles and revivals, the same marvelous results as found described in the Book of Acts.

The preacher's task in today's world has not changed: God has not changed. God still calls men to engage in conflict with evil: He still equips men with the power and the authority of His Spirit to do the job. Reason dictates that if one of these sentences be true, then the other must also be true. If our task today is the same as that which the New Testament church faced, then our equipment and spiritual power must be the same.

The man of God who is called and anointed of the Holy Spirit, and who will faithfully yield to the leading of the Spirit, has the same commission and enablement as was given to the disciples of old.

Simply stated, this has been our thesis. It may not be one with which every reader agrees and it may not be one fully explained, but it is one which is the honest opinion of this author's heart.

Just as in the Book of Acts and within the New Testament church, pentecostal preaching today will produce signs and wonders. It will change lives and bring revival. Pentecostal preaching is totally adequate for doing the task God has commissioned us to do in this day.

One of the abiding marks of the Pentecostal Movement has been its success in becoming indigenous in leadership and form on its many overseas mission fields. In addition, most North American and European based pentecostal churches have more adherents overseas than at home. Perhaps the best-known product of pentecostal missions has been the ministry of Paul Yonggi Cho in Seoul, Korea. In this article, excerpted from *Global Church Growth* (March-April 1984), Pastor Cho gives an inside view of a local church with 500,000 members.

9
The Secret Behind the World's Biggest Church

Paul Yonggi Cho*

Church growth has become one of the most noteworthy subjects in Christianity today. Before 1980, individual revival movements took place with such prominent figures as Billy Graham and Oral Roberts. More recently it appears that the individual revival movements have abated and revivals have burst forth in the local church. Each year has had its specific move of God. The healing movement in the 1960s; the charismatic movement in the 1970s; the church growth movement of the 1980s.

Following are four important steps to church growth which I have been teaching for the past years in overseas crusades.

Step One: Prayer

It is utterly impossible for a pastor to expect his church to grow without prayer. Many ministers today think the motivating power of church growth is in a particular system, or in a particular organizational structure. This is a wrong opinion. The motivating power behind church growth is fervent prayer.

Upon graduation from Bible school, I first pioneered a church in Bulkwang-dong, a suburb of Seoul. At that time, Bulkwang-dong was a very remote place where foxes slinked around at night. During the summer, more frogs than people came to the church services. Their noise greatly disturbed my preaching. To add to the difficulty, a long rainy period, known as the monsoon, took place in the summer.

---

* Dr. Paul Yonggi Cho, internationally known evangelist and pastor, is the founder and Senior Pastor of Full Gospel Central Church in Seoul, Korea. He also heads Church Growth International, a Church growth organization which publishes *Church Growth* magazine and annually trains thousands of pastors and church leaders. He is the author of *The Fourth Dimension, Successful Home Cell Groups,* and *More Than Numbers.*

At first my congregation consisted of only five people, and they were my family members.

My life as a new pastor was horrible and miserable. In fact, a couple of times I almost gave up pastoring the church. The only thing I could do in that difficult situation was to pray. Prayer became my solution as I sought and found peace only through fervent prayer. Every night I prayed until the early hours of the morning for the congregation to increase.

Due to the devastation following the Korean War, it was very difficult to evangelize. The church was expected to supply the people with financial and material needs, as well as the Word of God.

However, a change soon came to the church which caused it to grow. Some ruffians in the village threatened our church, saying that if I did not show them miracles, they would destroy the church building.

Meanwhile, there was a lady who had been suffering from paralysis for seven years. I started to pray for this lady in order to show the miraculous power of God to those who still believed in shamanism. One day as I was praying for her, I had a vision. I was fighting with a great serpent, and was finally able to cast it out "in the Name of Jesus." The very next day, this lady was marvelously healed.

The lady came to our church, and when the ruffians saw the change, they repented of their sins and accepted Jesus Christ as their Savior. It was not long before others in the village began to come to church and confess that truly God did exist. Naturally, the church began to grow rapidly.

A short time ago, while holding an interdenominational seminar for ministers, I was interviewed on television by Dr. McGavran of the Fuller Theological Seminary in California. During the interview I made the point that "without signs and wonders, the church cannot grow." The Fuller Theological Seminary offers a course in "Signs and Wonders." The students showed great interest in this particular course. Surely, signs and wonders have an important role in the growth of the church in today's world.

Now, I do not believe I have received a special gift from God. I just read the Word of God diligently and apply the principles contained therein to my own ministry. As a result, the Holy Spirit works through my ministry. I have seen souls saved, broken hearts healed, physical diseases touched by the power of the Holy Spirit. In addition, I have seen many people become successful after the Holy Spirit came into their lives.

One thing to remember is that signs and wonders can never take place without prayer. Therefore, ministers ought to pray more fervently and eagerly than any other person. I arise at five o'clock every morning and concentrate on praying for one or two hours. Unless I follow this pattern, there is no way I can continue to minister to people. When I am lost in prayer with the Lord, my soul becomes full of hope and encouragement, and my body feels as though I am in a state of ecstacy. This is the reason I admonish ministers to pray for one or two hours early in the morning. By keeping a consistent time, the result will show in the interpretation of the Word of God. To a pastor, the message being preached is like life. The right interpretation of the Word of God is the most important part of the message. How to interpret the Bible determines what to preach. What to preach determines the growth of the church.

Prayer helps to interpret the Bible in the right way. Nowadays, there are many pastors who do not interpret the Bible in the correct way. They are called humanistic ministers. Christianity is to be absolutely theocractic. The Gospel of Jesus Christ should not be used as a political tool. Up until this point, my ministry has been Bible-centered, and it will continue to be so in the future. Every Wednesday and Friday evenings I teach the Word of God chapter by chapter in an exegetical way; even on Sunday my sermon is mainly interpreting the Word.

At one time I neglected praying and used the Bible as a tool of philosophy. This was when our church was at Seodaimun before it moved to Yoido. On one particular morning, my subject was on "existentialism." After the service, an elderly lady came into my office with her gray-haired husband. I figured they were going to tell me how wonderful the service was, and how much they had been blessed by the sermon. To my surprise, the husband said, "Pastor Cho, I am a philosophy professor in college. My wife forced me to go to church with her. I came here today, and was really disappointed. Your preaching was just like a research paper that a freshman in college wrote. I did not come to church to listen to a philosophical lecture. I came to hear the Word of God."

After this experience, I was shocked and deeply regretted that my sermon had been such a disappointment. I determined anew to preach only the Bible, the wisdom and the knowledge of God. And, I began to pray harder than ever before.

In addition, by praying a close walk with God is experienced. God is love. That is why God wants to have loving communication with His people. Our fellowship with God becomes deeper and closer through the communion of the Holy Spirit. The pastors who have a deep fellowship with God have power in their ministry. By being filled with the Holy Spirit, your ministry will be overflowing with deep abundant truth from the living Word of God.

Being filled with the Holy Spirit is in direct proportion to prayer. There is no way to be full of the Holy Spirit without prayer.

It is because of prayer that the Full Gospel Central Church has been growing so phenomenally. The people in our church pray without ceasing. Every weekend at Prayer Mountain, about 10,000 people gather to intercede in prayer for souls to be brought into the Kingdom of God, for our church, and for themselves. Prayer is the motivating power to lead this big ship of the Full Gospel Central Church.

Step Two: Holy Spirit
The right relationship with the Holy Spirit is essential to becoming a successful pastor. One time I fell asleep while praying and had a dream. I heard God's voice saying to me, "Pastor Cho, do you want the people in your church to overflow?" "Yes, Lord." "Be filled with the Holy Spirit." "Lord, I am filled with the Holy Spirit."

There is a difference between being filled with the Holy Spirit and having the right relationship with *Him*. The person who has the right fellowship with the Holy Spirit is the person who is filled with the Holy Spirit, and should accept Him as a person. To have "koinonia" with the Holy Spirit, a person must have: (1) The relationship of fellowship; (2) The relationship of partnership; (3) The relationship of transportation. Many people fail to have fellowship with the Holy Spirit because they consider Him as an object instead of a person. The Holy Spirit is a person in the sense that He has knowledge, emotion and will.

The Holy Spirit is the spirit of action. I have discovered that when I have fellowship with Him, my ministry is fruitful. Every month there are countless new converts in our church.

Salvation is not possible by might nor by power, but only by the Holy Spirit. It is the Holy Spirit who gives hope to those in despair; comfort and peace to those in sorrow; life and vitality to those in anguish and agony; and healing to those suffering from diseases.

No matter how desperate and disappointing circumstances may be, if you have fellowship and partnership with the Holy Spirit, your church will grow exceedingly.

Step Three: Message
In one word, this message could be labeled, *Hope*.

I recall while a student in elementary school, many of the students passed out under the hot sun while doing morning exercises. This was due to lack of nutrition. The teachers would move the unconscious students to the shade beneath a nearby tree, and gently massage their faces with cool, refreshing water.

The message of a pastor has the same function as that cool water. Pastors are to lay the broken souls of those who have passed out because of sins, sorrow, afflictions, and meaningless lives, under the tree of God's love, and encourage them to build up a new life by giving them the message of living water through Jesus Christ. Where there is hope, there is faith. Only then can lives become meaningful. The Bible says: "Where there is no vision, the people perish" (Proverbs 29:18).

Many ministers have set up their pulpit in Mount Sinai to judge and condemn the souls of the men, instead of quenching their thirst. Why don't they give the Living Water to those who are thirsty? It would be a great tragedy if a pastor only judged the thirsty souls as to why they became so thirsty.

My message of hope is based on 3 John 1:2, "I wish above all things that thou mayest prosper and be in health, even as thy soul prospereth."

Some theologians claim that if a person asks God to bless him in a material sense, he is in a low spiritual state. They call it "prosperity religion." Is this wrong? Where can we go to be blessed if not to God? When God created the heavens and the earth and all the things that are in it, He also blessed man. "So God created man in his own image, in the image of God created He him; male and female created He them. And God blessed them, and God said unto them, be fruitful and multiply, and replenish the earth, and subdue it; and have dominion over the fish of the sea, and over the foul of the air, and over every living thing that moveth upon the earth" (Genesis 1:27-29).

The message of a pastor is to include God's blessings. Obviously, it is wrong to proclaim only material blessings. Above all, pastors must preach the redemption of Jesus Christ. Next they must proclaim the blessing in their own hearts and lives, and the blessings of good health. It is actually because Christ intended to bless us that He suffered and died. Yet, there are people restricting the work of redemption only to the salvation of souls. God wants us to be blessed materially, also. However, if a person directs his mind only to material blessings, it is fleshly desire, and greed which is idolatry.

Christians are to "seek first the kingdom of God and his righteousness; and all these things shall be added unto you" (Matthew 6:33).

The message of hope meets the needs of the people. God is the One who blesses us. As pastors preach this kind of message, their church will increase.

Step Four: Organization

One of the reasons churches do not grow is that ministers are only fishing with a rod and reel instead of using the net also. The net is the Home Cell System. In our church five or ten families belong to one home cell. The home cell leaders and section leaders work together in the home cells. Even if a pastor organizes the system very tightly, it would be of no avail unless the home cell and section leaders do their jobs faithfully.

At the Full Gospel Central Church, seminars for home cell leaders are held twice a year. Home cell leaders are trained in different ways. First, using the basis of biblical truth, we help them realize how important and crucial the role of leaders actually is. The Bible is taught very explicitly in order that each leader, in turn, may teach the Word of God correctly to members in his home cell.

Each home cell leader is required to complete a three-month course at our Bible School for Church Laymen and a six-month course at our Bible College for Church Laymen.

However, sometimes there will be tears and holes in the net. Perhaps a home cell leader is not leading his cell according to biblical truth, or is leading the cell astray. Of course, if a flaw is found in the net, someone has to repair it immediately. The pastor in charge of this particular district is responsible for the repairs. Nevertheless, pastors do their best in starting the home cell so that people may grow and yield fruit in the community.

One point to consider is that pastors must have goals to attain. The main reason why the majority of pastors fail in their home cell ministry is they have not taken proper care of the cells once they have been organized. It might seem hard to set weekly, monthly or even yearly goals, but it is essential for growth. I have watched dogs running a race. Their master puts a rabbit on a wire connected to a tractor so that the dogs can keep on looking at the rabbit while running the race. Our church always sets goals. This is one of the secrets to our growth.

Some people might be afraid the fellowship between pastors and congregation will be severed if the church grows too big. There is no need to worry about this situation, if the home cell system is well organized. Church growth is the will of God. The home cell unit can be considered as a small church. If a church becomes big, it can reach out to more people, and have a broader scope of evangelization.

Our church has over 100 missionaries serving overseas. Moreover, every day my telecasts are being aired in strategic cities throughout the Republic of Korea, and once a week in the United States. In addition, we have provided financial aid to building military churches, and have assisted over 300 churches in the countryside of Korea, and we have donated to many Christian organizations. This information is given to emphasize just how effective a large church can be in ministering to the glory of God. Our ultimate purpose, though, is winning souls.

My prayer is that churches all around the world may grow so that they can glorify God through their ministries.

Part Four

Pentecostals and the
Church Growth Movement

From *Bridges* to *Waves:*
Pentecostals and the Church Growth Movement

L. Grant McClung, Jr.

The title of this introductory essay is carefully chosen because it symbolizes more than a quarter century of events which have turned the course of evangelical missions and have also influenced the missionary policies of the pentecostal movement. *Bridges* is Donald A. McGavran's *The Bridges of God* (Friendship Press 1955), the book that technically set the Church Growth Movement in motion. *Waves* is C. Peter Wagner's *On The Crest of the Wave* (Regal Books 1983), one of the more recent and most popular literary products of the Church Growth Movement.

The twenty-eight year spread between McGavran's and Wagner's books have introduced research, documentation, publishing, and teaching on Church Growth which has revolutionized the shape of evangelical missions and has set the tone of their emphases for the future. During this time some significant events have taken place as products of the Church Growth Movement: the initiation of the *Church Growth Bulletin* (now known as *Global Church Growth*) in 1964; the establishment of the Institute of Church Growth (1961) and its subsequent move to Fuller Theological Seminary to become the School of World Mission (1965); the founding of Church Growth research groups, publishing companies, and organizations such as MARC—the Missions Advanced Research & Communication Center (1966), William Carey Library (1969), Institute for American Church Growth (1973), and the Charles E. Fuller Institute (1976); and the publishing of hundreds of academic studies, books, and articles on church growth.

What has been the relationship between the Pentecostal Movement and the Church Growth movement during this time? This essay reviews some related literature and traces the interrelationship of the two movements during the last quarter century, showing how they have interfaced with and influenced one another. To do this it will be helpful to notice some pre-McGavran voices which have called attention to the Church Growth dynamics of the pentecostals and to cite some of the contributions of Donald A. McGavran himself. In addition, the observations of other Church Growth proponents will be noted and attention will be given to the pentecostal response to the Church Growth Movement.

Pre-McGavran Voices

Though an extensive listing of all literary sources is not the intent of this essay, it is evident from even a cursory review of missions literature that pentecostals have been at the forefront of the missions advance in this century. McGavran and the Church Growth school of thought are to be credited for popularizing and analyzing pentecostal growth dynamics, but others were calling attention to the pentecostals (for various reasons!) before McGavran and his colleagues.

One of them was J. Merle Davis who wrote of pentecostals in his *How the Church Grows in Brazil* in 1943 (a World Missionary Council study). William R. Read says of Davis, "He was one of our first missionary statesmen to see the dynamic factors involved in the Pentecostal movement, and he called attention particularly to the rapid growth of the Pentecostal churches" (1965:123).

Davis studied the leadership styles, the message, training methods, and lower class audience of Brazilian pentecostals and concluded that they were "suited to the task of evangelizing the masses of Brazil" (1943:68). In his *Church Growth in Mexico,* McGavran cited the Church Growth conclusions of Davis and also called upon the insights of Eugene Nida's work on pentecostals (1963:119-120).

Davis was not only the pre-1955 observer of pentecostal church growth. Already in 1952, L.F.W. Woodford, then the Missionary Secretary of the British Assemblies of God, was able to report to the World Pentecostal Conference:

> Informative articles and references to pentecostal missionary work are now appearing from time to time in responsible missionary journals and magazines, including the *International Review of Missions* and *World Dominion,* the values and extent of the pentecostal contribution to world missions is thus receiving acknowledgement from these authoritative quarters. (Greenway 1952:50)

Had the pentecostals been just another isolated sect emphasizing controversial doctrines and inward-looking practices, their existence could have probably been ignored. The "inconvenient reality" of pentecostalism, however, was its pervasive expansion and presence around the world. The fact of their growth, says Noberto Saracco in a later *International Review of Missions* article, explains the attention given to them by Church Growth researchers:

> The reason there is so much talk about the Pentecostal Movement is not due to its emphasis on charismatic manifestations, nor to

divine healing, but to its amazing growth in the seventy-five years of its existence. . . . Evangelism occupies a central place in the ministry of the Pentecostal churches. The other manifestations revolve around it. (1977)

McGavran and the Pentecostals

Commonly regarded as "The Father of the Church Growth Movement," Donald A. McGavran was deeply influenced in the early 1930s by the writings of a Methodist bishop, J. Wascom Pickett. In 1936, McGavran and Pickett (both missionaries in India at the time) teamed with A.L. Warnshuis and G.H. Singh to produce *Church Growth and Group Conversion* (later revised by William Carey Library, 1973). By the time of his *The Bridges of God* in 1955, McGavran was firmly convinced of the people movement approach to missions as opposed to the traditional missions station approach.

It was also along this time that McGavran was beginning to analyze the growth of pentecostal churches. This writing does not attempt to document the chronological progression of McGavran's mention of pentecostals in his writings. In reference to the title of his article, "What Makes Pentecostal Churches Grow?" (*Church Growth Bulletin,* January 1977), McGavran said, "The question underlined above has animated my mind since the early sixties . . ." (1982:97). As early as 1961 when he established the Institute of Church Growth on the campus of Northwest Christian College in Eugene, Oregon, McGavran had accepted pentecostals as research associates there (McClung 1983e:31).

In 1963, McGavran (along with John Huegel and Jack Taylor) wrote *Church Growth in Mexico* and devoted Chapter 11 to "The Pentecostal Contribution" (1963:113ff). He referred to pentecostals as "evangelicals" and noted the unfortunate choice of some denominations to "shut themselves off" from pentecostal churches. He quoted from Bishop Newbigin of the United Church of South India who had earlier said:

If any Church believes in the deity of Jesus Christ and the authority of the Bible and manifests the fruits of the Spirit, we are on dangerous grounds to question its validity. (1963:113)

"By that standard," says McGavran, "each Pentecostal denomination is a sound Church indeed! Continued Pentecostal growth forces old-line denominations to consider whether the Pentecostals may not have a valuable contribution to make" (1963:113-114). McGavran went on to claim that the most prominent of the pentecostal contributions was its belief "that God Himself, through the Holy Spirit, personally guides and directs each disciple of Christ" and that this "principle of *spontaneous action under the control of the spirit of Jesus as revealed in the Scriptures* lies at the heart of the Pentecostal faith" (1963:114-115).

Just two years later, in the March, 1965 issue of *Church Growth Bulletin,* McGavran initiated a series of articles on "Notable Missions Leaders on Church Growth" and introduced a pentecostal as the first writer. It was

Robert T. McGlasson, then the Foreign Missions Secretary of the Assemblies of God, who wrote on "The Mission of The Church." "Dr. McGlasson," said McGavran in his introduction, ". . . has something important to say about church growth. We are glad to have his article as the first in this series" (1977:42). This was an early event in the publication of the *Church Growth Bulletin* which McGavran had started just the preceding year.

In the January, 1968 issue of *Church Growth Bulletin* McGavran broke precedence in order to favorably comment on the report from the eighth triennial meeting of the Pentecostal World Conference (this was after Read's study on Brazil in 1965 but before the Read, Monterroso, and Johnson report of 1969—both had favorable conclusions on pentecostal growth). Responding to J. Philip Hogan's report on the international pentecostal gathering in Rio de Janeiro, in July, 1967, McGavran said:

> *Church Growth Bulletin* does not publish accounts of great denominational gatherings, but we have departed from this rule in the case of the Rio Conference solely because the Pentecostal family of Churches has had such notable growth in so many countries. We congratulate the Pentecostals and ask God's richest blessings to rest upon them as they multiply the Gospel throughout the earth. (1969:277)

By 1970 McGavran had produced his greatest work, *Understanding Church Growth* (Eerdmans, later revised in 1980), and in it did not hesitate to favorably commend pentecostals. He spoke of the "vitality and growth of Pentecostal sections of the Church," "Pentecostal fire," and of "the enormous growth of the Pentecostals. . . ." He noted that the "rapid growth" of pentecostal churches in Brazil and Chile "has startled and encouraged the missionary world" (1970:13, 113, 349, 161).

In 1973, McGavran paused near the decadal anniversary of the *Church Growth Bulletin* and reflected upon "five happenings which have great meaning for the advancement of the Gospel," saying that among the multitudinous events reported around the world, these "stand out like mountain peaks" (1977:366). Among the five (which also included the upcoming International Congress on World Evangelization, the spread of Church Growth thinking across America, the "workshop explosion" in "Latfricasia," and the advancement of Asian missionary societies) was pentecostal-style "faith healing" campaigns (1977:376-377).

McGavran had introduced a pentecostal in a leading *Church Growth Bulletin* article in 1965 (1977:42-44). By the time of the January, 1977 issue, he devoted the entire issue to pentecostals with his own lead article, "What Makes Pentecostal Churches Grow?" (1982:97ff). He examined five growth factors including: "utter yieldedness to the Holy Spirit"; God the Holy Spirit acting powerfully through ordinary Christians; the use of connections—bridges—between newly saved pentecostals and their unreached friends in the world; the belief in and ability to deal with demons and evil spirits; and the use of innovative and adventurous patterns of Church growth (1982:98-99).

Within five months, McGavran returned to the pentecostals, commending them for getting "serious about the evangelization of the three billion" (1982:121).

That part of those unreached three billion live in North America and that the pentecostals have a contribution to make here has also been recognized by McGavran. In a recent interview with the author he spoke of the widespread "religion" of secularism in North America and said, "It is here that the Pentecostal church—with its tremendous emphasis upon God the Holy Spirit acting right now in Society—is needed" (McClung 1983e:31-32). He went on to emphasize that pentecostals would "do a wonderful job" among the unreached ethnic populations coming into the United States. Of these peoples, he said:

> They come over here, and they are not secularized. When they come, they believe in miracles. They confront Secularism, and there is a vacuum there. I am inclined to think that if the Pentecostals would stress signs and wonders in the ethnic community, they could win them in a big way. (McClung 1983e:34)

Because of his pragmatic approach to Church Growth and his theological foundation which causes him to seek for ways to find "God's lost children," Donald A. McGavran has pointed to pentecostal growth as exemplary for the evangelical world. He is to be credited as a bridge-builder between pentecostals and others who are fulfilling the Great Commission of our common Lord.

Church Growth Observers

A large part of Donald McGavran's genius in forming the Church Growth Movement was his ability to attract to himself persons of high caliber who joined him in Church Growth research and writing. At the original Institute of Church Growth in Eugene, Oregon, McGavran recruited anthropologist Alan R. Tippett. Later, when the Institute moved to the Fuller campus, McGavran brought in Ralph D. Winter, Arthur Glasser, C. Peter Wagner, Charles Kraft, and J. Edwin Orr to form the initial School of World Missions faculty.

McGavran encouraged team research into pentecostal growth. With John Huegel and Jack Taylor he wrote *Church Growth in Mexico* and included a chapter on "The Pentecostal Contribution" (Eerdmans 1963). This was soon followed by a ground-breaking study of Brazil which had a large portion devoted to pentecostal growth in that Latin American country. It was William R. Read's *New Patterns of Church Growth in Brazil* (Eerdmans 1965). Alan R. Tippett said in his "1970 Retrospect and Prospect" that Read's study, "opened up the whole area of Pentecostal church growth for our consideration—a new dimension which turned out to be highly significant" (McGavran 1977:50).

Read found five significant patterns of growth among Brazilian pentecostals. He said that they were urban, and that they made good use of strategic centers of population. Thirdly, he said that their growth was dependent upon sociological factors and that, fourthly, they had a wide geographical distribution. Finally, he observed that the pentecostals were following Pauline patterns of church planting (1965:126-131).

Read's research stirred great interest in Latin American pentecostal growth patterns. A follow-up study was commissioned by McGavran and the School of World Mission. Read was joined by Victor M. Monterroso and Harmon A. Johnson and together they produced *Latin American Church Growth* (Eerdmans 1969). McGavran called it a "monumental study" and it has since become a standard reference volume on church growth in Latin America. The pentecostal story is woven throughout the book and Chapter 21 is a significant analysis of pentecostal growth.

What Read, Monterroso, and Johnson had done for the academic world, C. Peter Wagner accomplished for the wider evangelical church audience. Wagner's *What Are We Missing?* (formerly titled *Look Out! The Pentecostals Are Coming,* Creation House 1973) not only was extensively used as a textbook in leading seminaries and Bible colleges across the country, but became a catalytic and wide-read introduction for many church leaders into the phenomenon of pentecostal growth. It was also highly instructional to North American pentecostals who had not realized some of the growth dynamics of their Latin brethren to the south.

Wagner, who has done much to inform the evangelical world about pentecostals and to instruct the pentecostals in Church Growth principles, has long been a friend to pentecostals. Recently, he said:

> Through the years I have become very close to Pentecostals. Why? Primarily because I am a student of church growth: and, no matter where I look around the globe, I find that Pentecostal churches are leading the way in rates of increase. (1982:4)

Before writing *What Are We Missing?,* Wagner had already served in Latin America as a missionary for many years and had also become trained in Church Growth research by McGavran himself. He recalled how God led him to contact the pentecostal churches and said, "I had to find out why God seemed to be blessing these churches" (1973:12). As a result, he was able to discern some valuable lessons for the rest of the evangelical church world which has been indebted to him since. He, along with McGavran and the other research colleagues, was a forerunner in bringing the Church Growth and Pentecostal Movements closer together. In reflecting recently on the "Characteristics of Pentecostal Church Growth," Wagner observed:

> If the Lord tarries, Pentecostalism will undoubtedly go down in future history as the most significant religious phenomenon of the twentieth century. (1982:5)

A further Church Growth proponent who should be mentioned is Jim Montgomery. Montgomery found Church Growth dynamics among pentecostals in the Philippines much like Wagner's conclusions from Latin America. His book, *Fire in The Philippines* (Creation House 1975), highlighted the growth of the Foursquare Church in the Philippines and added another excellent entry into the growing body of literature on pentecostal growth. He has also been instrumental in bringing pentecostal growth to the attention of Church

Growth students through his editorship at *Global Church Growth*. His insightful articles have brought the best of pentecostal lessons to Church Growth readers (McGavran 1982:253ff).

Church Growth advocates in Canada are aware of the efforts of Dennis M. Oliver and the publication *His Dominion* (formerly *Church Growth: Canada*). Oliver, a Church Growth disciple and graduate of the Fuller School of World Missions, has exposed his readers to the Church Growth principles arising from pentecostal growth in Canada, particularly among the Pentecostal Assemblies of Canada (1974 Volume 1, No. 2:4-5; 1975 Volume 2, No. 3:8-15; 1980 Volume 7, No. 1:11-15). He and his colleagues have found and published examples of solid growth from Canadian pentecostal case studies.

The Pentecostal Response

In the lead article, "What Makes Pentecostal Churches Grow?" (January, 1977 *Global Church Growth*), McGavran noted that he and his colleagues began serious research into this issue in the early 1960s. From that time until his article, he noted, of the more than 150 serious researchers at the Fuller School of World Missions, several had been concerned with the growth of the pentecostals (1982:97). Presently, the total number of School of World Missions dissertations and theses numbers more than 450, and there continues to be a growing list of researches both about and by pentecostals. Pentecostals themselves have come to the School of World Mission and reflected upon issues pertinent to their own growth (Chelliah 1981; Daniel 1977; De Wet 1981; Elmore 1981; Gaxiola 1978; Goble 1975; Pomerville 1982; Shinde 1974; and others).

Pentecostals have also responded to Church Growth teaching by writing articles of their own in *Global Church Growth* (McGavran 1969:232-235; 1977:42-44; 451) and *His Dominion* (Oliver 1974; 1975; 1980). In addition, pentecostals have called upon the insights of the Church Growth Movement in their own publications (Thomas 1983; Champion, Caldwell, and Leggett 1968; Jones 1978; Graham 1983; Wagner 1982:4-9).

Though benefiting from each other in a parallel (some would say semi-symbiotic) relationship, neither the Church Growth Movement nor the Pentecostal Movement would say that they have been the cause for each other's acceptance and diffusion. The Pentecostal Movement has, in a sense, benefited from the Church Growth Movement's recognition. On the other hand, the Pentecostal Movement has encouraged the Church Growth Movement and has been admired as a model by its researchers. McGavran and his colleagues would be the first to consent:

> . . . a lot of growth is going on in the world that is not the direct result of the church growth school of thought . . . look at the Pentecostal churches of the world. Many of them were getting astounding growth before they heard of the church growth school of thought.

> Church growth simply takes the dreams and aspirations and methods of good missionaries and effective evangelists and throws a spotlight on them and says, "Look, this is working." (McGavran 1976:76)

Pentecostals, on the other hand, would like to have more input as to where the spotlight ought to be placed. One of the basic concerns of pentecostals with the Church Growth Movement, for example, has to do with the underlying, foundational reasons for the growth of the pentecostal movement. Pentecostals fear that the Church Growth Movement may tend to overemphasize the socio-anthropological explanations for the growth of pentecostalism. This is the position of outsiders to *both* movements (Hollenweger 1972; Bloch-Hoell 1964; Epinay 1969; Damboriena 1969; Willems 1967; Samarin 1972) who, unfortunately, have influenced some Church Growth thinking.

Pentecostals are concerned with too much emphasis given to "environmental factors" which can produce growth (McGavran 1980:159, 184) and to the use of pentecostal "methodology" even while discounting the pentecostal doctrine and experience.

Glover Shipp, for example, reported on the Brazilian Assemblies of God when they passed their three million mark. He noted that there are aspects of Assemblies' doctrine and practice which are unacceptable to other evangelicals. But, he said:

> Let us utilize in our own efforts every possible biblical method of this rapidly expanding movement. Many of these methods are perhaps unpolished by our standards yet are highly successful. In so doing, maybe God will grant us the same degree of growth with which He has blessed our brothers of the Assemblies of God. (Global Church Growth 1981 January-February:86)

C. Peter Wagner has said that non-pentecostal churches can "pentecostalize" themselves without compromising their own particular doctrines. "In other words," he asserted, "non-Pentecostals might do well seriously to consider the possibility of behaving more like Pentecostals, even if they do not choose to believe like them" (1973:39).

In more recent times, however, Church Growth proponents are finding a new emphasis upon the Holy Spirit and signs and wonders in Church Growth (*Christian Life* 1983). Pentecostals would claim that their growth is more than the convergence of sociological receptivity factors. Pentecostals themselves do not discount receptivity theory and generally appreciate the insights from the Church Growth Movement. They have the advantage, however, of interpreting their own growth dynamics from the *inside out* (Zimmerman 1975; Champion, Caldwell, Leggett 1968:114ff; Hughes 1968:63ff; Gee 1963; Hodges 1965; 1972:142ff; 1977; Hogan 1975; Douglas 1975:242ff). Parts two and three of this work (on Theology and Practices) demonstrate pentecostals' self-evaluation and analysis of their growth.

Repeatedly, pentecostals have affirmed:

> . . . the reason for progress in missions is that the Pentecostal
> people endeavor both in preaching and experience to give the place
> to the Holy Spirit which the New Testament indicates should be
> given.
>   The Pentecostal missionary movement is prospering for
> the very reason that it is Pentecostal. Some recent writers
> have attempted to show that the results Pentecostal churches
> experienced on the foreign field could be achieved by simply
> adopting some of the practices of Pentecostals which are
> most appealing to the masses without necessarily beˆɔming
> "Pentecostal" in experience. It is questionable that one could find
> a Pentecostal who would agree with this premise. (Hodges
> 1977:35-36)

Pentecostals do not claim to have a monopoly on the Holy Spirit. In fact,
they have taken positive positions on the Charismatic Movement and the new
developments of the Holy Spirit in our time (Thomas 1983:9-11). They react,
however, toward interpretations of their growth that tend to give explanations
not holding the primacy of the Holy Spirit.

Pentecostal missiologist Paul A. Pomerville has addressed this issue and
other concerns of pentecostals in his very significant doctoral dissertation,
"Pentecostalism and Missions: Distortion or Correction?" He has emphasized,
"Among the reasons for the phenomenal growth of Pentecostalism in the world,
the Pentecostal baptism of the Spirit must be given primary attention"
(1982:289). Pomerville, and other pentecostals, would agree that Church
Growth is complex and that there are many contributing factors involved (De
Wet 1981:10; Douglas 1975:242ff). He admits:

> A common error on the part of the Pentecostals is to attempt to
> explain church growth in terms of one dimension—the Holy Spirit.
> But perhaps an equally deceptive error made by non-Pentecostals is
> the underestimation of that dimension of church growth, specifically
> the dynamic of the Pentecostal experience itself. (1982:351-352)

This is not to imply that non-pentecostal writers have ignored the
dimension of the Holy Spirit. As already mentioned, the Church Growth
Movement has been informed not only by pentecostal practices but by
pentecostal beliefs. This has been a growing process. It is interesting to note that
when one searches the indices of all *three* consolidated volumes of the *Global
Church Growth,* he makes the following discoveries: in the first two consolidated
volumes (1969 and 1977) there are only three index references to pentecostals
and *no* index references to the Holy Spirit. By the time of the third consolidated
volume (1982) there are *fourteen* references to pentecostals and *twenty-two*
entries under "Holy Spirit." On the other hand, Church Growth thinking is also
finding its way into more pentecostal circles. There is reason to believe that both
movements will continue to edify and instruct one another.

In summary, pre-McGavran voices were calling attention to the Church Growth practices of pentecostals in the 1940s and early 1950s. At the outset of the Church Growth Movement, Donald A. McGavran determined that one of his primary goals would be to find out "what makes pentecostal churches grow." He was joined by Church Growth proponents who made discerning observations about pentecostal growth. Pentecostals have responded by interacting with the Church Growth Movement and emphasizing particular areas that they feel are indispensable reasons for their own growth. At the same time, they have been informed and helped by the insights of the Church Growth thinking.

As the missionary movement of world pentecostalism gained prominence, it became a phenomenon studied by sociologists, anthropologists, churchmen, and secular journalists. The religious world was faced with the fact that the pentecostals had come to stay. In other quarters, missionary strategists were asking themselves the question posed by Donald A. McGavran in the following essay. Though he was not the first to study the pentecostals, McGavran was one of the first missionary strategists to tell the evangelical world they had lessons to learn from their pentecostal brethren. He is to be credited for bringing pentecostal thought and practice to his colleagues through his editorship of the *Church Growth Bulletin* (now known as *Global Church Growth*). His article is from the January, 1977 issue which is devoted entirely to pentecostal church growth.

10
What Makes Pentecostal Churches Grow?

Donald A. McGavran*

The tremendous growth of Pentecostal congregations and denominations in many countries of the world, but especially nominally Christian lands, has led church growth thinkers in all six continents to ask: *"What makes Pentecostal churches grow?"*

Church Growth Bulletin devotes this issue to two recent Pentecostal case studies, along with my comments presented here, that deal with this question.

It is not enough to answer that many Pentecostal missionaries are as fruitless as some non-Pentecostals—though this is true. Nor are superficial replies, which allege that Pentecostals are emotional or slipshod in their methods and therefore grow, worthy of consideration. These answers are based on denominational pride, not solid evidence. Nor, we believe, is it true that speaking in tongues gives power to grow. There are too many cases of congregations—both among Pentecostals, Anglicans and other charismatics—full of Christians who speak in tongues and don't grow.

The question underlined above has animated my mind since the early sixties and lay at the bottom of the continent-wide survey of Latin America which issued in the authoritative 1968 volume *Latin American Church Growth* by Read, Monterroso and Johnson. Professor Wagner too has probed the problem in his volume *Look Out! The Pentecostals Are Coming.* Of the more than 150

Known as the "The Father of the Church Growth Movement," Donald A. McGavran served as a missionary in India for thirty-two years under the United Christian Missionary Society (1923-1955). With the publishing of *The Bridges of God* in 1955, McGavran initiated the Church Growth Movement and subsequently founded such entities as the Institute of Church Growth, the *Church Growth Bulletin,* and the School of World Mission at Fuller Theological Seminary. He is the author of scores of Church Growth articles and books including *Understanding Church Growth* and *How Churches Grow.* He is the Dean Emeritus and Senior Professor of Church Growth and South Asian Studies at the Fuller School of World Mission.

serious researches done at the School of World Mission in Pasadena, several have been of the growth and non-growth of Pentecostal denominations in Latfricasia. The other researches allowed us to see pentecostal growth in perspective—against other denominations which grew and did not grow.

Out of it all, I tender the following lessons which God is teaching us through our pentecostal brethren. I set down this incomplete and partial list hoping to stimulate more thought among all Christians and to encourage our pentecostal friends to greater and more focused harvesting. No one of these factors is solely responsible. The combination of factors—different in every case—is what brings about growth. If readers will carefully read the two articles in this issue which tell of growth of pentecostal congregations in resistant populations, they will find most of these lessons amply illustrated.

1. Pentecostals emphasize utter yieldedness to the Holy Spirit, and believe that God stands at our very elbows, knocking at the door of our hearts, speaking in our intuition and dreams. Pentecostals believe that God our Heavenly Father is instantly available, *and powerful.* He is simply waiting for the soul to open the door. This common Christian doctrine is believed by all denominations, but pentecostals appear to believe it more than most others.

2. Pentecostals teach that God the Holy Spirit acts powerfully through ordinary Christians. God is not limited to those with college or theological degrees. He has chosen the weak and often foolish things of this world to put to shame the wise, the strong, and those of long educational pedigrees. Factor 1 and factor 2 combine to liberate power *in* and to give power *to* all kinds of Christians whether they be fishermen, carpenters, housewives, dockhands, indentured laborers and allegedly "inferior" races ("the things that are not" 1 Corinthians 1:28).

3. Common Christians—*soon after they become disciples of the Lord*—have multitudinous good *connections* with friends and relatives among Buddhists, Hindus, Jews, materialists, secularists, agnostics and other worldly people. It is along these *connections,* these bridges of God, that the Gospel flows. Those who have been Christian for many years, or who grew up in Christian homes and have married Christians and have few intimates among the worldly, do not have such connections and so are not evangelistically potent. Old pentecostal congregations find the same thing operative in them. It is the new congregations which are potent. Pentecostals have more new congregations than most denominations—and *trust them more.*

4. Pentecostals accept the fact that most men and women today believe that demons and evil spirits (varying forms of Satan and dark thoughts) do invade them, bind them, and rule over them. Pentecostals believe that the mighty name of Jesus drives out evil spirits and heals all manner of sickness. The secular scientific "knowledge" which makes most western Christians cringe at the thought of faith healing (Penicillin, yes. Prayer, no), has been renounced by pentecostals, particularly new converts. Again and again the initial rushes of pentecostal growth have come where men and women in bondage to Satan have been freed by the mighty name of Jesus.

5. Again and again old line denominations (sometimes called "main line")

are locked into some non-reproductive pattern of Christian life. They adopted this back in the 19th century when the Gospel was first preached in those parts and the "educational-good-deeds approach buttressed by rich mission services," was the only way in which missionaries could stay on and work. Old line companies find this pattern respectable and dear (the dear old shoe syndrome) and continue the pattern. They dig up verses of Scripture to prove it biblically, and dignify it by much theological argument. They canonize it. Pentecostals by way of contrast (like the Methodists between 1780 and 1880 and the Presbyterians around 1600) tend to be innovative and adventurous and observe what patterns God is blessing to the conversion of sinners and the growth of His Church, and to using those. They are more flexible and adaptable than many "soundly Christian denominations."

Non-pentecostals may please take note that none of the lessons mentioned in any way offend their doctrines of polities. Seeking to spread the Gospel in these ways is equally possible to all Christian denominations.

Pentecostals may note that in many places they themselves through failure to practice these principles are not getting growth. The Assemblies of God in Taiwan, to which the T'ung-hwa congregation belongs, is a very small denomination. It has around 1,000 communicants today. Pentecostals (and charismatics in main line denominations too) need to remember that when increasing maturity brings increasing sterility, the Holy Spirit is not pleased—no matter how correct the theology, how sound the cultural approach, and how often they speak in tongues. God wants His lost children found. The ripe harvest in Sri Lanka and Taiwan call loudly for God's obedient servants to multiply there the kinds of evangelism God has blessed to the increase of His Churches.

Because of their exciting and productive growth around the world, the pentecostals have been close to the heart of the Church Growth Movement. Any serious student of church growth has had to come to terms with the universal presence of the Pentecostal Movement. One of the Church Growth proponents who has had the most contact with and expertise on the pentecostals has been C. Peter Wagner. Wagner's *What Are We Missing?* (formerly *Look Out! The Pentecostals Are Coming,* Creation House 1973) was the single most catalytic publication in the 1970s that popularized the Church Growth dynamics of the Pentecostal Movement. But Wagner and his colleagues have not only admired the pentecostals, they have been faithful friends who have warned pentecostals of dangers which may hinder or halt their growth. His following article, excerpted from *The Penetecostal Minister* (Summer, 1982) is must reading for pentecostals and for outsiders who would emulate pentecostal growth dynamics.

11

Characteristics of Pentecostal Church Growth

C. Peter Wagner*

Are pentecostal churches the most rapidly growing group of churches in the world? If they are, why? What are some of the most prominent characteristics of pentecostal church growth?

The editor of *The Pentecostal Minister* should be commended for asking an outsider to address these questions in his journal. I know that it is risky business to ask a relative stranger to take a look at family affairs, and I will attempt to be a good steward of this responsibility. However, I do plan to tell it like it is. As I see it, pentecostals are showing some ominous signs of subtly drifting away from some of the very qualities which have made them great, and these need to be mentioned.

Actually, I am not a very distant outsider. I am a born-again child of God, baptized in the Spirit, and thus part of the same spiritual household. I am growing in my faith, conscious of my spiritual gifts, and thanking God for the privilege of addressing Him in a language that I never learned. But I am a member of neither a Pentecostal nor a Charismatic church. I am an active, involved member of a Bible-believing Congregational church and teach in an interdenominational seminary.

---

* C. Peter Wagner is the Donald A. McGavran Professor of Church Growth at the Fuller Theological Seminary School of World Mission. He was a missionary to Bolivia for sixteen years before joining the Fuller faculty in 1971. A prolific writer, he has authored or edited more than twenty-five books including *Your Church Can Grow, Your Church Can Be Healthy* and, more recently, *On The Crest of the Wave* and *Leading Your Church to Growth.* He is an internationally known expert on church growth and one of the leading proponents of the Church Growth Movement.

Pentecostal Church Growth

Through the years I have become very close to pentecostals. Why? Primarily because I am a student of church growth; and, no matter where I look around the globe, I find that pentecostal churches are leading the way in rates of increase. A recent study of the growth of United States' denominational families, for example, has shown that pentecostal churches are growing at a DGR (decadal growth rate) of 48%, far ahead of all others. Second on the chart is the Seventh-Day Adventist denomination at 26% DGR. For comparison, Southern Baptists are growing at 17% DGR (the same as Mormons), and Lutherans at minus 5% DGR, while the entire U.S. population is growing at 9% DGR.

Korea as a nation is enjoying the most rapid church growth in the world. While churches of other denominations are growing as well, the largest church there and in the world is the Full Gospel Central Church, a pentecostal church. As of this writing, it has more than 200,000 members and is adding over 5,000 new ones per month. In Africa a pentecostal evangelist using a tent which accommodates 10,000 has found it much too small. He is taking delivery from an American contractor of a tent which will seat 35,000! In Latin America after World War II, about 35 years ago, pentecostals comprised only an estimated 20% of evangelical Christians. Now, over 70% of Latin American evangelicals are pentecostals, with the figure running over 90% in Chile.

To say that this growth is phenomenal is an understatement. The pentecostal movement is less than 100 years old, young as such movements go. Only 50 years ago it was still being classifed by many along with Jehovah's Witnesses, Mormons, and Christian Science as a false cult. Now, being a Pentecostal is an "in" thing among many Christians, and the stature, reputation, and dignity of the group continue to grow. If the Lord tarries, pentecostalism will undoubtedly go down in future history as the most significant religious phenomenon of the twentieth century.

What is behind this awesome growth?

First and foremost, pentecostal growth, as all bona fide church growth, is a sovereign work of God. Paul said that although he plants and Apollos waters, it is God who gives the increase (see 1 Corinthians 3:6). Jesus said, "I will build my church" (Matthew 16:18). It is His Church, and He is the builder. To God and God alone be the glory!

But the same God is the underlying cause of Episcopal, Mennonite, Presbyterian, Lutheran, and any other kind of church growth, as well as pentecostal growth. Why is it, then, that pentecostals seem to grow more vigorously? The full answer to that question is complex; but, for the purpose of this article, I am going to attempt to simplify it by selecting as carefully as I can what I consider to be the four most salient characteristics of pentecostal growth. Not that other churches do not also share some of these qualities—they do. But none, it seems to me, have combined all four quite as well as pentecostals have. Pentecostals are usually characterized by churches of purity, prayer, power, and the poor. Let me develop each one of these.

Churches of Purity

Pentecostal churches have a tradition of purity in three key areas: belief in the Bible, Christian doctrine, and lifestyle.

The Bible is a treasured book for pentecostals. The authority of the Scriptures is final. Pentecostals believe that what the Bible says is the Word of God, no questions asked. The great theological debates of the last century which have eroded confidence in the Bible among large segments of Christendom have scarcely touched pentecostals. If pentecostals have erred at all, they may interpret the Bible too literally in places. but that is hardly a dangerous error any more than having too many clothes on when you are caught in a mountain snowstorm. Too many clothes may be cumbersome, but too few could cost you your life.

Research in church growth has shown that the more literally the Bible is interpreted, the more likely the church is to grow. One reason, then, that pentecostal churches are growing is that they hold firm to biblical purity.

Sound doctrine, which goes along with biblical authority, has also contributed to the purity of pentecostal churches. While it is true that pentecostals have differed among themselves on secondary doctrines, they have agreed on the basics. Unlike many other denominations, they have never lost touch with the Gospel. They firmly believe that sin has alienated human beings from God and that Jesus Christ came to die on the Cross to pay the price for sin once and for all. The good news is that salvation and eternal life are available to all who repent of their sin, turn to Jesus in faith, and open their heart to the regenerating work of the Holy Spirit. The bad news is that those who have not believed in Jesus Christ do not have eternal life. When they die, they go to a Christless eternity. Because this truth has gripped the hearts of most pentecostals, they join with the apostle Paul in declaring, "Woe is unto me, if I preach not the gospel!" (1 Corinthians 9:16). No wonder pentecostal churches grow!

Christian lifestyle is a third mark of pentecostal purity. For most pentecostals conversion is a radical, life-changing experience. Separation from the world is demanded at the new birth. No drinking, no smoking, no drugs, no extramarital sex, no cussing, and no gambling are common lifestyle characteristics among pentecostals. Some groups add others such as no dancing, no gold, no bikinis, no rock music, no movies, no card playing, no sports, and no buying on Sunday. On the positive side, pentecostals usually go to church three or four times a week, read the Bible daily, pray before each meal, and give at least ten percent of their income to the Lord.

It may seem to some that such strictness could be an obstacle to church growth. Just the opposite. It is a well-known fact that the stricter the religious obligations and the higher the level of commitment demanded on its members, the more vigorously a church grows. Watering down the Christian lifestyle to conform to society in general may appear to have some short-term benefits for growth, but over the long haul it will surely turn people away from the church. The pentecostal pendulum, fortunately, is still over on the strict side.

Churches of Prayer

This section on prayer will be relatively short. The shortness, however, does not reflect the lack of importance of prayer for the growth of the church. It simply reflects the lack of research. I know that prayer is closely related to church growth, and I have set as one of my research goals for the eighties an attempt to discover just how and why this is true.

However, even though I do not know as much as I wish I knew about the subject, I do know that pentecostals are praying people. The kind of prayer that requires the active, energetic participation of each person (as contrasted to liturgical prayers that require very little personal involvement) is a universal characteristic of pentecostal people in their churches, their family circles, and their private devotions. Praying in tongues undoubtedly helps this greatly. It frequently establishes an intimate contact with God that is otherwise much more difficult to establish and maintain. Through the years I have noticed that in interdenominational meetings the person called upon to lead the group in prayer is frequently the pentecostal.

Intimacy with God is reflected not only in formal prayers, but also in revelatory manifestations of the Spirit such as prophecies, including what many call a word of knowledge (which I consider a type of prophecy). This kind of direct contact with the Holy Ghost is a tremendous force for growth and is most consistently prominent in pentecostal churches.

If I may be permitted a personal anecdote, some years ago I was helping our Congregational church through the process of planting a new daughter church. We retained a firm to do a demographic study so that we would be sure we located the new church in the right place. As I recall, the service cost us about $7,000. While we were still in the process of this project, I was invited to dinner at a friend's house. Pastor Jack Hayford of the Church of the Way in Van Nuys, the largest church of the Foursquare Gospel in the country, was also a guest. He mentioned in passing that they were planting a new church in Valencia, and I asked him how they went about selecting Valencia as the location. "Oh," he said, "I was driving along the freeway by Magic Mountain when all of a sudden I got a warm feeling in my chest, and the Lord said, 'Plant a new church in Valencia.' " I told him that it was much cheaper to be a Pentecostal than a Congregationalist!

Churches of Power

Closely related to the intimacy with God attained through prayer is the frequent manifestation of supernatural signs and wonders in Pentecostal churches. Probably the greatest contribution that Pentecostalism has made to Christianity in general is restoring the reality of the miracle power of the New Testament. Such power had been absent among the other churches for so long that when it appeared in Pentecostalism around the turn of the century the only way many traditional Christians could handle it was to declare it a heresy and classify Pentecostals as a false cult. Most Christians are smarter now, and God has forgiven them for the past.

Although I am still in the process of studying this, it does seem to me that one of the major purposes, if not the major one, of signs and wonders in the New

Testament was to attract the attention of unbelievers and to draw them to Jesus Christ and to the kingdom of God. Time after time in the book of Acts, signs and wonders are related to vigorous church growth. Acts 5:12-16 is typical of many other passages: "Many miracles and wonders were being performed among the people by the apostles . . . more and more people were added to the group—a crowd of men and women who believed in the Lord."

Worldwide, Pentecostal churches grow when the Holy Spirit is free to manifest His miracle power through believers. An amazing phenomenon of modern times is the explosive growth of churches in Mainland China during the Mao era. When the missionaries were driven out in 1949 and 1950, an estimated one million Protestant Christians remained in China. Through 30 years of the harsh persecution, through the brutality of the Cultural Revolution, with no Bibles, pastors, or church buildings, the church did not wither away as many feared it would. Instead it grew vigorously so that estimates of believers in China now run from 25 million to almost 50 million. How did this happen? All the answers are not yet in, but one thing we know for sure is that a major factor was God's immediate supernatural work of healings, casting out of demons, and miracles. While the thousands of house-churches that have been springing up cannot be claimed for Pentecostals or for any other denomination, my hunch is that most of them will turn out to be more like Pentecostals than any other modern branch of Christianity.

Not only do Pentecostals believe in miracle power, they also believe in soul-winning power. Sharing the faith is a constant way of life for Pentecostals. They believe that God wants to use them to win souls, and He does. When I consult with many denominations, I have to start by convincing them that the gospel is worth sharing and that God wants churches to grow. Not so with Pentecostals. It never occurred to them to question it. Pentecostals are possibility thinkers—their faith level is high. They believe in evangelism, and they believe in church growth. They trust God for great things, and God honors their faith. Pentecostal churches are churches of power.

Churches of the Poor

The God of the Bible is a God who loves the poor. It is true that He loves all people, including the rich; but, if we take the Bible seriously, we know that He has a special bias for the poor. Because of this, God is going to make sure that the poor have a strong witness for Christ. Back in the eighteenth century the Anglican Church in England had abandoned the poor, so God raised up the Methodist Church. When the Methodists came to America, they ministered to the poor with circuit riders going from cabin to cabin out on the frontier. But one hundred years later, the Methodists had become middle-class, and God raised up the Holiness/Pentecostal movement to minister to the poor once again.

Check it out. Almost all Pentecostal preachers now in their sixties or seventies were born in poor homes, and many younger ones were also. This is one of the strongest characteristics of Pentecostal growth. Research has shown that the working class people of the world are more receptive to the gospel than the higher classes. Furthermore, God reserves a special blessing for His servants who preach the good news to the poor, and Pentecostals have been receiving this blessing through the years.

But this observation leads me to my final section in which I want to elaborate on what I said up front; namely, that there are some ominous signs that Pentecostals may subtly be moving away from the very things that have contributed to their growth for 80 years. Many different factors are entering into this process, but most of them can be classified under the following: *the burning desire for respectability.*

Dangers of Respectability

I have argued that Pentecostal churches are growing steadily and strongly because they are churches of purity, prayer, power, and the poor. If they remain that way, they will remain strong. But cutting any of these characteristics off will be like cutting off the hair of Samson. Unfortunately, I think Delilah with her scissors may be lurking right around the corner.

Especially since World War II ended, 35 years ago, Pentecostals have been gaining respectability rapidly. Being persecuted and classified with the Jehovah's Witnesses now seems like an unreal bad dream. General superintendents and general overseers are now officers in the National Association of Evangelicals. They get invitations to the large international congresses. For the older generation it is a great relief to be able to mix with other leaders interdenominationally after taking nothing but abuse for so many years. The younger generation knows no different—weren't Pentecostals *always* respectable, just like Lutherans and Presbyterians?

All this is to the good. Behold how good and how pleasant it is for brethren to dwell together in unity. But it has its problems—especially for church growth. One price of respectability is that you will continue to be accepted so long as you do not stress your doctrinal distinctives. For Pentecostals this means keeping a low profile on Baptism in the Holy Spirit, the initial evidence of speaking in tongues, hallelujahs and amens from the audience, miraculous healings and exorcisms, prophecies/words of knowledge, and many more. But these are some of the very characteristics that have enabled Pentecostals to grow three or four times faster than the other groups they are trying to gain respectability from.

Some have rationalized by saying that we will keep a low profile while we are working with our brethren from other persuasions, but we will let loose when we get back with our own. It sounds good in theory. And it probably worked for a couple of decades. But if I am not mistaken, the attitude is now creeping into Pentecostal churches themselves. As an example, I was interested to see the very first lead article published in Volume 1, Number 1 of *The Pentecostal Minister.* It ran for nine pages with three prominent Pentecostal leaders discussing "The Church of God Minister in the '80s." The most I could find was one sentence that stressed a Pentecostal distinctive: Bob Lyons said, "Our worship services are . . . open to the move of the Holy Spirit in our midst, and we allow him to lead, guide, and direct the service." Hallelujah! But—one sentence in nine pages? The entire balance of the interview could have been taken from the Baptists or the Nazarenes, and no one would have known the difference.

Behind all this is a phenomenon called redemption and lift. When poor people become Christians and allow God to clean up their life, they frequently do not remain poor. But, as the Methodists learned, rising to middle-class respectability can easily get a church out of touch with the poor they originally came from. This hasn't completely happened to Pentecostals, but it has happened enough to hoist yellow flags all over the place. If the Pentecostals abandon the poor, God will raise up someone else to minister to them and the rate of growth of Pentecostal churches will surely begin to drop.

One of the measuring sticks for redemption and lift is the denominational educational system. As Pentecostals who were born poor rise socially and economically, they desire better educational opportunities for their children than they themselves had—so they establish colleges. When their children graduate from college, they are irretrievably middle-class. Over the decades this can and usually does shift the focus of outreach and church growth from the poor to the middle class.

Another measuring stick involves requirements for ministers. Most of the old-time Pentecostal preachers were either self-educated or they learned by being an apprentice to another pastor. Then, when the colleges came, more and more were college graduates. Ministers were considered more respectable if they went to college. Then the process escalates until graduate schools are established. Currently, the Church of God, the Assemblies of God, and the Pentecostal Holiness Church are about at this point. Down the line a two-tiered ministry is likely to develop. Those who go to graduate school will subtly be thought of as superior to those who do not, and they will be elected to influential denominational policy-making positions. It may take a few decades, but the well-meaning declarations of the present leaders (who have not gone to graduate school) that no formal educational requirements will be made for ordination into the ministry may begin to erode and eventually disappear altogether. A study of the Methodist church will show that it can happen. It will be devastating for church growth if it does.

By this time some are saying, "Hey! Wagner has stopped preaching and gone to meddling." Well, then, let me conclude with a list of concrete suggestions that can keep Pentecostals on track as the global leaders in making church growth happen:

1. Hold purity high. I do not see much change as yet in biblical authority or doctrine, but I do detect some watering down of the Christian lifestyle as distinctly separated from the world around. Keep strict, and God will bless.

2. Depend on prayer and fasting as your spiritual core. Keep channels open for intimacy with God through tongues and prophecies.

3. Ask God to show His power through signs and wonders as He did in the early days of the Pentecostal movement. Publicize testimonies of those who have been blessed through miracles. Not enough is said about healing any more. If I am not mistaken, only one author, David L. Lemons, addressed the issue of healing in the entire first year of publication of *The Pentecostal Minister*.

4. Maintain a passion for souls. Keep witnessing and outreach in the forefront of all church programs.

5. Never allow educational requirements to substitute for spiritual gifts as the basis for ordaining new ministers.

6. Vigorously plant new churches and exalt the bivocational minister. There's nothing wrong with earning money from a secular job while you're building a new church.

7. Curse "the demon of respectability." Be willing to be fools for Christ's sake. Do not allow association with other Christians to water down Pentecostal distinctives of doctrine or practice.

The last two decades of the twentieth century hold incredible promise. I believe that they will see the greatest harvest of souls in the history of the Christian Church. My prayer is that, as Pentecostals have led the way in reaping the harvest over the past two decades, they will maintain this leadership with even greater power as we move into the future for the glory of God.

Part Five
Future Cautions and Challenges

Introduction
Another 100 Years?
Which Way for Pentecostal Missions?

L. Grant McClung, Jr.

The Pentecostal Movement began with explosive dynamism at the turn of this century and has not retreated since. Early pentecostal missionaries went everywhere preaching the gospel. They were captivated by an eschatological urgency and filled with the assurance that God had divinely ordained them for "last days ministry." Eventually, the movement began to consolidate and organize into structures which would allow for a wider diffusion of its message. Subsequently, the combined communities of nominal pentecostal bodies and adherents of the charismatic movements are estimated to total some 120 million members (one million for each of the original 120 in the Upper Room!).

Three of the leading North American pentecostal bodies—the Assemblies of God, Church of God, and Pentecostal Holiness—have had organized missions outreaches for more than seventy years. They were preceded by the Pentecostal Missionary Union in England and by other pentecostals in Scandinavia. Thus, the Pentecostal Movement as a whole is nearing its centennial (the Church of God, the oldest of the North American denominations, marked its centennial in 1986). It is appropriate, therefore, to ask whether or not there will be *another* one hundred years for pentecostal missions.

In doing that, this essay will be guided by three considerations that bear upon the question, "Which way for pentecostal missions?" Initially, it will be seen that among pentecostals there is a *commitment* to the future. Secondly, there are *cautions* which are a concern to pentecostals. Finally, the *challenges* which face pentecostal missions will be examined.

Future Commitments

Nearing a century of ministry, the pentecostals now have a history. They can turn to past accomplishments under the blessing of God and feel a sense of heritage. Though reflecting on the past and enjoying their present growth, most pentecostal groups are not content to remain there. They are optimistic about the future and are committed to the continued perpetuation of the movement.

Optimism. Pentecostals are faced with structural institutionalization and other parasitic detractions which plague the growth of movements. Yet, in the face of those obstacles, there seems to be a mood of optimism among pentecostal leaders, a mood which is typified in the faith statement of Melvin L. Hodges: "We see great things ahead" (1978:97). As Thomas F. Zimmerman has noted, pentecostals are grateful for the events of the day of Pentecost and amazed at the rise of the twentieth-century Pentecostal Movement, but feel that "the best days are not in the past. They are in the future" (1975:12-13).

As a whole pentecostals have not laid down their missionary mandate. Though expressing gratitude for the wider charismatic awakening among the historic and evangelical churches, pentecostals continue to feel that God has commissioned them with a message for the last days. Pastor Jack Hayford spoke recently of a "new anointing" upon the churches and projected that:

> . . . the world can be changed through intercessory prayer with spiritual warfare, followed by forthright evangelism and a self-giving stewardship of our lives to every nation . . . the Word of God confirms our history and challenges our present. Let us take it as the guarantee of our future—a vision He will fulfill. It is written that he will. (Pedersen 1981, Volume 18, No. 2:14)

At the movement's mid-century mark, pentecostal emissary David J. du Plessis reported with optimism on the "Golden Jubilees of Twentieth-Century Pentecostal Movements" (1958:193-201). Twenty-five years later his enthusiasm had not waned:

> I have said in the last decade that the churches are being stirred, now, look for the nations to be stirred. And I see signs in Africa and in other places where nations are being stirred by this charismatic life in the church. (Robeck 1983:5)

That scores of reports from every quarter are regularly coming to pentecostal periodicals is evidence of a "stirring." In a recent issue of *SOW* (*Save Our World*) magazine, Church of God field superintendents from South Africa, South America, the Far East, Europe, and other regions, gave solid reports of revival and growth, especially among young people (Moree 1983:7-10). The reports, typical of most major pentecostal missions operations, are more than "verbal fog" but are documented by statistics and by validations from outside observers.

Pentecostals are not only dreamers but realists. They see the reality of adverse political conditions and economic strain. However, these realities often result in unprecedented open doors (Moree 1983:10). As pragmatists, pentecostals take advantage of these receptivity factors and move with God into new opportunities for growth. For example, South African pentecostal leader M. L. Badenhorst has reported:

> I believe Southern Africa, including the nearby countries as well as South Africa, is entering a phase of revival with a spiritual awakening throughout the area. Churches which were almost empty a short while back are now filled and overflowing with worshippers. In our planning, we are moving with God to take advantage of these times of refreshing. Optimism prevails in the churches, and we are expecting great things from God. (Moree 1983:7-8).

Perpetuation. Pentecostal missions have been able to maintain perpetuity and growth primarily because of their commitment to leadership training, indigenous churches, and church planting (Wagner 1973:89ff; Brumback 1961:342-343; Enns 1971:236; Pomerville 1982:357). This pattern continues today as a thrust for the future (Mitchell 1982:380).

Pentecostals have also been able to capitalize upon the growing spiritual awakening among young people. Reporters who cite revivals in many parts of the world are quick to observe, "God is moving among the young people" and that leaders have "tapped into this promising development" (Moree 1983:9-10).

Though research is still needed to determine the missions awareness and involvement (on a career basis) among this generation of pentecostal young people, general trends indicate a good level of participation in youth missions programs (Denison 1983; Hand 1978; Graham 1983).

The major pentecostal bodies have also seen the necessity of recruitment and training of career missionary personnel. Already in 1943 the Assemblies of God initiated a series of informal conferences which became known as the "School of Missionary Orientation" (Menzies 1971:246-247). Other denominations have had missions emphases in their Bible school curriculums and have instituted internship programs for new appointees. More recently, the Assemblies of God have launched the "Missionary-in-Training" program (Graham 1983 August: 8-11). They, along with the Church of God, have initiated seminary level training for candidates, furloughing missionaries, and national church leaders (McClung 1983d).

For pentecostals, there is a commitment to the future.

Future Cautions

If there be a commitment, there is also a concern among pentecostals that they proceed in the right direction, not departing from some distinctions which have contributed to their growth.

A sign of pentecostal maturation and the move into ecclesiastical acceptance on the sect-church continuum has been a growing inclination toward self-criticism. As John Thomas Nichol has observed in his *Pentecostalism:*

One of the most significant indications that the maturation process has commenced in a sect might be, then, when it shifts its critical attention from others to itself. As one reads the literature that has been produced by Pentecostals, especially during the past two decades, one becomes aware that they have begun to evaluate themselves rather critically. (1966:234)

As a result, one sees introspective articles from insiders such as Charles W. Conn's "Can Pentecostalism Survive?" (1983:57-63) and David A. Womack's "The Future of the Pentecostal Movement" (1968:87-95). For pentecostals, the future may be guaranteed, but it is not, in the words of Melvin L. Hodges:

... without its problems and dangers.

There is a danger of the suppression of the Church on the part of ungodly governments within the Christian countries such as has occurred in Russia and China.

There exists the danger that the Pentecostal movement will become ingrown and be more concerned with its own blessings than in evangelizing the world.

A great danger exists that the Church will become less Pentecostal in experience while holding to certain forms of Pentecostal worship and doctrine. There is the danger of human element taking too important a place so that the divine is crowded out. There always exists the danger of losing our love and cooling off spiritually.

There is the danger that some of the churches planted by our missionaries overseas may be content with the status quo, and only seek to keep the machinery running instead of aggressively completing the work of evangelism that God has entrusted to them.

Of course, there is always the danger that the Church will compromise with the world and compromise its convictions. We desire to encourage fellowship with all true Christian bodies, but we must be alert that our united effort with other groups do not cause us to compromise our own particular mission to the world.

Against these dangers, we can only urge that we all seek a deep humility before God and not trust in the arm of flesh. Further, we must be sure that our doctrines and practice remain Bible-based rather than representing the best thinking of prominent men . . . we must constantly reaffirm our complete dependence upon the Holy Spirit in order to accomplish the work of God, and seek that true spiritual experience will be reborn with each new generation. (1974:36-37)

Concerns. From this writer's perspective, there seems to be five main areas of concern among pentecostals in regard to missionary expansion. These warrant intense investigation to determine their relationship to the future of pentecostal missions.

First, there is a concern over *loss of spiritual ardor.* Pentecostals mean it as more than rhetoric when they warn against the potential loss of pentecostal passion (Conn 1983:58; Womack 1968:92). They carry "a profound sense of spiritual concern" (Champion, Caldwell, and Leggett 1968:10) for their future and express the need of "a new anointing for a new day" (Edvardsen 1982:8).

Secondly, there is the danger of *drifting toward theological "slippage."* This has already been introduced in the former quote from Assemblies of God missiologist Melvin L. Hodges who subsequently warned in 1977 of the encroachment of universalism and liberal theology in his *A Theology of the Church and Its Mission: A Pentecostal Perspective.* Pentecostals, with all their dramatic growth and subsequent strength, are not immune to the dangers of losing their biblical ideology which has been at the heart of their movement. They must remind themselves, at any cost, says Norman L. Correll, of the "all-consuming knowledge that people will spend eternity in hell unless they accept Christ as their personal Saviour" (Graham 1984 March:9). This, and other theological foundations, must not be eroded.

In the third place, there is the danger of a *departure from an emphasis upon world evangelization.* Toward the end of his fruitful ministry both as an analyst of and spokesman for world pentecostalism, Donald Gee stated that the health of the Pentecostal Movement had been directly due to its emphasis upon world evangelization. He warned against a departure from this stand and noted that the Irvingites, British predecessors of the modern Pentecostal Movement, and the movement surrounding Alexander Dowie in Zion, Illinois, slipped into fanaticism and eventual obscurity because they became ingrown, neglecting the Great Commission (1963:91ff). Pentecostal missiologists serve a prophetic role to the rest of their pentecostal colleagues since their insistence upon world evangelization serves as a check upon the survival of the movement. Their ministry is typified by Hodges's admonition, "Any church that defaults on its missionary obligation is on its way to obscurity as far as the plan of God is concerned" (1974:33).

A fourth danger signal has been observed more by outsiders than by pentecostals themselves and, from a church growth standpoint, represents a threat to the vitality of the movement. It is the *potential neglect of the masses.* Though not accurate in all their assumptions, writers such as Robert Mapes Anderson (*Vision of the Disinherited: The Making of American Pentecostalism,* Oxford University Press 1979) and Liston Pope *(Millhands and Preachers* Yale University Press 1942) have documented the humble social origins of modern pentecostals. This has been no secret to pentecostals themselves, who, until recently, have prided themselves as not being "of this world," often meaning not being like the "rich folks in the uptown churches."

This perception was true, says theologian Walter J. Hollenweger, himself a former pentecostal, up to the Second World War. Hollenweger's view of the Church of God is most likely typical of the majority of contemporary pentecostal churches, particularly in North America and Europe:

Since then, a steady rise on the social scale has altered the sociological position of the Church of God. Other Pentecostal groups, particularly of Negro Pentecostals, have taken over its function. . . .

The Church of God has rapidly developed into a middle-class church. Its rigorist understanding of salvation has been modified, and it has adopted the patriotic values of the American middle class. (1972:59)

Pentecostal scholar Vinson Synan says that the trends toward upward mobility began even earlier than World War II. "By 1930," he said:

. . . there were many signs that indicated the trends that the pentecostal movement would follow in the future. It was clear by that time that the great appeal of the pentecostal religion would be to the lower classes, but that as the lower classes rose on the economic scale, the pentecostals would rise with them. The advent of pentecostal churches as middle-class institutions would come, not by converting members of the middle class, but by entering it *en masse* from below. (1971:200)

As a result of this new hospitable climate, pentecostals have gained respectability and seem to welcome it (Conn 1977:xxvii).

The inherent danger of moving out of the "social cellar," however, is that pentecostals will move away from the masses of winnable and receptive people. As a result, their rapid rate of growth could wane. Donald A. McGavran has warned against this "Halting Due to Redemption and Lift" and devotes an entire chapter to this problem in his magnum opus, *Understanding Church Growth* (1980:295ff). In a recent interview with the author, he sounded a warning to the Church of God, and to pentecostals in general. "Fear," he said, "even as you fear death, getting 'sealed off' into respectable churches which grow only by biological and transfer growth" (McClung 1983e:35).

McGavran's successor, C. Peter Wagner, has cautioned pentecostals against the "burning desire for respectability," and warns that with it comes a slowing rate of church growth (see Wagner's article, "Characteristics of Pentecostal Church Growth" in Part Four).

These concerns are especially vital in the Third World, where pentecostals are enjoying burgeoning growth. "The future belongs to the masses in Brazil," states researcher William R. Read, who also claims:

The Assemblies of God is a Church of and for the masses, and as long as it continues to minister to their needs it will grow, for in Brazil the future belongs to the Assemblies. (1965:143)

Whether that statement is as true today as it was almost twenty years ago is of vital importance to pentecostal trends in Latin America and around the world. This concern must be addressed.

Finally, a fifth danger for pentecostal missions is the *infiltration of institutionalization.* Early pentecostal missions were marked by spontaneity and a fluid dynamism. These strengths, unchecked and unchanneled, became weaknesses when they tended toward doctrinal naiveté (Synan 1971:111) and financial immaturity (Conn 1959:24-25). Later efforts toward consolidation and organization helped the pentecostal missionary cause (see Introduction under Part One: Historical Perspectives).

Though consolidation, structures, and organizations were necessary (and are biblically founded), they were never intended to drift toward the institutionalization and bureaucratization which plague pentecostal denominations today. Canadian pentecostal scholar Ronald Kydd says that organization for organization's sake was shunned in early pentecostalism:

> It is interesting to note that when we raise the question of organization, we are touching upon what was perhaps the paramount fear of the early Pentecostal. With the possible exception of the devil, himself, I have not found anything in the sources which is condemned with the passion that organization is. (1983:28)

Pentecostals need to re-examine how much organization for organization's sake is really necessary.

That questions of structure are already upon the minds of pentecostal denominational leaders is evident (Thomas 1983:8-9). From 1980-1984, for example, the Church of God underwent a massive self-evaluation under the direction of a General Study Commission. The Pentecostal Holiness Church has also completed a missions "Self-Study Report" (Underwood 1984). A tendency toward institutionalization is a threat to all of the mainline pentecostals.

Certainly one of the key items on the pentecostal missiological agenda will be the matter of structure and the avoidance of institutionalization. Pentecostal organizations that may have become overweight with bureaucratic overload will need to look for ways to maintain a lean and efficient missions thrust into the twenty-first century.

Prescriptions. If pentecostals have projected concerns and dangers, they are not without proposed solutions. Missiologist Paul A. Pomerville gave pentecostals a five-fold prescription that will help them take a fresh look at the Book of Acts for a trinitarian theology of mission, to give priority to Great Commission missions while concentrating on the receptive, to adopt a holistic view of mission while maintaining the priority of the evangelistic mandate, to emphasize church planting under the peculiar dynamic of the pentecostal experience, and to respect independency movements in the Third World (1982:353-360).

David A. Womack offers seven suggestions which "ought to assure the continuation of the Pentecostal nature of our church" (1968:94). These include: a commitment to apostolic doctrine; participation in apostolic experiences such as water baptism, the Baptism of the Holy Spirit, and the Lord's Supper; the maintenance of a proper worship atmosphere which allows for apostolic experiences; encouraging daily prayer and Bible reading and keeping Bible exposition central in the pulpit; the involvement of families of the local church in regular home prayer meetings; keeping a clear sense of missionary purpose before the people, reminding them of the Great Commission obligations; being ready at all times for the imminent coming of the Lord (1968:94-95).

Charles W. Conn agreed with Pomerville and Womack that the continuity of the Pentecostal Movement is centered in a constant adherence to the Scriptures and to the basic beliefs and tenets distinctive to pentecostalism. In addition, he said that there must be critical and honest self-evaluation, periodic times of renewal, and the flexibility "to adjust our course in order to keep on target" (1983:62-63).

Pentecostals are committed to the future but are also cautious that they proceed in the right direction, not departing from the essentials that have led to their inception and expansion.

Future Challenges

Numerous challenges face pentecostal missions as they look to the future. A large part of the challenge will be to rethink their history and motivation and face the concerns and threats to their own perpetuity. They will need to decide what the Holy Spirit is placing on their agenda and, under His direction, formulate strategies appropriate to God's vision for them. Among many things, two broad issues will need to be addressed in pentecostal missions: the people to be reached; and the people to reach them.

The people to be reached. Since Ralph D. Winter's landmark address on the cross-cultural dimensions of the unfinished task of world evangelization (at the International Congress on World Evangelization in Lausanne, Switzerland, in July, 1974) evangelical missions have been constantly called to the challenge of the massive blocs of non-Christian peoples and the thousands of unreached people groups among them.

Pentecostals have begun to take up this challenge. Regularly, the terms "unreached people," "hidden people," and "people groups" are making their way into pentecostal missions publications (Pedersen 1982; Graham 1983; Moree 1983). This, according to Leland Edwards, Director of Missions International for the Foursquare Church, is a "Renewed Vision." Speaking about the Foursquare Church, Edwards said:

> . . . we have set a goal to reach a minimum of 100 hidden people
> groups by the end of this decade. It means literally reaching that
> many more "nations" scattered around the world without any
> viable church amongst them and amongst whom the Gospel really
> has not penetrated. (Pedersen 1981 October:2)

He made these remarks in the guest editorial of a special issue of *Foursquare World Advance* devoted to the cause of unreached people.

Edgar Coombs, Special Assistant to Dr. Edwards, said in the same issue of *Advance* that this commitment to reach unreached people is a way of "pushing back darkness" and noted that for more than fifty years Foursquare workers "have been pushing back the darkness among the world's forbidden frontiers. Many of the first Foursquare missionaries sent to the field by our founder, Aimee Semple McPherson, went to some of the most primitive untouched people groups of the world" (Pedersen 1981 October:3).

The Assemblies of God are regularly highlighting the unfinished task as it relates to unreached people groups. Their January, 1983 issue of *Mountain Movers* from their Division of Foreign Missions called attention to their "Focus for the 80s" under the title of "New Frontier Evangelism." J. Philip Hogan, Executive Director of the division, recounted the many countries where the Assemblies of God have strong, thriving churches but reminded his readers of many peoples who have no witness of the gospel:

> "New Frontier Evangelism" is a term we have coined as an expression of our determination to penetrate the masses of unreached peoples. Four major blocs are of primary concern: the Chinese, Hindus, Muslims, and tribal peoples. These together total over half the world. (Graham 1983:4)

In publications, conferences, planning sessions, and schools, pentecostals are catching the vision for unreached people.

Pentecostals are also aware that the remaining task of world evangelization will be completed primarily in the cities. They have been traditionally urban on the mission field. It is interesting that on the eve of the twenty-first century there is a parallel to some of the events which accompanied the rise of pentecostalism at the outset of the twentieth century. Bloch-Hoell, for example, says that twentieth-century pentecostalism arose on the scene during a time of massive immigration, industrialization, and growth of cities which accompanied the emergence of this century (1964:9). In a sense, pentecostals are now faced with some of the same challenges that were before them in the early 1900s.

Accordingly, they now speak of "urban targets" (Underwood 1984:137). Cecil B. Knight, then General Overseer of the Church of God, told a group of his denominational missions colleagues in 1978:

> We must not be deterred by mounting obstacles such as finance or scarcity of land. Starting congregations with small cells in homes and rented quarters is still a viable approach to the invasion of cities. On the other hand, mass campaigns and such efforts need to be launched when feasible. By all means, we must reach the great cities of the world. (White 1978:5)

One of the organizations actively seeking the redemption of the cities is Youth With A Mission (YWAM), one of the largest and fastest growing interdenominational missions in the world. Though now broadly evangelical-charismatic, YWAM began with traditional pentecostal roots. Its founder and director, Loren Cunningham, is a former Assemblies of God minister (Wilson 1971) and many of its early core leadership came from the classical pentecostal movements. One of Cunningham's early recruits was Floyd McClung (a former Church of God minister) who has intitiated Urban Missions, a division of Youth With A Mission, in Amsterdam, Holland. Urban Missions is a program of urban evangelization and church planting in several world-class cities. Its long-range objective is "to send pioneering teams to the world's 300 great cities. It is projected that a minimum of 5000 workers are needed to accomplish this objective" (McClung 1982:60, 64).

Two of the key missiological issues for the 80s are on the pentecostal agenda: unreached peoples and cities. These are the people to be reached.

The people to reach them. In order for the Pentecostal Movement to have continued expansion and a wider effectiveness in reaping the harvest, it will have to concentrate on ways of motivating, recruiting, training, and deploying a greater "force for evangelism." Pentecostals should build on their present momentum in three areas: the increasing of career missionary personnel; the forming of new missions structures; and the proliferating of Third World missions agencies and personnel.

North American pentecostal missions have been among the leaders in establishing early indigenous leadership on their foreign fields, yet recognize that the day of the western missionary is far from being over. "Our help is needed," says Melvin L. Hodges, "until Jesus comes" (1974:33). Thus, pentecostal missions leaders are continuing to find ways to *increase career missionary personnel.*

The Assemblies of God, for example, in an effort to "grow their own missionaries," have launched their "Missionary-in-Training" program in order to facilitate missionary recruitment (Graham 1983 August:8-11).

The International Church of the Foursquare Gospel has adopted four major missions goals as a part of their "Advancing Through the '80s" emphasis. One of them is to increase their North American missionary personnel on the field from 100 currently to 185, and to develop a short-term missions program "to release scores of people into special overseas assignments" (Pedersen 1982).

Secondly, *pentecostals must look into the feasibility of forming new missions structures,* whether within or outside of denominational organizations. Initially, these structures seem to fall into three categories: denominational programs and departments; interdenominational faith missions; and missions programs from unaffiliated evangelists.

1. Denominational. Pentecostal denominations have well-developed departmental missions structures. Recently, they have been launching new efforts from within their denominations. The Assemblies of God have MAPS, a program of lay involvement using professional skills in short-term assignment such as building projects. Their youth department has Ambassadors in Mission (AIM) as a short-term missions experience (Graham 1983). Likewise, the Church of God has initiated their "Tentmaking" program for laymen, and Summer Training and Evangelism Partners (STEP) for their youth (Polen 1983). The Pentecostal Holiness Church aims at working in foreign cities through their "Operation Antioch" and Urban Church Training Centers (UCTC) (Underwood 1984).

2. Interdenominational. A second type of structure which has grown within the ranks of the Pentecostal Movement has been the interdenominational

faith mission such as Youth With A Mission, already described. Pentecostal denominations and groups like YWAM will need to find areas of cooperation and mutual support. Several vital questions about missions structures face pentecostals. For example: Should there be more separate pentecostal missions? Will there be joint missions endeavors and structures formed out of the Pentecostal World Conference or the Pentecostal Fellowship of North America (PFNA)? Will there be room for sodality-type missions movements *within* denominations, yet separate from the administration of denominational missions departments? Will new styles of missions approaches such as community living be an option for pentecostal denominations or other interdenominational or independent pentecostals? Will there be a growth in the formation of missions agencies among adherents of the charismatic movement? Reflections upon questions like these will help pentecostals carry out their mandate in the future.

3. Unaffiliated evangelists. A tnird issue to consider when dealing with the question of structures is that of the missions ministries and programs which have grown up around the ministries of unaffiliated evangelists. "Unaffiliated"is used in the broad sense because in reality some evangelists are technically licensed by a mother organization. For all practical purposes, however, they are basically directing their own ministries.

Missions movements have sprung up around the ministries of pentecostals like Gordon Lindsay (Christ for the Nations) and T.L. Osborn. More recently, brethren such as Morris Cerullo, Kenneth Hagin, and Jimmy Swaggart have been instrumental in developing overseas ministries. In addition, media outreaches such as The 700 Club have now taken on an international flavor. What do these "unaffiliated"structures mean for penteeostal missions? How can they be used in recruiting and deploying missions personnel? What is their function in church planting and leadership training? Are they focusing upon unreached peoples? Are they tending toward institutionalization? Answers to these questions need to be formulated and analyzed in order to further the pentecostal missionary cause.

A third main goal for pentecostal missions in the future should be the *proliferation of Third World missions agencies and personnel.* Pentecostals in the areas of Latin America, Africa, and Asia should be encouraged and allowed by older North American pentecostal brothers to develop their own sending agencies and appoint their own missionaries.

There are signs that this is already happening. As part of their "Goals for the 1980s," for example, the Pentecostal Holiness Church is encouraging each national church to form its own missions department (Underwood 1984:137).

The real strength of the contemporary Pentecostal Movement has moved to the Third World and they are moving ahead in many areas. Assemblies of God theologian Russell P. Spittler has predicted that "the first truly indigenous Pentecostal theology will emerge from the Third World, specifically Latin America, within 10 years"(1983:17). Since our Third World brethren are taking the lead in church growth, theologizing, and effectively struggling with issues of social justice, then may they also thrust the world Pentecostal Movement forward by sending forth cross-cultural laborers into the harvest! May they join other Third World evangelicals and charismatics in bringing about what missiologist Lawrence E. Keyes has called *The Last Age of Missions* (William Carey Library 1983).

Which way for pentecostal missions? The answer to that question is found in the positive commitment that pentecostals have to their own future. Their survival, direction, and success will depend upon how they deal with the concerns that are before them and how effectively they embrace their future challenges.

Until recently, most Church Growth literature about pentecostals was written by outside observers. Now, with missiological strategists like Paul Pomerville, pentecostals are analyzing, delineating, and articulating growth factors seen from an *insider's* perspective. Here, Pomerville summarizes pentecostal growth and proposes five "pentecostal prescriptions" and contributions for the future growth of the Church universal. His insights are drawn from his doctoral dissertation, "Pentecostalism and Missions: Distortion or Correction?" (Fuller Theological Seminary School of World Mission 1982).

12
The Pentecostals and Growth

Paul A. Pomerville*

Like the growth picture of any group the dynamics of Pentecostal growth are complex. A common error on the part of Pentecostals is to attempt to explain church growth in terms of one dimension—the Holy Spirit. But perhaps an equally deceptive error made by non-Pentecostals is the underestimation of that dimension of church growth, specifically, the dynamic of the Pentecostal experience itself. . . .

In order to understand Pentecostal missions strategy the Pentecostal's value for the Word and Spirit must be in focus. The issue of biblical authority determines the basic configuration of the Pentecostal's approach to missions. They are people of "The Book." While some may question their *use* of The Book, their hermeneutics, nevertheless Pentecostals seek to be led by Scripture as well as by the Spirit in their missions efforts. Their textbook for missions strategy often boils down to the Book of Acts. At first, this appears to be myopic; but . . . it is a crucial focus for missions strategy. From that textbook the Holy Spirit emerges as Supreme Strategist of mission. Therefore, even apart from their own motivating Pentecostal experience with the Spirit, they seek to be led by the Spirit in mission as the early church was in the Acts.

Both by experience and biblical focus, therefore, Pentecostals are characteristically "people of the Spirit" also. Their contemporary experience with the Spirit is found in the Book of Acts; they see that experience playing a significant role in the ongoing of mission in the Acts. Therefore, it becomes an important part of their contemporary missions strategy. As an enablement for witness it is crucial for the continuation of mission. Whole churches are thereby

---

* Missiologist Paul A. Pomerville served his first term as an Assemblies of God missionary in Indonesia. His second term was on the staff of ICI, the International Correspondence Institute, in Brussels, Belgium. He is a 1982 graduate of Fuller School of World Mission (Ph.D.), and the author of *The Third Force in Missions*.

mobilized in mission by that "missionary spirit" that indwells the church. Pentecostal missiologists examine Paul's strategy and observe him planting churches, training leaders, and trusting the Holy Spirit to equip and develop the church in its native setting. Therefore, it is this "biblical pragmatism" which characterizes Pentecostal missions strategy, and leads Pentecostals to emphasize that which they find in Scripture in their missions approach. *The first Pentecostal prescription for growth would be to suggest a fresh look at the Book of Acts in the quest for a thorough-going trinitarian theology of mission.*

What do Pentecostals find in Scripture which accounts for their phenomenal growth? That is to say, what emphases in strategy do they find in Scripture, in addition to the dynamic of the Pentecostal experience itself? The previous discussion of the "Kingdom and the poor" accounts for a major Pentecostal growth dynamic. Pentecostals have a clear view of the priority of mission—the proclamation of the gospel. The role of evangelism, therefore, is crucial for Pentecostal mission theology. They pursue this priority of mission, focusing on those who are receptive to their message. This, Wagner believes, is the key to unlocking the phenomenal growth of Pentecostals in Latin America (Wagner 1973:65). Because they are responsive, more often than not, the poor are the focus of Pentecostal missions efforts. The Pentecostal finds himself in "fertile" soils, but not by design; it is by a "biblical pragmatism." A response to the gospel is interpreted as an indication of the leading of the Spirit. After all, it is not his ministry to prepare persons for the gospel? Is not a response to the gospel an indication of his working and leading (Wagner 1973:68-69)?

Furthermore, the Word is often confirmed by the signs following. This is the Pentecostal expectation among the majority of the unevangelized—the Animists; this approach amounts to effective evangelism. This in itself may be a factor of growth equal to that of the concentration on the responsive. The world view and Christian experience of the Pentecostal is appealing and effective in the power-encounter with Animists. The phenomenal growth of the African Independent Church Movement is proof of this factor. This may point to the need of the people of God to be confirmed by both the inward and outward witness of the Spirit. "Focus on the receptive" may appear to be overly pragmatic, but it was the strategy of Jesus (Luke 8:37; 9:5, 53-56; 10:8-12; 15:7). This principle of receptivity also emerges from the Kingdom motif. The twofold sign of the Kingdom (preaching of the gospel, and the confirming signs of the Spirit) is, in fact, characteristic of Pentecostal missions strategy. Phenomenal growth is explicable in terms of the above configuration of growth dynamics. *The second Pentecostal prescription for growth would be to give a priority to Great Commission missions in the power of the Spirit, with an expectation of the Spirit's charismatic confirming ministry while concentrating on the receptive.*

However, the priority of evangelism should be pursued while not losing sight of the biblical, holistic view of mission. *The third Pentecostal prescription for growth concerns the necessity for a holistic view of mission, but with a priority on the evangelistic mandate.* Evangelism's relation to "service" or the cultural mandate must be held in biblical tension. Witness and service should both be involved in missions practice. However, the biblical priority was seen to be evangelism. They are distinguished mandates. There is merit in the idea that the best way to fulfill both mandates is to pursue Great Commission missions. . . .

Concerning the growth of Pentecostal churches among the poor, the Pentecostal poor are attracted more by the "comprehensive message" than they are by the "comprehensive approach." It is precisely at this point, the comprehensive Pentecostal message, that the charismatic community appeals to the "common man." The Pentecostal's recognition that he or she has an important part, a ministry, in the local Body of Christ, due to the enabling and equipping of the Holy Spirit, helps him or her to achieve a dimension of fulfillment that is possible to even the "poorest of the poor." Rather than an upward social mobility being the point of attraction for purposes of social power, the upward spiritual mobility for purposes of humble service is the point of attraction.

The phenomenon of "redemption and lift" is often noted in Church Growth studies (McGavran 1970:261). The gospel brings the life of God which permeates all of the dimensions of human life. McGavran states:

> When Christ comes in, man becomes a new creation. He repents and turns from his sins. He gains victory over pride, greed, laziness, drink, hate, and envy. He ceases quarreling with his neighbours and chasing women. He turns from litigation to constructive activity. He educates his children. He learns what God requires of him, and worships regularly. He becomes a more effective human being. . . .
>
> The fellowship of the Church buoys him up. The brethren gather at his bedside to pray for him in sickness. He reads or hears the Bible and realizes that God is for him and is available to him. He realizes he is a son of God and begins to act as such—begins to live for others. His community, in which many others have accepted Christ, becomes a better and better place to live. (1970:261)

To emphasize this sociocultural lift that accompanies redemption is not a "cop out" on social concern and the cultural mandate. First, it is to differentiate between the evangelistic and cultural mandates in terms of the priority of mission. Second, it recognizes that to accomplish the former is to bring into being the true potential for the fulfillment of the latter. The local church itself, as a community of believers and individuals, becomes the focal point for the fulfillment of the cultural mandate in its own community. Wagner notes that the social change brought about by Pentecostals in Latin America is significant. However, it is "indirect" in nature. But he attributes their priority on evangelism and the indirect social transformation that evolves from this as a positive factor in their phenomenal growth (Wagner 1973:138-140).

Another Pentecostal growth dynamic in connection with the above is that the evangelism priority is directed toward *church planting* (Wagner 1973:53-63). Great Commission missions is conceived in terms of integrating those who are evangelized into churches. Where there are not churches they should be planted.

Evangelism is to go beyond the mere proclamation of the gospel in geographical locations to persuading men and women to commit their lives to Christ and become members of a local church. Furthermore, for Pentecostals evangelism does not stop with believers integrated into the church. The whole church is to be mobilized in witness. The integration of the believer leads to his or her orientation to the Christian life and worship by Bible training, then this leads to ministry in the Body and ministry outside of the Body in terms of witness in the local community. The Pentecostal *experience* (not doctrine alone), however, is the major dynamic in this mobilization of the church (Wagner 1973:34-35, 80), not the quality and depth of training, nor the organizational expertise of the Pentecostal. *The fourth Pentecostal prescription for growth concerns an evangelism directed toward church planting, the view of the local church as the Holy Spirit's instrument for world evangelism, and the Pentecostal experience as a primary dynamic for its mobilization in witness.*

The cruciality of this church-centeredness relates to the fulfillment of mission in the world. At the same time the emphasis on its instrumentality does not cause a denigration of its essence. It is to say that the church, or the New Testament people of God, are a major means by which God accomplishes His special mission in the world (1 Peter 2:4-10; Hebrews 8:8-10). The Church as the New Israel, the new people of God, is a major biblical theme (Genesis 12:1-4; Exodus 19:4-6; Mark 11:12-14, 20-25; 12:1-12; Romans 11:16-24; John 15; cf. Psalms 80:8-16; Isaiah 5:1-7; 1 Peter 2:9-10). The Church is by heritage, by Spirit (it is infused with a missionary spirit), and by command (Matthew 28:19; Romans 16:26) a missionary community. The church is under the mandate of Christ, and is thrust out by the indwelling missionary Spirit to disciple peoples wherever it exists. Therefore, it must be planted among every ethnic group. Multiplying congregations is the means for world evangelism. Melvin Hodges states:

> Each local church . . . becomes a living cell of the Body of Christ,
> and God's agent for the bringing of the message of reconciliation to
> its community. Therefore church-planting and church growth (cell
> multiplication) are of supreme importance in Christian mission.
> (1972:144)

Churches become home bases for further sending missions. The "strawberry vine" principle, or mother-church principle, is prominent in Pentecostal church planting strategy (Wagner 1973:61). . . .

The fifth major Pentecostal prescription for growth, one that is crucial for the growth of the Christian faith in the non-western world, is that independency movements must be respected. They represent a major missiological issue in the last part of the twentieth century. Their recognition and nurture could be decisive for the evangelization of the so-called resistant blocks of unevangelized peoples. The western contribution to these movements cannot be made, the Pentecostal contribution included (which is significant), until the movements are treated with respect. Respect must be shown toward their Pentecostal expression of Christianity;

it must be viewed positively in the context of the New Testament, as well as against the background of indigenous religion. Central to giving this respect is a trust in the working of God the Holy Spirit in their Christian experience and in their efforts to express an indigenous form of the Christian faith.

Pentecostals have long been noted for their pioneering efforts among unreached tribes and people groups. More recently, most leading pentecostal groups have joined the "unreached peoples" emphasis of the Lausanne Movement and the EFMA and IFMA. One of the first groups to see the strategic importance of "hidden people" was the International Foursquare Church. Dr. Jack Hayford's article is indicative of challenges now being presented in the missions publications of pentecostal denominations. It is drawn from the *Foursquare World Advance* (October 1981), the missions magazine of the Foursquare Church.

13
Hidden But Not Unreachable

Jack Hayford*

Among other signs of renewal, the work of the Holy Spirit in the Church today is being manifest by an increased refinement in missionary strategy. More are gaining expanded insight into the scope of the Great Commission, and its implications in the complex population structures of our global society.

Jesus' command to go to every nation (*ethnos,* Matthew 29:19) is elaborated in Acts 1:8, "unto the utmost place" (*eschatos*); and finally expounded in the vision of John, found in Revelation 5:9, as he describes the redeemed coming from "every tribe (*phule*), tongue (*glossa*), people (*laos*) and nation (*ethnos*)." Here is scriptural evidence that the Holy Spirit has literally ransacked our language to confront us with adequate and specific terminology indicating the detailed nature of our assignment to evangelize *everyone.*

We all recognize our call to go to "all the earth," but our going is given more specific guidance than merely that we cross national boundaries. The words of the Bible emphasized above precisely show that every people group—tribal group, language group, ethnic group—is to be reached, and align us more closely with God's heart when we discover it.

It is not adequate to say, for example, "We have sent missionaries to Bolivia." A more probing perspective is in the question: "How many of its sixteen tribal groups have been reached?" Bolivia includes many separate "peoples" who are "hidden" from view if we lump them in the whole. As a case in

---

* Dr. Jack Hayford is the Senior Pastor of Van Nuys Foursquare Church, commonly known as The Church on the Way, in Van Nuys, California. He has been among the first pentecostal supporters of the Lausanne Covenant since its adoption in 1974. Hayford is a noted conference speaker and radio and television personality as well as the head of Living Way Ministries. He is the author of *Prayer Is Invading the Impossible* and *The Church on the Way.*

point, these Bolivian groups of people vary in population from the largest, about 1,000,000 Quichuas, to an actual count of 258 Indians of the Chacobo tribe. Thus in looking at Bolivia's 5½ million population, our prayer directive and evangelism concerns gain refinement.

And it is not only the noting of tribal groups which help us discover our task with greater precision, but within every nation are distinct cultural groups whose collective uniqueness and life style often create barricades to evangelism unless we are sensitized to their distinction. For example, one distinct "hidden people" within our own North American continent are those who live and work in the race tracks of the land. They are virtually a people unto themselves, and there are more than 50,000 of them. They are not at all unreachable, but their special arena of life tends to "hide" them from our awareness, and thereby from our concerned prayer and loving outreach.

Since true intercessory prayer is spiritual warfare at its most demanding level, it is important to know how to take aim when you go into battle. Knowing how to pray for hidden people is more than a matter of intellectual analysis. Perceiving different cultures, recognizing the barriers to specialized penetration in ethnic settings, is often the key to awakened compassion in concern and passion in prayer. Recently, I experienced this sharpening of focus in prayer while perusing P.J. Johnstone's *Operation World*.[1] I was praying for the desert nation of Chad, in north central Africa. Factual information quickened the pulse of my prayer: "The Quaddai," I read, "800,000 people in 17 tribes are largely Muslim . . . unwilling to receive the Gospel but slowly responding to the loving care of medical and agricultural missionaries seeking to alleviate their suffering in this drought prone area." My heart leapt with Jesus' words, *"I was hungry and you gave me meat . . ."* (Matthew 25:35), and I was moved to pray for those people and the missionaries who are seeking to establish a beachhead through love and service.

With these above thoughts in mind, perhaps you might benefit as I have through taking these steps in learning to pray for "hidden people" groups of the world:

Pray first for the Holy Spirit to give you direction as to a nation or geographic region to make as your focus. Praying for the world begins with praying for a part of it. You may find guidance coming in varied ways. One man I know was given the name of a province in China which he had never heard of. He had to find it on the map to verify it existed, yet the Holy Spirit had whispered it to his heart while he prayed. Another person I know said, "I decided to pray for Germany—East and West—because my family background is German." Both received direction, but in very different ways.

Though the use of available materials, such as the annual *Unreached Peoples,*[2] look up those hidden people groups who occupy that area the Lord has put on your heart. There are just over 200 nations in the world, but there are nearly 17,000 definable people groups. The hidden ones are those whom we have been unable to yet penetrate with the Gospel. Isn't it logical that this may be because we have not yet saturated that culture with prayer?

Discovering the panorama of peoples present in the geographic area of your concern, and learning something of their life and their need, will stir prayer . . . and open doors of evangelism.

Footnotes

1 STL Publications, P.O. Box 48, Bromley, Kent, England.
2 David C. Cook Publisher, Elgin, Illinois.

Though criticized for unduly seeking the miraculous, pentecostals have been very pragmatic about the matter of signs and wonders as they relate to world evangelization. For pentecostal missionaries, signs and wonders are seen as the necessary fulfillment of the Great Commission of Jesus Christ and should normally accompany the Spirit-anointed preaching of the gospel. What role will the miraculous play in reaching the yet unreached population blocs of our world? For South African evangelist Christiaan De Wet, signs and wonders are an indispensable part of the advancement of the kingdom into new territory, especially those under the influence and domination of such belief systems as Animism and Islàm. De Wet's article is from Chapter 8 of his Fuller School of World Mission Master's thesis "Signs and Wonders in Church Growth" (Fuller Theological Seminary School of World Mission 1981).

14
The Challenge of Signs and Wonders in World Missions for the Twentieth Cenutry

Christiaan De Wet*

I get excited when I think of the tremendous opportunity that we have of reaching the millions who are still in the utter darkness of sin and misery and slavery of Satan. Some theologians are very pessimistic and they say that the age of missions is over. I think the devil says Amen to that.

No, it is not over! We are now stepping over the threshold of a mighty new wave of evangelism that is going to shake the foundations of hell and harvest millions of precious souls for the kingdom of God.

This is the best time ever to reach out to a lost world for the proclamation of the gospel than ever before in the history of mankind. Better, and more important that anything else, God is eager to move by His Spirit and to touch whole nations with His saving power.

Whenever and wherever the gospel is proclaimed, God is ready to demonstrate His power and to confirm His Word through signs and wonders. Seeing the millions of people that have been reached for Christ directly through signs and wonders, I have no alternative but to believe that signs and wonders will be one of God's choice missiological strategies to reach the lost. . . .

Most of those who have used this same strategy through the years have reaped plentifully and have seen tremendous church growth. Again I want to stress that we ought not to look at signs and wonders as an end in itself, but rather as a means to an end. Yes, surely, we do want to see people blessed through the healing of their sicknesses, but someday they will die in any case. However, the saving of a lost soul from hell has eternal value.

* Christiaan De Wet is a pastor and evangelist with the Apostolic Faith Mission, South Africa's oldest pentecostal denomination. As an active pentecostal missionary in South Africa, he has been personally involved in the ministry of signs and wonders in evangelism.

I am positive that God will also bless other strategies in the harvesting of the unreached, but with not nearly as much fruit as signs and wonders.

No other strategy holds a bigger challenge for reaching the millions of Animists, to break the resistance of the millions of Muslims, to destroy the strongholds of Marxism than a ministry of signs and wonders.

A Challenge to Reach the Animistic World

In 1973 Alan Tippett predicted that "animism" will be a spent force" in the following ten to twenty years and that at least 200 million people would be "ripe unto harvest" for Christianity (1973:5).

I share this view with Tippett. As has been stated previously,the animistic worldview sees the world wholistically. They see the spiritual forces as having ready access to their world. Their life is one of trying to live harmoniously with these spiritual beings. In this attempt their lives become totally bound up with regulations, rules, taboos, sacrifices and rituals that will help them maintain this harmony. Because these spirits are sometimes good and sometimes bad, often capricious and unpredictable, it is extremely difficult to maintain this harmony.

Dollar estimates that there are about one billion people who are animistic in their worldview (1981:140). One billion people are tired of the empty promises of the witch doctors, the shamans and sorcerers; tired of living in constant fear day in an day out. They are exhausted in their efforts to please the ancestral spirits and to try and keep the evil forces at bay.

To them the message of a powerful God who breaks the chains of sin and degradation, whose blood protects His people, who demonstrates His power by healing them, who cares for people, is like the cool breeze of the evening wind. No wonder that among animistic societies people by the thousands attend healing campaigns. They are not interested in a God who can only save them from a future judgment and who only prepares for them a place in heaven for the future. What really appeals to them is a God who can heal and protect and give them peace of heart now, and who also saves them from hell and prepares for them a place in heaven.

Some argue that so many attend these campaigns because they do not have many medical doctors to tend to their needs. There might be an element of truth in it, but certainly it is not the whole answer. We get the same phenomena where thousands attend such campaigns in, for example, South Africa or America, where there are ample medical facilities. Yes, the sensational might attract some, but I wonder sometimes if there is not also deep down in the Westerner's heart that something that cries out, "Show me that powerful Jesus of the Bible that can heal and do miracles! Not the powerless Jesus that some preachers and theologians are preaching." People want to serve a God who can really meet their needs, even if it takes a miracle to do so!

And what if that which Tippett believes happens, and that animism becomes a "spent force"? Who will reach these people as they get more educated and disillusioned with the ancestral spirits? All of a sudden there will be millions of people who will be in a spiritual vacuum. Will we leave it to the more than eager Communists to fill their hearts with Marxism?

People who are raised in animistic societies are accustomed to the supernatural because they are familiar with the spirit world, be it good or evil spirits. A ministry of signs and wonders will reach these people by the millions for Christ.

A last point I want to make is this. The fear of the spirits among animistic people is most evidenced in times of sickness. When Jesus heals them in a campaign, it is not only a physical blessing for them, but also a spiritual victory. For them He then becomes "Christus Victor," the most powerful God that they really want to serve.

But what about the most unresponsive segment to be reached by the gospel of Jesus Christ today, the Muslims?

A Challenge to Reach the Muslims

For years now the Muslims have been regarded as one of the hardest and most resistant groups to reach with the gospel of Jesus Christ. Don McCurry, Director of the Samuel Zwener Institute, states that, "Muslims may constitute the largest single block of unreached people in the world. Of the three billion unreached, 24% were Muslims" (1978a:13). This represents one out of every six persons.

Many Christians who have long been praying for Islam have been greatly encouraged by the people movements to Christ that have occurred among the Muslims in Indonesia since the abortive communist coup in 1966. Islam has always been resistant to Christianity, but what has taken place in Indonesia may be indicative of a new day dawning for Christian outreach to the Muslim world. Donald McGavran is quite optimistic concerning this and feels that within the near future they are going to become responsive in great numbers. He believes that:

> After Muslims have tried substitutes of various sorts, they will become responsive—to communism or to Christianity—in very large numbers. They, too, are men and cannot live in a faith-vacuum. (1970:224)

McCurry also holds this view. "There are many, many signs that point to a coming harvest" (1970b:188).

One is very grateful for the fact that Muslims are becoming more and more responsive to the gospel of Jesus Christ. However, I believe that there is a bridge towards the Muslims that has not been used enough. The biggest bridge towards reaching Muslims is a powerful ministry of the Holy Spirit, which must be evidenced by mighty signs and wonders and exorcisms, a ministry that will be a demonstration of the resurrected Christ's glory and power.

Because a big part of Islam is also animistic, the felt needs of both groups are very much the same. "His (Islam) is dominated by the 'evil eye,' by sickness and death, by sorcery and curses. Not by quranic Islam but by animistic Islam, and the hunger of the heart it constantly discloses" (Glasser 1978:137). Just as is the case with the animistics, they need a God who can really protect them and set them free from evil spirits.

This is the reason why charismatic evangelists in Pakistan have such huge success among the Muslims. Praying for the sick and exorcizing demons in rural villages, they have been literally besieged by Muslims in need (Fraser 1978:169).

Different people that have been working among the Muslims report good success as a result of signs and wonders. Musk tells of an official in high Islamic circles in Egypt that turned to Christ when his sick little child was miraculously healed. His conclusion is that Islam needs to discover that Christ can heal, can give power, can defeat demons, can speak supernaturally to man to guide him (Musk, 1978:213). In response to this article by Musk in *The Gospel and Islam,* somebody wrote:

> . . . that Christians in Muslim lands must show that they believe in miracles as a major and integral part of their daily lives, and argued that no missionary should be sent to the Middle East who does not believe in the miracles that can be performed through the power of the Holy Spirit. Many readers concurred with Mr. Musk that "power encounter"—practical applications of the power of Christ over sickness, evil spirits, and superstition— is the best approach to adherents of "popular Islam." (Musk 1978:223)

Bashir Abdol Massih tells about a born-again orthodox priest whom God is using mightily in Muslim evangelism in the Middle East. Among the key factors contributing to his success are miracles. "Miracles were present as a persuasive mover of the Muslim will and as part of his religious logic, for he is a firm believer in the supernatural" (Massih 1978:91).

Don McCurry testifies that, "In Egypt, through healing and exorcisms, Muslims are 'seeing' the power of Christ and believing" (1978b:186).

Who can still doubt that signs and wonders can be positively used in reaching countries for God's kingdom? It does not matter whether it is an animistic or Islamic or communistic or Western country. The fact is that they can be reached!

I believe that today's churches, mission agencies, missionaries, pastors, evangelists and ordinary laypeople are confronted by the biggest challenge ever to reach a lost world for Christ. The harvest is ripe and ready to be gathered. God wants to send out His messengers with a special unction of the Holy Spirit to confirm His glorious message of hope and salvation through signs and wonders.

One may argue, "But we do not have anybody in our church that has the gift of healing or of miracles." Then it is high time that you start praying and waiting upon the Lord to impart the gifts to somebody. When you start praying, very soon God will wake up somebody who will have the ministry of signs and wonders.

One can also argue, "Our church is not really interested in the outwardly signs, we confine ourselves to the deeper spiritual things." In that case you will just happily have to watch how the Pentecostal churches keep on growing and growing and winning the world for the Lord.

No, God does not want to use only the Pentecostal churches! We thank God for what He is doing through them, but He wants to use every available vessel in bringing in the harvest. . . .

May it be the prayer of us all: ". . . grant to thy servants to speak thy word with boldness, while thou stretchest out thy hand to heal and signs and wonders are performed through the name of thy holy servant Jesus" (Acts 4:29-30).

Most Assemblies of God historians have agreed that the Assemblies of God was formed as a missions organization. This pentecostal denomination has a positive self-image of itself as a body that God has raised up as an instrument, an agency, a channel to evangelize the world. In its self-evaluation, the Assemblies of God has expressed a concern for a constant spiritual revitalization and a perpetual commitment to world evangelization. This is the tone of the "Declaration at St. Louis," an Assemblies of God statement that returns to foundational elements in the church's history: mission, evangelism, the supernatural working of the Holy Spirit, and charismatic worship. The "Declaration" was adopted at the 1968 Assemblies of God Council on Evangelism in St. Louis, Missouri. It is excerpted from *Our Mission in Today's World* edited by Richard Champion, Edward S. Caldwell, and Gary Leggett (Gospel Publishing House 1968).

15
Declaration at St. Louis
Assemblies of God

Recognizing the end times in which we live and the evident hand of God which has rested upon the Assemblies of God for these times, and having engaged together in prayerful study in this Council on Evangelism concerning God's purpose in the world today and our place in His purpose, we make the following declaration.

Declaration

Because the Assemblies of God came into being as the Holy Spirit was poured out in prophetic fulfillment at the turn of the century and a body of like-minded Pentecostal believers voluntarily joined together in worship, ministry, and service; and

Because the Assemblies of God has accepted the Bible as the inerrant Word of God and has declared it as the whole counsel of God, giving emphasis to the full gospel; and

Because the Assemblies of God has grown rapidly both at home and abroad and has continued to experience the blessing of God as it has sought to do His will and to be an instrument of divine purpose; and

Because the Assemblies of God determines to remain a body of believers responding fully to the divine working in these last days; therefore, be it

Declared, That the Assemblies of God considers it was brought into being and built by the working of the Holy Spirit as an instrument of divine purpose in these end times; and be it

Declared further, That the Assemblies of God recognizes God's purposes concerning man are:

1. To reveal Himself through Christ to seek and to save that which was lost.
2. To be worshiped in Spirit and in truth.
3. To build a body of believers in the image of His Son; and be it

Declared further, That the Assemblies of God recognizes that its mission is:

1. To be an agency of God for evangelizing the world.

2. To be a corporate body in which many may worship God.

3. To be a channel of God's purpose to build a body of saints being perfected in the image of His Son; and be it

Declared further, That the Assemblies of God exists expressly to give continuing emphasis to this mission in the New Testament apostolic pattern by encouraging believers to be baptized in the Holy Spirit, which enables them:

1. To evangelize in the power of the Holy Spirit with accompanying supernatural signs,

2. To worship God in the fullness of the Spirit,

3. To respond to the full working of the Holy Spirit in expressing His fruit and gifts as in New Testament times, edifying the body of Christ and perfecting the saints for the work of the ministry.

Response

Leaders: In response to this declaration of mission of the Assemblies of God, we affirm that God is not willing that any should perish but is revealing Himself through Jesus Christ and is seeking to save the lost, calling man to Himself in Christ.

Congregation: This we affirm!

Leaders: We affirm that God desires to build a body of believers in the image of His Son, separating them unto Himself.

Congregation: This we affirm!

Leaders: We give ourselves to be an agency of God for evangelizing the world through Jesus Christ.

Congregation: We give ourselves to Him for this mission.

Leaders: We give ourselves to be a spiritual body in which man may worship God in the beauty of holiness and may be separated unto Him.

Congregation: We give ourselves to Him for this mission.

Leaders: We give ourselves to build a body of saints being perfected in the image of His Son, conforming unto Him.

Congregation: We give ourselves to Him for this mission.

Leaders: We dedicate ourselves to Spirit-filled living and teaching, to encourage believers likewise to be baptized in the Holy Spirit, knowing this will enable us to evangelize in the power of the Spirit with signs following.

Congregation: We dedicate ourselves to this mission.

Leaders: We dedicate ourselves to be filled with the Spirit so we will worship God in the fullness of the Spirit and minister before Him in spirit and truth.

Congregation: We dedicate ourselves to this mission.

Leaders: We dedicate ourselves to respond to the full working of the Holy Spirit, praying He will use us mightily even as He worked in the New Testament Church, granting expression of fruit and gifts and ministries for the edifying of the body of Christ.

Congregation: We dedicate ourselves to this mission.

Leaders: This purpose of God and this mission of the Assemblies of God we affirm this day, and to this mission we dedicate ourselves, praying always to be kept in the faith, to evangelize in the power of the Spirit, to worship in spirit and in truth, and to conform to the image of His Son—so help us God!

Congregation: To this purpose of God and to this mission of the Assemblies of God we give ourselves this day—so help us God!

Founded on August 19, 1886, the Church of God (Cleveland, Tennessee) has the distinction of being North America's oldest pentecostal denomination. Throughout its history, this organization has been characterized by a strong missions emphasis. Typical of most North American pentecostal denominations, the Church of God has more members outside of North America than within the continent. The Church of God has sought to maintain a focus on evangelism and world missions through international gatherings such as the 1983 International Congress on World Evangelism. The following covenant was adopted by unanimous response at the congress in Cleveland, Tennessee, on August 12, 1983, and was subsequently published in all Church of God publications.

16
A Covenant on World Evangelization

Church of God
(Cleveland, Tennessee)

We, the delegates to the International Congress on World Evangelism, have gathered as followers of our Lord Jesus Christ. We come from many diverse cultures and countries; but we are united in the communion of the Church of God and in His universal Church by the common bond of the redemptive act of God in Jesus Christ. Participation in this Congress has heightened our awareness of our history and our destiny. We have been humbled, therefore, by the realization that God has favored us with His salvation and has entrusted us with His ministry in the world. While recognizing the significant accomplishments of other missions agencies, we feel compelled to acknowledge the extraordinary blessings of God upon the international ministries of the Church of God. Developments in the modern missionary movement and unparalleled growth in missions activity around the world compel us to respond.

We Respond with Thanksgiving

We praise God for what He is doing in the world today and acknowledge it to be the sovereign work of the Holy Spirit. We rejoice that the Church of God is an international communion with vibrant national churches which are sending missionaries to other cultures while effectively evangelizing their own people.

We thank God for the worldwide outpouring of the Holy Spirit and for the role He has allowed the Church of God to play in world evangelization (Romans 1:8; 16:26; Ephesians 1:10-12; Revelation 7:9).

We Respond with Concern

In spite of the significant advances of the modern missionary movement over the past two hundred years, we are sobered by the immensity of the unfinished task:

171

- To our world of 4.8 billion, a half million people are being added every day.
- Some three billion are still untouched with the Gospel message.
- At least 16,750 identifiable people groups are without a Christian witness.

We are concerned that the missionary force is still woefully inadequate and that only a small fraction of the Church of God membership is involved directly in cross-cultural ministry (Matthew 9:36-38; Jeremiah 3:14; Luke 10:2; John 4:35).

We Respond with Commitment

Because we are grateful to God and because we are concerned about our world, we respond in humility by committing ourselves to a "world Christian" lifestyle:

A submitted lifestyle that brings all goals and ambitions under the Lordship of Jesus Christ;

A biblical lifestyle that seeks to conform our lives to God's purpose and will revealed in the only infallible rule of faith—the Bible;

A separated lifestyle that recognizes the obligations of being in the world without conforming to its way of thinking and living;

A dedicated lifestyle that transcends any political-economic system and seeks to channel resources to areas of need rather than amassing them for our own personal comfort and security;

A cross-cultural lifestyle that appreciates the dignity and value of all people and seeks to communicate the gospel to them in terms of their own cultural context;

A cooperative lifestyle that affirms our solidarity with all committed followers of Jesus Christ regardless of their culture or nationality and that recognizes our unity (not uniformity) in the body of Christ;

An anticipatory lifestyle that expectantly awaits the return of our Lord who gave us the Great Commission in the context of His promise to return (Matthew 28:18-20; Luke 19:13; 24:47-49; John 13:34, 35; 17:15-18; Acts 1:8; Romans 12:1, 2).

We commit ourselves to crossing cultural barriers in order to go to the unreached peoples of the world—whether in our own country or abroad. We commit ourselves to raising missions awareness and support among Christians in our own culture. We commit ourselves to a lifestyle which will sustain this resolve in ourselves and encourage it in others. In view of these challenges and commitments, we confess our own weakness and inadequacy and reaffirm our dependence on God in the task of world evangelization.

References Cited
Annotated Bibliography of Pentecostal Missions

L. Grant McClung, Jr

Introduction

This Annotated Bibliography of Pentecostal Missions is primarily concerned with the history, theology, and practices of the Pentecostal Missionary Movement. Its focus is upon pentecostal *missions,* mainly from North America. Though concerned primarily with the mainline pentecostal movements and denominations, there are a few entries related to the charismatic movement and cross-cultural ministry (Dollar 1981, Jones 1976, Harper 1965, and others).

The bibliography is preliminary, not exhaustive. Most of its entries are *books.* There are a few references to magazine or journal articles.

Finally, it should be noted that extensive pentecostal literature holdings are available for researchers through various pentecostal publishing houses and such centers as the Assemblies of God Archives in Springfield, Missouri; the Pentecostal Research Center in Cleveland, Tennessee; and the Holy Spirit Research Center at Oral Roberts University in Tulsa, Oklahoma.

The references cited in this book are incorporated into the main body of the annotated bibliography.

Annotated Bibliography

1938 *A Survey of the Assemblies of God in Foreign Lands.* Springfield, Missouri. Foreign Missions Department of Assemblies of God. 59 pages.

Anderson, Robert Mapes
1979 *Vision of the Disinherited: The Making of American Pentecostalism.* New York: Oxford University Press. 334 pages.

Chapter 6, "Apostles and Prophets," gives a biographical cross section of 45 selected American pentecostal leaders from 1909-1914. Good leadership selection study, which also provides insights into the missions consciousness of the early leaders. The bibliography is very helpful.

Key Words
young, rural, southern, blue collar, low economic status

Apostolic Faith Mission
1965 *A Historical Account of the Apostolic Faith.* Portland, Oregon: Apostolic Faith Mission. 304 pages.

Part VI (Chapters 22-29) traces the foreign missionary work of this trinitarian pentecostal group.

Key Words
Scandinavian countries, Africa, West Indies, Newfoundland, Lebanon, Japan

Arrington, French L.
1978 *Divine Order in the Church.* Cleveland, Tennessee: Pathway Press. 183 pages.

A study of 1 Corinthians from a pentecostal perspective. See Chapter 7 on spiritual gifts.

Key Words
unity of the Spirit, diversity of gifts, mutual interdependence, orderly worship

Arscott, Lindsay
1971   *Forward in Faith*. Kingston, Jamaica: Hallmark Publishing Ltd. 44 pages.

Area case study. The story of the New Testament Church of God in Jamaica (Cleveland, Tennessee).

Key Words
1925, conflict, persecution, Bible school, pentecostal preaching

Aspinall, H. Raymond
1973   *The Brethren Church in Argentina: A Church Growth Study*. Pasadena: Fuller School of World Missions. 128 pages. SWM Thesis.

Short section comparing the Assemblies of God begins on page 31.

Key Words
1909-American Assemblies of God, 1921-Canadian Assemblies of God, Tommy Hicks, masses, lay participation and leadership

Atter, Gordon F.
1962   *The Third Force*. Petersborough, Ontario, Canada: The College Press. 314 pages.

See chapters 7, 10, 18. Chapter 8 has biographical sketches, with photos, of some 45 pentecostal pioneers from the United States, Canada, and Great Britain.

Key Words
revivals, denominations, training institutes

Baker, H.A.
1937   *God in Ka Do Land*. Mokiang, Yunnan, China: The Adullan Reading Campaign. 118 pages.

Phenomenal accounts of an indigenous people movement among the Ka Do aboriginal tribe in Western China. Interesting reading on spontaneous physical manifestations of the Holy Spirit.

Key Words
mass movement, prophecy, trances, physical manifestations, trembling and shaking, prostrations, dancing in the Spirit, laying on of hands, young

Barratt, Thomas Ball
1927   *When the Fire Fell*. Norway: Alfons Hansen & Sonner. 229 pages.

Personal experiences of an early pentecostal pioneer.

Key Words
Norway, America, India, Copenhagen, Lewi Pethrus

Barrett, David B.
1982 *World Christian Encyclopedia*. New York: Oxford University Press. 1010 pages.

Make use of the extensive indices to locate pentecostals or denominations by name. Refer also to the dictionary section to "pentecostals."

Bartleman, Frank
Two Years Mission Work in Europe: Just Before the World War 1912-14. Privately published by the author. 60 pages.

Travel experiences of one of the Azusa Street alumni.

Key Words
British Isles, France, Norway, Sweden, Holland, Germany, Switzerland, Denmark, Finland, Russia

1924 *Around the World by Faith*. Privately published by the author. 81 pages.

Travelogue of a 1910 world trip by one of the original Azusa Street pioneers. Fascinating reading.

Key Words
faith, sacrifice, revival, preaching, contacts

1962 *What Really Happened at 'Azusa Street'?* 96 pages.

This book was originally published in 1925 under the title *How Pentecost Came to Los Angeles*. Bartleman, one of the original eyewitnesses of the 1906 Azusa Street revival, gives an inside glimpse into the dynamics of the movement. There is a close connection made between Azusa Street and the 1904-1905 revival in Wales (as related by the correspondence of Evan Roberts in Wales).

Key Words
prayer, repentance, revival, gifts of the Spirit, worldwide spread

Bennett, Charles T.
1971 *Tinder in Tabasco: A Study of Church Growth in Tropical Mexico* Pasadena: Fuller School of World Mission. 234 pages. SWM thesis.

See index under "Apostolic Church," "Assemblies of God," "Church of God," "Pentecostals" for history of pentecostal origins and growth.

Key Words
healing, poor people, Van Nuys, California, pastor-oriented

Bloch-Hoell, Nils
1964 *The Pentecostal Movement*. Oslo: Universetforlaget. 255 pages.

Originally written from the author's Norwegian/European experience. The English edition has been expanded to take the American and

British aspects into consideration. Chapter 6 is devoted to foreign missionary work. The appendix has short biographies of four pentecostal leaders (Barratt, Bjorner, McPherson, Pethrus).

Key Words
eschatology, revival, dynamic, Scandinavia, World Pentecostal Conferences, xenolalia (see Index)

Booze, Joyce Wells
1980 *Into All the World: A History of Assemblies of God Foreign Missions.* Springfield, Missouri: Assemblies of God Division of Foreign Missions. 74 pages.

A five-lesson course designed to facilitate missions awareness and participation in local AOG congregations. Includes 8 biographies of early AOG missionary pioneers.

Key Words
beginnings, organizations, biographies, new frontier evangelism

Bowdle, Donald N., Editor
1980 *The Promise and The Power: Essays on the Motivations, Developments, and Prospects of the Ministries of the Church of God.* Cleveland, Tennessee: Pathway Press, 332 pages.

A *Festschrift* honoring Charles W. Conn at the anniversary of his ten-year tenure as president of Lee College in Cleveland, Tennessee. The first two chapters, on evangelism and missions, are relevant to this bibliography.

Key Words
historical roots, American Indian ministries, "Double in a Decade," the Lay Movement, World Missions Department, indigenous leadership, Master Plan of Education

Brumback, Carl
1947 *What Meaneth This?* Springfield, Missouri: Gospel Publishing House. 352 pages.

Written by an insider. Somewhat apologetic and polemical in nature. However, it provides insight into pentecostal theology in the 1940s.

Key Words
Pentecost, evidence, objections, tongues

1961 *Suddenly . . . From Heaven: A History of the Assemblies of God.* Springfield, Missouri: Gospel Publishing House. 380 pages.

One of the best known histories, later updated by Menzies. See Chapter 25 and Appendix E—"Foreign Missions Survey."

Key Words
biographies, national workers, indigenous, Bible schools, literature

Bruner, Frederick Dale
1963 *The Doctrine and Experience of the Holy Spirit in the Pentecostal Movement and Correspondingly in the New Testament.* Hamburg: Evang.—Theologischen Fakultat der Universitat Hamburg. Two volumes, 667 pages.

Bruner's dissertation, later revised as *A Theology of the Holy Spirit* (Eerdmans, 1970). Doctrinal in nature. Though strongly critical of the pentecostal movement ("Pentecostalism is heresy with vitality") Bruner's resources are valuable. Note Chapter One, the Appendix to Chapter Two, and the bibliography.

Key Words
background, theology, doctrine, Baptism of the Holy Spirit, gifts of the Spirit, exegesis

1970 *A Theology of the Holy Spirit.* Grand Rapids: William B. Eerdmans, Publisher. 390 pages.

A revision of his 1963 dissertation, Bruner's work is primarily doctrinal/theological. Part One (Chapters 1-4) provides historical/theological backgrounds to the international spread of the movement. One of the most valuable assets of the book is the extensive bibliography.

Key Words
self-perspective, world mission, pentecostal interpretation of their mission, backgrounds, systematic theology

Buntain, D.N.
1956 *The Holy Ghost and Fire.* Springfiela, Missouri: Gospel Publishing House. 97 pages.

Author is a former executive of the Pentecostal Assemblies of Canada.

Burke, Todd and DeAnn
1977 *Anointed for Burial.* Plainfield, New Jersey: Logos International. 259 pages.

The story of Khmer Church in Cambodia before the forced evacuation of missionaries.

Key Words
healings, power encounter, miracles, frontier missions

Campbell, Joseph E.
1951 *The Pentecostal Holiness Church in 1898-1948.* Franklin Springs, Georgia: Pentecostal Holiness Church. 573 pages.

Fifty-year history of one of the oldest American pentecostal denominations. Later updated by Synan's history (*Old Time Power)*. See pp. 344-359 for history of foreign missions.

Key Words
T.J. McIntosh, China 1907, Bishop J.H. King, E.M. Spooner—Africa

Carver, E. Earl
1972 *Showcase for God: A Study of Evangelical Church Growth in Puerto Rico.* Pasadena: Fuller School of World Mission. 254 pages.

SWM thesis. Author is from Church of God (Anderson, Indiana). See pp. 153-173 for discussion of various pentecostal groups, including the Pentecostal Church of God, Church of God (Cleveland, Tennessee), Assemblies of God, and Church of God of Prophecy.

Key Words
ministerial training, home meetings, laymen, rural evangelism, sacrifice, transfer growth

Cary, Lovell R., Compiler
1976 "Far East Leadership Seminar." Hong Kong: Church of God World Missions Asian Department. 153 pages.

Collected papers and essays from a strategy/leadership seminar sponsored by the Church of God.

Key Words
"Double in a Decade," church growth, communication, revolution, leadership responsibility, "How Jesus Trained The Twelve," youth and evangelism, Christianity and Marxism, accreditation and education

Champion, Richard, Edward S. Caldwell, and Gary Leggett, Editors
1968 *Our Mission in Today's World: Council on Evangelism Official Papers and Reports.* Springfield, Missouri: Gospel Publishing House. 217 pages.

Proceedings of a historic Assemblies of God meeting in which ". . . we re-examined our reason for being and redefined our goals" (Thomas F. Zimmerman).

Key Words
mission of the church, revival, leadership, church, priorities, evangelism, church growth, Declaration at St. Louis

Chandy, V.
1981 *The Discipling of Muslims in Sri Lanka* (Unpublished master's thesis). Pasadena: Fuller School of World Mission.

Chelliah, Zechariah
1981   *Missiological Strategy for the Assemblies of God in Tamil Nadu*
(unpublished doctoral dissertation). Pasadena: Fuller School of World
Missions. 387 pages.

Area case study. Chapter 2 deals with the early beginnings of
the Assemblies of God. Part II has good analysis of growth patterns
and roadblocks to future growth. Part III suggests strategies for the
future.

Key Words
church planting, road blocks, social system, castes, ethnic compositions,
little conversion growth, homogeneous unit principle, unreached peoples

Cho, Paul Yonggi
1979   *The Fourth Dimension.* Plainfield, New Jersey: Logos International.
186 pages.

Faith teaching by the pentecostal pastor of the world's largest church.

Key Words
faith, the spoken word, rhema

1981   *Successful Home Cell Groups.* Plainfield, New Jersey: Logos
International. 176 pages.

First-hand experience about the organization of home cell groups.

Key Words
evangelism, how to, Holy Spirit, lay leadership, obstacles, unlimited
church growth

1983   "The Evangelist and the Life of Faith." Address to the International
Conference for Itinerant Evangelists, Amsterdam, Holland. July 12-21,
1983.

Key Words
Hebrews 11:1-6, filled with the Holy Spirit, revelation of the Holy Spirit,
the faith life, vision and faith, fasting and prayer

1984a   *More Than Numbers.* Waco, Texas: Word Books. 531 pages.

Church Growth thinking with theological and practical insights.

Key Words
laity, cell system, media, kingdom of God, revival, the future

1984b   "The Secret Behind the World's Biggest Church," in *Global Church
Growth,* James H. Montgomery, Editor. Volume XXI, No. 2
(March-April).

Written by the pastor of the world's largest church, Full Gospel Central Church of Seoul, Korea.

Key Words
prayer, the Holy Spirit, message, organization

1984c *Prayer: Key to Revival.* Waco, Texas: Word Books.

Christian Life Magazine and C. Peter Wagner, Editors
1983 *Signs and Wonders Today.* Wheaton, Illinois: Christian Life Magazine. 79 pages.

The reprint of the original *Christian Life* issue on the Fuller Seminary experimental course Signs, Wonders and Church Growth. Also included is a thirteen-session study with questions and applications.

Key Words
historical evidences, biblical basis, C. Peter Wagner, John Wimber, around the world, healing, miracles, Vineyard Christian Fellowship, teaching

Clanton, Arthur L.
1970 *United We Stand: A History of Oneness Organizations.* Hazelwood, Missouri: The Pentecostal Publishing House. 207 pages.

The reader should note each section for the particular foreign missions record and statistics for each individual oneness pentecostal group. Note the biographical sketches of eleven selected leaders (page 183).

Key Words
Jesus' Name, oneness, merger, world outreach

Clark, Elijah Columbus
c.1946 *Marvelous Healings God Wrought Among Us.* Cleveland, Tennessee. Church of God Publishing House. 160 pages.

Testimonies of healing among early Church of God leaders.

Coggins, Wade T., Compiler
1977 "Reports of the Annual Mission Executives Retreat." Washington, D.C.: Evangelical Foreign Mission Association. 134 pages.

Two reports by Assemblies of God contributors: Melvin L. Hodges, "Apostolic Missions Today," and Joseph Kilpatrick, "Combined Media in Education and Communication."

Key Words
Acts 1:8, the task, the Holy Spirit, spiritual preparation, signs and wonders, prayer, International Correspondence Institute (ICI), video, film, literature, extension education

Conference Advisory Committee

1961 *The Sixth Pentecostal World Conference.* Toronto, Canada. Conference Advisory Committee. 59 pages.

Reports and messages from the sixth Pentecostal World Conference in Jerusalem, 1961. Includes greeting from Israeli Prime Minister David Ben-Gurion. Conference theme: "Pentecost—Then and Now." 2,595 delegates from over 40 countries.

Key Words
sermons, first-century pentecost, twentieth-century pentecost

Conn, Charles W.

1955 *Like a Mighty Army Moves the Church of God.* Cleveland, Tennessee: Church of God Publishing House. 380 pages.

Denominational history of the Church of God (Cleveland, Tennessee), America's oldest pentecostal church (1886). See Index under "Foreign Missions." Note: A revised version has been published (1977 Pathway Press).

Key Words
missions board, organization, Bible schools, J.H. Ingram, amalgamation, indigenous, revival

1956 *Pillars of Pentecost.* Cleveland, Tennessee: Pathway Press. 141 pages.

Apologetic type material written by an insider.

Key Words
fundamental, holiness, evangelistic zeal, biblical, Baptism of the Holy Ghost

1959 *Where the Saints Have Trod: A History of Church of God Missions.* Cleveland, Tennessee: Pathway Press. 312 pages.

Although in need of updating and revision, this denominational survey shows how America's oldest pentecostal church has spread. Includes tables and an index.

Key Words
early "faith" missions, pioneers, abortive beginnings, J.H. Ingram, organization, Bible schools

1975 *A Balanced Church.* Cleveland, Tennessee: Pathway Press. 183 pages.

A pentecostal view of ecclesiology and the gifts of the Spirit.

Key Words
Trinity, church, fruit of the Spirit, gifts of the Spirit, the ministry gifts

1983   "Can Pentecostalism Survive?" in *The Pentecostal Minister*. Volume 3, Number 3 (Fall).

This article, written by an insider, delineates the requirements for the endurance of the Pentecostal Movement.

Key Words
Pentecostal distinctives, twenty-first century, scriptures, beliefs and tenets, self-appraisal, renewal

Conway, Frederick James
1982   *Pentecostalism in the Context of Haitian Religion and Health Practice.* Ann Arbor: University Microfilms International. 284 pages.

Though not related to the history of pentecostal missions, Chapters 7 and 8 are interesting from the standpoint of pentecostal theology and practice as it confronts such elements as voodoo (power encounters).

Key Words
power, confrontation, spirit possessions, divine healing

Cook, Robert F.
c.1930 *A Quarter Century of Divine Leading in India.* Travancore State, South India: The Church of God in India. 72 pages.

Personal accounts from the pioneer ministry of a Church of God missionary earlier influenced by Azusa Street.

Key Words
Azusa Street, Baptism of the Holy Spirit, healings, Bible schools

1955   *Half a Century of Divine Leading and 37 Years of Apostolic Achievements in South India.* Cleveland, Tennessee: Church of God World Missions. 257 pages.

Chronicles of an early pentecostal pioneer missionary, influenced by Azusa Street, who went to India in 1913.

Key Words
miracles, healings, prayer, faith, Bible schools, deliverance

Corum, Fred T., Compiler
1981   *Like as of Fire: A Reprint of the Old Azusa Street Papers.* Collected by the author. 160 Salem Street, Wilmington, MA 01887.

Much in the original documents of how the pentecostals were spreading to other countries in the early days of this century. Good book list in the introduction. Sample headlines of *The Apostolic Faith* are listed below under "key words."

Key Words
Beginning of World Wide Revival, Pentecost Both Sides of the Ocean, In the Last Days, Everywhere Preaching The Word, Pentecost in Many Lands

Cross, James A.
1966 "Glossolalia: Its Value to the Church" in *The Glossolalia Phenomenon,* Wade H. Horton, Editor. Cleveland, Tennessee: Pathway Press, 304 pages.

Written by a pentecostal author.

Key Words
first-century church, twentieth-century church, revival, growth, world outreach, empowerment, convincing of the unbeliever

Damboriena, Prudencio
1969 *Tongues as of Fire: Pentecostalism in Contemporary Christianity.* Washington D.C.: Corpus Books.

One of the better surveys. Note Chapter 8, "Pentecostal Missions: A Survey," and Chapter 9, "Missions and Ecumenism." Pentecostal missions by continent and country.

Key Words
evangelical force, financial support, expansion, Brazil, Baptism of the Holy Spirit, strategy, methodology, social action

Daniel, Christopher J.
1977 *Church Growth—Its Dynamics and Strategy: A Challenge to the Church in Sri Lanka Today.* Pasadena: Fuller School of World Mission. 124 pages.

SWM thesis. See pp. 49-51 on the Assemblies of God and the Ceylon Pentecost Mission. Section VIII (p. 105ff.) describes the author's move into the pentecostal movement.

Key Words
divine healing, Smith Wigglesworth, Walter Clifford, Baptism of the Holy Spirit, signs and wonders, power

1977 "Signs and Wonders in Sri Lanka," in *Church Growth Bulletin.* Volume 13, Number 3 (January).

Key Words
open air preaching, Baptism of the Holy Spirit, healing, exorcism, training ministry, church planting

1978 *Indentured Labour and the Christian Movement in Sri Lanka.* Pasadena: Fuller School of World Mission. 242 pages.

SWM dissertation. Parts 2 and 3 relate the contribution of pentecostal churches toward reaping the harvest among this people group. Interesting section on power encounter (Chapter 7).

Key Words
Church Growth principles, animism, power encounter, "blood," "cross," demons, conversion, Holy Spirit

Davadason, S.
1978   *Indian Missionary Societies* (unpublished doctoral dissertation). Pasadena: Fuller School of World Mission.

Davidson, C.T.
1976   *Upon This Rock.* Cleveland, Tennessee: White Wing Publishing House and Press, 3 volumes, 2,457 pages.

A massive history of the Church of God of Prophecy. See Volume 3 for most information on their foreign missions work.

Key Words
Barbados, India, Bermuda, Mexico, West Indies, England

Davis, J. Merle
1943   *How the Church Grows in Brazil.* New York: World Missionary Council. 167 pages.

William R. Read says of Davis, "He was one of our first missionary statesmen to see the dynamic factors involved in the Pentecostal movement, and he called attention particularly to the rapid growth of the Pentecostal churches" (1965:123). One of the earlier International Missionary Council studies.

Key Words
economic and social base, indigenous, pentecostal churches, masses, Church of God

De Leon, Victor
1979   *The Silent Pentecostals: A Biographical History of the Pentecostal Movement among the Hispanics in the Twentieth Century.* Privately published by the author. 206 pages.

A record of the cross-cultural growth of Hispanic Assemblies of God ministries primarily in the Southwest USA.

Key Words
Bible institute, H.C. Ball, Texas, New Mexico, Colorado, California, Hispanics, district organization

Denison, Barry Reed
1983 "An Evaluation of the Effectiveness of the ORU Summer Missions Program in Fulfilling its Statement of Purpose" (unpublished research paper). Tulsa, Oklahoma: Oral Roberts University School of Business. 70 pages.

The author notes in his abstract, "The ORU Summer Missions Program holds a strategic role in the fulfillment of ORU's purpose and founding commission. This paper sought to audit the performance of the Summer Missions Program in fulfilling its purpose."

Key Words
review of literature, changes in participants, cross-cultural communication, missionary motivation, missionary call

De Silva, Ranjit
1979 *Discipling the Cities in Sri Lanka: A Challenge to the Church Today.* Pasadena: Fuller School of World Mission. 272 pages.

SWM thesis. Pentecostal churches are among 70 churches and 19 denominations researched for the years 1969-1978. See page 92ff.

Key Words
Bible schools, transfer growth, working class people, healing miracles

De Wet, Christiaan Rudolph
1981 *Signs and Wonders in Church Growth.* Pasadena: Fuller School of World Mission. 156 pages.

SWM thesis. See index under pentecostals, Assemblies of God, Apostolic Faith Mission of South Africa, Foursquare Church, Full Gospel Central Church, Gifts of the Holy Spirit, etc.

Key Words
North American healing evangelists, Tommy Hicks, healings, power encounter, Foursquare growth, Azusa Street, Morris Cerullo, Navajos

Dollar, Harold
1981 *A Cross-Cultural Theology of Healing.* Pasadena: Fuller School of World Mission. 319 pages.

SWM dissertation. Chapters 12 and 15 deal with the historical roots and growth of pentecostalism and the pentecostal model of healing. Chapter 16 considers the charismatic model.

Key Words
Azusa Street, emphasis on the supernatural, manifestations, healing, growth

Douglas, J.D., Editor
1975 *Let the Earth Hear His Voice.* Minneapolis: World Wide Publications. 1,471 pages.

Among some of the pentecostal/charismatic papers and responses at ICOWE (Lausanne, 1974) are from Philip Hogan (p. 242), Larry Christenson (p. 273), Herman H. tu Welle (p. 725), and Loren Cunningham (p. 958).

Key Words
Sovereignty of Holy Spirit, spiritual gifts, miracles vs. modern man, young people

du Plessis, David J., Editor
1949 *Minutes of the Second Pentecostal World Conference.* Cleveland, Tennessee. David J. du Plessis, Secretary. ca. 100 pages.

Proceedings of the second World Pentecostal Conference in Paris, 1949. One hundred fifty-six delegates; 320 observers from 30 countries; evening meetings attended by 1,500 to 2,000 people.

Key Words
organization, unity, polity, Manifesto, secretary, advisory committee

du Plessis, David J.
1958 "Golden Jubilee of Twentieth Century Pentecostal Movements" in *International Review of Missions,* Volume 47 (April, 1958, pp. 193-201).

An excellent mid-century internal appraisal by an authoritative pentecostal leader.

Key Words
Holy Spirit, personal experience, 1906-1908, power, masses, Assemblies of God, Church of God, Pentecostal Assemblies of Canada, indigenous movements, Pentecostal World Conference, statistics

1972 *The Spirit Bade Me Go.* South Plainfield, NJ: Bridge Publishing, Inc.

1977 *A Man Called Mr. Pentecost.* South Plainfield, NJ: Bridge Publishing, Inc. 247 pages.

The story of one of the most prominent pentecostal-charismatic leaders today.

Key Words
Apostolic Faith Mission, dialogue, Roman Catholics, World Pentecostal Conference

Duggar, Lillie
1964   *A.J. Tomlinson: Former General Overseer of the Church of God.*
Cleveland, Tennessee: White Wing Publishing House. 807 pages.

Written by the personal secretary to this early Church of God of
Prophecy leader. Interesting travelogue from Tomlinson's early mission
journey (Chapters 9-13) plus glimpses of his theology of mission. Good
photos from the original days.

Key Words
Holy Ghost, Bahamas, Bermuda, preaching, "the power"

Durasoff, Steve
1969   *The Russian Protestants: Evangelicals in the Soviet Union 1944-1964.*
Rutherford: Fairleigh Dickenson University Press. 312 pages.

Chapters 5, 9, 11, 12 deal with Pentecostals.

Key Words
Voronaev, Odessa, tongues speaking, polemics

1972   *Bright Wind of the Spirit: Pentecostalism Today.* Englewood Cliffs, NJ:
Prentice-Hall, Inc. 276 pages.

See Chapter 6, "The Global Explosion of Pentecostalism" (pp. 77-112).

Key Words
Pentecostal Fellowship of North America (PFNA), National Association
of Evangelicals, David J. du Plessis, indigenous, Donald Gee, China,
World Pentecostal Conference, T.L. Osborn, William Branham

1972   *Pentecost Behind the Iron Curtain.* Plainfield, N.J.: Logos International
128 pages.

As its title suggests, the book is a country-by-country report of
pentecostals in key Eastern European nations. Of interest is the start of
pentecostal churches through a returned Russian immigrant to the
United States. Interesting reading.

Key Words
young people, pioneers, sacrifice, revival, radio, literature

Edwardsen, Aril
1982   "New Anointing For a New Day" in *Church Growth,* Paul Yonggi Cho,
Editor. Volume 1, No. 1 (Summer/Fall).

Edwards, Fred E.
1971   *The Role of the Faith Mission: A Brazilian Case Study.* South Pasadena:
William Carey Library. 139 pages. SWM thesis on church growth in
Brazil.

Key Words
indigenous pentecostal churches, Italian people movement, Gunnar
Vingrin, Daniel Berg

Elliot, William W.
1971 "Socio-cultural Change in a Pentecostal Group: A Case Study in
Education and Culture of the Church of God in Sonora, Mexico."
Unpublished doctoral thesis. The University of Tennessee.

Elmore, Ralph M.
1981 *Discipling Inner City Peoples: Models for Church Growth Among
Ethnic Groups in Los Angeles.* Pasadena: Fuller School of World
Mission. 152 pages.

SWM thesis written by a pentecostal author. See Chapters 4-6. A good
section on the history of Aimee Semple McPherson and Angelus Temple.
Case study shows how a pentecostal church adapts to American urban
cross-cultural ministries.

Key Words
Foursquare Church, extension and bridging growth, urban ethnics, inner
city, changing community

Engelsviken, Tormod
1975 "Molo Wongel: A Documentary Report on the Life and History of
the Independent Pentecostal Movement in Ethiopia 1960-1975"
(unpublished research project). Oslo, Norway: The Free Faculty of
Theology. 223 pages.

Key Words
history, Scandinavian Pentecostal Missions, literature, revival, growth,
persecution, imprisonment

Enns, Arno
1967 *Profiles of Argentine Church Growth* (unpublished master's thesis).
Pasadena: Fuller School of World Mission.

1971 *Man, Milieu and Mission in Argentina.* Grand Rapids: Eerdmans
Publishing Company. 258 pages.

Especially note Chapters 5, 15, 16, 17, 18.

Key Words
Assemblies of God, church growth trends, Tommy Hicks, "de-
intellectualizing," participation, leadership

Epinay, Christian Lalive d'
1969 *Haven of the Masses: A Study of the Pentecostal Movement in Chile.*
London: Lutterworth Press. 263 pages.

A CWME/WCC publication from their World Studies of Churches in Mission series. Good academic field study with sociological emphases. Chapters 1 and 2 tell how the pentecostal movement spread to Chile.

Key Words
David Trumbull, Methodists, schism, W.C. Hoover, social change, pentecostal explosion. Note: Also available in Spanish under Lalive d'Epinay, Christian, *El Refugio de las Masas*

Ervin, Howard M.
1972 *This Which Ye See and Hear: A Laymen's Guide to the Holy Spirit.* Plainfield, New Jersey: Logos International. 112 pages.

Written by the author of *These Are Not Drunken As Ye Suppose* who, at the time of this publication, was a professor at Oral Roberts' University. See Chapters 4 and 13.

Key Words
witnessing, the pentecostal imperative, pentecost and eschatology

Ewart, Frank J.
1975 *The Phenomenon of Pentecost. A History of the Latter Rain.* Hazelwood, Missouri: World Aflame Press. 207 pages.

A revision of Ewarts original account (1947—also in Fuller library). See Chapters 11-13.

Key Words
Canada, China, India

Ezzo, Elsie Bolton
1969 *Bought for a Dollar.* Springfield, Missouri. Gospel Publishing House. 95 pages.

Popular-style mission stories from the daughter of the Reverend and Mrs. Leonard Bolton, Assemblies of God pioneers to China.

Key Words
idols, poverty, power encounter

Faupel, David W.
1972 *The American Pentecostal Movement: A Bibliographical Essay.* The Society for Pentecostal Studies. 56 pages.

Though somewhat dated, this is an excellent research tool.

Key Words
world surveys, classification of American pentecostal groups, theological distinctives, missions, homiletics and sermons, apologetics

Fisher, Robert E., Editor
1983   *Pressing Toward the Mark.* Cleveland, Tennessee: Pathway Press.
176 pages.

See Chapter 4 by Carl Richardson "The Impetus of Anointing" (an important distinctive in pentecostal missions/preaching).

Key Words
Old Testament, New Testament, power, preaching, unction, indispensability

Flora, Cornelia Butler
1976   *Pentecostalism in Columbia: Baptism by Fire and Spirit.* London: Associated University Presses. 288 pages.

Sociological case study. Excellent bibliography.

Key Words
social change, lower class, solidarity movements, United Pentecostal Church, internal structure, pentecostal women

Flower, Alice Reynolds
1962   *Grace for Grace.* (Privately published by the author.) 430 Woodridge Street, Springfield, Missouri.

Fraser, David A.
1978   "An 'Engel Scale' for Muslim Work," *The Gospel and Islam,* Don McCurry, Editor. Monrovia: MARC.

Frodsham, Stanley H.
1946   *With Signs Following: The Story of the Latter-Day Pentecostal Revival.* Springfield, Missouri: Gospel Publishing House. 279 pages. Revised Edition.

One of the earlier, and better, descriptions of how the movements beginning in Topeka, Kansas, and Los Angeles spread to the world. Early apologetic for the movement.

Key Words
revivals, Christian and Missionary Alliance, Canada, Europe, Pentecostal outpourings in history, scriptural

1973   *Smith Wigglesworth: Apostle of Faith.* Springfield, Missouri: Gospel Publishing House. 158 pages.

Biography of a pentecostal pioneer. Excellent reading.

Key Words
revival crusades, world travel, miracles, healing, prayer

Furman, Charles T.
1950 *Guatemala and the Story of Chuce.* Cleveland, Tennessee. The Church of God Publishing House. 46 pages.

First-hand report on the beginning of the Church of God in Guatemala.

Key Words
Indians, twenty year review (1920-1940), opposition

Garlock, Henry B.
1974 *Before We Kill and Eat You.* Dallas: Christ for the Nations. 128 pages.

Story of an early Assembly of God pioneer to Liberia. Foreword by C.M. Ward.

Key Words
spontaneous leading (of the Holy Spirit), dreams, power encounter

Gaver, Jessyca Russell
1971 *Pentecostalism.* New York: Award Books. 286 pages.

Gaxiola, Manuel Jesus
1978 *A History of the Apostolic Church of the Faith in Christ Jesus in Mexico: 1914-1974.* Pasadena: Fuller School of World Mission. 197 pages.

SWM research project. A Church Growth history by a Mexican pentecostal leader. It connects the Los Angeles revival of the early 1900s with the founding of Mexico's oldest pentecostal denomination.

Key Words
immigrants, 1914, organic growth, training, structures and organization

Gee, Donald
c.1932 *To the Uttermost Part.* The Home Missionary Reference Council of the Assemblies of God in Great Britain and Ireland. 26 pages.

A general summary of "The Missionary Results of the Pentecostal Movement in the British Isles" (subtitle) up to ca. 1932.

Key Words
British pentecostal movement, Assemblies of God, Sunderland, China, Tibet, India, indigenous principle

1949 *The Pentecostal Movement.* London: Elim Publishing Co. 236 pages.

Although written primarily about and for Britishers, Gee's history shows the Transatlantic connection to Americans at Azusa Street and gives interesting background to early pentecostal efforts in various European countries.

Key Words
Azusa Street, The Pentecostal Missionary Union, Bible schools, Assemblies of God, The Elim Pentecostal Alliance, European Pentecostal Conference, World Pentecostal Conference

1961 *Toward Pentecostal Unity.* Springfield, Missouri: Gospel Publishing House.

Formerly published as *All With One Accord,* a collection of short articles from Gee. Short section (five pages) on the training of leaders in the pentecostal movement through Bible schools.

1962 *Concerning Spiritual Gifts.* Springfield, Missouri: Gospel Publishing House. Revised Edition. 119 pages.

A classic pentecostal Bible study which views spiritual gifts mainly from the background of 1 Corinthians 12-14.

Key Words
"Are Spiritual Gifts for Today?", abuses, fruit of the Spirit, Bible studies, Bible, the miraculous

1963 *Spiritual Gifts in the Work of the Ministry Today.* Springfield, Missouri: Gospel Publishing House. 101 pages.

Originally presented as the L.I.F.E. Bible College Alumni Association Lectures in 1963. See Chapter 5, "Spiritual Gifts and World Evangelization."

Key Words
spiritual gifts, tongues, Baptism of the Holy Spirit, apostles, deliverance, Pentecostal Revival, Holy Spirit, divine energy, preaching

1967 *Wind and Flame.* Croydon, England. Heath Press, Ltd. 315 pages.

Incorporates and updates *The Pentecostal Movement* (1949) through 1964.

Key Words
World Pentecostal Conferences, phenomenal growth, Tommy Hicks, Full Gospel Business Men, younger leaders emerge, world-wide scope

1972 *Now That You've Been Baptized in the Spirit.* Springfield, Missouri: Gospel Publishing House. 175 pages.

An editing together of two former writings (*After Pentecost* and *The Ministry Gifts of Christ*).

Key Words
Christian maturity, after Pentecost, revival, gifts, ministries, world evangelization

George, Thackil C.
1975 *The Growth of the Pentecostal Churches in South India.* Pasadena: Fuller School of World Mission. 133 pages.

SWM thesis. The founding and comparative study of five pentecostal churches in Southern India. Comparison is also made between these and those of Latin America.

Key Words
Church of God, Assemblies of God, Indian Pentecostal Church of God, theology, Church Growth, Latin America, structures, laity

1976 *The Life and Growth of Churches in Bangalore.* Pasadena: Fuller School of World Mission. 320 pages.

SWM dissertation. Succinct account of denominations and congregations in Bangalore, India. The Assemblies of God and other pentecostal groups are discussed.

Key Words
Anglo-Indians, Malayalees, English services, transfer growth, redemption and lift

George, William T.
1983 "Church Growth: The Dimension of the Holy Spirit," in *The Pentecostal Minister.* Volume 3, Number 3 (Fall).

Key Words
at work in the world, conviction, leading of the Holy Spirit, overseeing, empowering

1984 *Leadership Training in The Church of God in Mexico.* Pasadena: Fuller School of World Mission. 131 pages.

Gerlach, Luther P. and Virginia H. Hine
People, Power, Change, Movements of Social Transformation. New York: Bobbs-Merrill Co. 257 pages.

Classic study of two movements: the pentecostals and the Black Power movement. See Chapter 1.

Key Words
"faith missionaries," indigenous lay leadership, Black pentecostals, college campuses, "hidden" pentecostals, glossolalia

Glasser, Arthur F.
1978 "Power Encounter and Conversion from Islam," *Gospel and Islam,* Don McCurry, Editor. Monrovia: MARC.

Glasser, Arthur F., and Donald A. McGavran
1983   *Contemporary Theologies of Mission.* Grand Rapids: Baker Book House. 251 pages.

Two brief, but very significant, pages on the pentecostal movement.

Key Words
joyous song, vivid story, biblical realities, "person-centered," "the dark side of the soul"

Glazier, Stephen D., Editor
1980   *Perspectives on Pentecostalism: Case Studies from the Caribbean and Latin America.* Washington, D.C.: University Press of America. 195 pages.

Good to scan for various pentecostal methodologies and field practices. Papers originally prepared for the 1977 annual meeting of the American Anthropological Association.

Key Words
healing, exorcism, modernization and development, power, capitalism, Catholics, diversity

Goble, Phillip E.
1975   *Messianic Judaism: A Biblical Apologetic With a View to Liturgical Reform.* Pasadena: Fuller School of World Mission. 172 pages.

SWM thesis by an Assembly of God "messianic synagogue" planter. Cross-cultural principles from a pentecostal perspective.

Key Words
messianic synagogue, Judaism, Gentiles, covenant, Shabbat, Seder

1981   *Everything You Need to Grow a Messianic Yeshiua.* Pasadena: William Carey Library. 298 pages.

Contextualized missiology for Jews from a pentecostal "messianic synagogue" planter.

Key Words
contextual theology, leadership training, preaching, Messianic Jewish Day School, deprogrammers

Golder, Morris E.
1973   *History of the Pentecostal Assemblies of the World.* Indianapolis: Pentecostal Assemblies of the World. 195 pages.

Some of the most interesting parts of this history are a brief biography of Azusa Street pioneer W.J. Seymour (a black leader) and early photos of Seymour's house and the Azusa Street mission in Los Angeles. Page 178ff. discusses the "Foreign Missionary Department."

Key Words
integrated, women, India, West Indies, Liberia

Goodman, Felicitas D.
1972 *Speaking in Tongues: A Cross-Cultural Study of Glossolalia.* Chicago: The University of Chicago Press. 175 pages.

Cross-cultural field observations of glossolalia from an anthropological-linguistic point of reference. Most interesting is the brief section on xenoglossolalia. The bibliography is also valuable.

Key Words
universal characteristics, psychological factors

Graber, Robert M.
1979 "The Pastor and Evangelism-Missions" in *And He Gave Pastors: Pastoral Theology in Action.* Springfield, Missouri: Gospel Publishing House. 629 pages.

A contemporary Assemblies of God view of the relationship of the pastor and the ministry of evangelism/missions.

Key Words
evangelism, pastoral evangelism, missions, Lausanne, The Great Commission, the missions convention (local church)

Graham, Beverly, Editor
1983 *Mountain Movers.* Springfield, Missouri: Assemblies of God Division of Foreign Missions. Volume 25, Number 1 (January).

The missions monthly of the Assemblies of God. This special issue highlights new frontier evangelism.

Green, Hollis
1972 *Why Churches Die.* Minneapolis: Bethany Fellowship. 219 pages.

Greenway, H.W., Editor
1952 *World Pentecostal Conference—1952.* The British Pentecostal Fellowship. 76 pages.

Proceedings of the Third World-Pentecostal Conference in London, 1952.

Key Words
David du Plessis, Donald Gee, Leonard Steiner, foreign missions, pentecostal literature, pentecostal Bible schools

Hamilton, Florence Olivia
1965 *To the Ends of the Earth.* Franklin Springs, Georgia: Advocate Press. 133 pages.

Autobiography of a Pentecostal Holiness missionary to Asia.

Key Words
China, education, World War II, refugees, Thailand

Hand, Marcus V.
1978　*Put Your Arms Around the World.* Cleveland, Tennessee: Pathway Press. 112 pages.

Church of God author writes to inspire world vision.

Key Words
cities, population, careers, missionary, action

Hargrave, Vessie D.
1970　*The Church and World Missions.* Cleveland, Tennessee: Pathway Press. 125 pages.

Written by a missions executive as a church workers training course in missions.

Key Words
purpose of missions, preparation of missionaries, prayer, finances

Harper, Michael
1964　*Power for the Body of Christ.* Fountain Trust.

1965　*As At The Beginning: The Twentieth Century Pentecostal Revival.* London: Hodder and Stoughton. 128 pages.

Thumbnail sketch of some key figures in the pentecostal-charismatic movements.

Key Words
Azusa Street, Charles Parham, Frank Bartleman, W.J. Seymour, T.B. Barratt, Alexander Boddy, Smith Wigglesworth, Donald Gee, David du Plessis, Dennis Bennett, Demos Shakarian

Harrell, Jr., David Erwin
1975　*All Things Are Possible: The Healing and Charismatic Revivals in Modern America.* Bloomington, Indiana: Indiana University Press. 304 pages.

Text and background for SWM course, Signs and Wonders and Church Growth. See index under "missions, foreign" for interesting reading on how the healing and charismatic revivals spread to other parts of the world. Note also "Evangelism and Ecumenicity," p. 93ff.

Key Words
T.L. Osborn, overseas crusades, "native evangelism," Tommy Hicks,

Gordon Lindsay, Lester Sumrall, Full Gospel Business Men's Fellowship International, Morris Cerullo, Jimmy Swaggart

1985 *Oral Roberts: An American Life*. Bloomington, Indiana: Indiana University Press.

Harris, Ralph W.
1973 *Spoken by the Spirit*. Springfield, Missouri: Gospel Publishing House. 127 pages.

Documented accounts of "other tongues" from Arabic to Zulu. A pentecostal argument for the value of "xenoglossolalia"—speaking in other tongues identified as known languages. Many of the instances have to do with missions and cross-cultural evangelism.

Key Words
See "The Value of Glossolalia."

Hastie, Eugene N.
1948 *History of the West Central District Council of the Assemblies of God*. Fort Dodge, Iowa: Walterick Printing Company. 207 pages.

History of early missionaries (1911-1913) sent from this area (Iowa-Missouri) *before* the AOG actually organized a missions department. This one district sent 43 missionaries in 36 years to some ten different fields. See Chapter 13.

Key Words
British East Africa, Egypt, Agnes Crouch, the "Busy Bee" plan, India

Hayford, Jack W.
1977 *Prayer Is Invading the Impossible*. South Plainfield, New Jersey: Bridge Publishing, Inc. 150 pages.

1982 *The Church on the Way*. Plainfield, New Jersey: Logos International.

Hedlund, Roger E.
1970 *The Protestant Movement in Italy: Its Progress, Problems and Prospects*. South Pasadena: William Carey Library. 257 pages.

SWM thesis. See the Part III case study of the Assemblies of God and also "pentecostals" in the index. Good Church Growth insights (charts and diagrams).

Key Words
poor people, Fascist persecution, growth, membership, lay leaders, potential

Hodges, Melvin L.

1953 *The Indigenous Church.* Springfield, Missouri: Gospel Publishing House. 157 pages.

One of the earlier pentecostal statements on the subject. Interesting appendices.

Key Words
self-government, self-propogation, self-support, developing leadership, hindrances, relationships

1957 *Build My Church.* Springfield, Missouri: The Foreign Missions Department of the Assemblies of God.

A manual on indigenous church principles for national pastors.

1964 *Spiritual Gifts.* Springfield, Missouri: Gospel Publishing House. 28 pages.

Short booklet on the nature and function of spiritual gifts from the view of a pentecostal missiologist.

Key Words
spiritual revival, gifts and ministries, function of the gifts, baptism in the Holy Spirit, limitations, physical manifestations

1965 "Creating Climate for Church Growth," "Developing Basic Units of Indigenous Churches," "Administering for Church Growth." Three chapters in *Church Growth and Christian Mission,* Donald A. McGavran, Editor. (See McGavran 1965.)

1972 "Polarization and Harmony," in *Church/Mission Tensions Today,* C. Peter Wagner, Editor, Chicago: Moody Press. 128 pages.

Missions and church relationships in the view of an Assemblies of God writer.

Key Words
relationships, national leadership, polarization, harmony, case studies

1972 "A Pentecostal's View of Mission Strategy" in *Eye of the Storm.* Donald McGavran, Editor. Waco, Texas: Word Books. 299 pages.

Assembly of God author. Hodges's article is from pp. 142-149.

Key Words
Holy Spirit, biblical methodology, church, laymen, indigenous principles

1973 *A Guide to Church Planting.* Chicago: Moody Press. 95 pages.

A "how-to" guide to church planting written by an Assemblies of God missionary and missions executive.

Key Words
message, Holy Spirit, new converts, developing leadership, social
responsibility

1974 "Pentecostal Movements in Missions" (unpublished class syllabus).
Springfield, Missouri: Assemblies of God Graduate School. 37 pages.

The course relates the effect of the Pentecostal movement on world
missions.

Key Words
purpose of Pentecost, church planting, case studies, pentecostal leaders,
leadership training, miraculous, laymen, worship, persecution, problems,
supernatural evangelism, organizational patterns, the charismatic
movement

1977 *A Theology of the Church and Its Mission: A Pentecostal Perspective.*
Springfield, Missouri: Gospel Publishing House. 185 pages.

Written by a leading Assemblies of God missiologist. See Chapter 3,
"The Holy Spirit and The Church" and pp. 137-140 (on miracles).

Key Words
theology, Holy Spirit, church, social concern, organization

1978 *The Indigenous Church and the Missionary.* South Pasadena: William
Carey Library. 99 pages.

A sequel to *The Indigenous Church* (1953, 1971). This version addresses
more directly the problems and opportunities of the expatriate
missionary himself.

Key Words
missionary partnership, New Testament missions, missionary relationships, missionary finance, goals

Hodges, Serena
1956 *Look on the Fields.* Springfield, Missouri: Gospel Publishing House.
201 pages.

Hoffnagel, Judith Chambliss
1978 "The Believers: Pentecostalism in a Brazilian City." Unpublished
doctoral dissertation. Indiana University. 285 pages.

Doctoral dissertation done as a case study. Good bibliography.

Key Words
profile, Assemblies of God, leadership, women and youth, recruitment
and discipline

Hogan, J. Philip
1975   "Observations Based on Experience in Ninety-Five Countries" in *Church Growth Bulletin.* Volume 12, Number 1 (Third Consolidated Volume) (September).

Key Words
city evangelism, church planting, communication, participation, expect results, training

Hohensee, Donald Wilhelm
1975   *Church Growth in Burundi.* Pasadena: Fuller School of World Mission. 153 pages.

SWM thesis. Pages 94-102 describe the beginnings of the pentecostal movement in Burundi through Swedish pentecostals.

Key Words
"outschools," power encounter, Bible school, self-supporting, people movement

Hollenweger, Walter J.
1971   *Die Pfingstkirchen: Selbstdarstellungen, Dokumente, Kommentare.* Stuttgart, West Germany: Evangelisches Verlagswerk. 480 pages.

History, theology of the pentecostal movement in many countries, submitted by a variety of national authors. Non-German readers will profit from an address list (pp. 365-377) of pentecostal churches and leaders in some 60 countries.

Key Words
history, practices, fundamentalism, conversion, healing, Baptism of the Holy Spirit, ecumenical

1972   *The Pentecostals.* London: SCM Press Ltd. 572 pages. (Translation of *Enthusiastisches Christentum*)

Chapters 3 and 4 describe the rise of the two largest U.S. pentecostal groups—the Assemblies of God and the Church of God (Cleveland, Tennessee). Chapter 5 gives a broad survey of the roots of the movement in various continents and regions of the world. The most valuable portions are the bibliography (37 pages), index, and appendices.

Key Words
spontaneous, persecution, independent churches, movement, World Pentecostal Conference

1980   "Charismatic Renewal in the Third World: Implications for Mission," in *Occasional Bulletin,* Volume 4, Number 2.

Horton, Wade H.
1973   *Unto the Uttermost.* Cleveland, Tennessee: Pathway Press. 279 pages.

Sermons, missionary stories and biographies, statistics, missions travelogues and personal experiences of a former Church of God missions executive and General Overseer. Includes a number of biographical sketches of early pentecostal missionaries.

Key Words
world tours, sermons, missionary personalities

Hughes, Ray H.
1968   *Church of God Distinctives.* Cleveland, Tennessee: Pathway Press. 135 pages.

Church training course written by a well-known pentecostal leader. See Chapter 3 "The Evangelism Distinctives."

Key Words
doctrine, healing, spiritual gifts, evangelism, worship, government and polity, holiness

1981   *Pentecostal Preaching.* Cleveland, Tennessee: Pathway Press.

See Chapter 9, "The Uniqueness of Pentecostal Preaching."

Key Words
power, Baptism of the Holy Ghost, faith, healing, spiritual gifts, prophesy

Hummel, Charles G.
1978   *Fire in the Fireplace: Contemporary Charismatic Renewal.* Downers Grove, Illinois: Inter Varsity Press. 275 pages.

See index under "pentecostals," "spiritual gifts" and under pentecostal leaders by name (Oral Roberts, Demos Shakarian, etc.). Also Chapter 5 on "Pentecostal Theology."

Key Words
pentecostal theology, history, baptism of the Holy Spirit, tongues

Humphrey, Peggy
1966   *J.H. Ingram: Missionary Dean.* Cleveland, Tennessee: Pathway Press. 158 pages.

Missionary biography of the man who, more than anyone else, helped spread the ministry of the Church of God to numerous fields.

Key Words
missionary ambassador, amalgamation, travel, Holy Spirit, miracles

1968 *Paul C. Pitt: Beloved of the Chinese.* Cleveland, Tennessee: Pathway Press. 124 pages.

Interesting biography, with photos, of an early Church of God medical missionary pioneer in China. Some interesting power encounters (pp. 44-70).

Key Words
medicine, healing, power encounter, persecution

Hunter, Charles and Frances
1981 *How to Heal the Sick.* Kingwood, Texas: Hunter Books, 215 pages.

Of particular interest for mission researchers is the reprint of a prophecy given by Tommy Hicks in 1961. Hicks is the evangelist best known for the pentecostal breakthrough in Argentina in which he was instrumental.

Key Words
visions, healing, anointing with oil, casting out devils, faith, "creative miracles"

Hunter, Harold D., Editor
1983 *Pastoral Problems in the Pentecostal-Charismatic Movement.* Cleveland, Tennessee: The Society for Pentecostal Studies. ca. 200 pages.

Proceedings and papers from the thirteenth annual meeting of the Society for Pentecostal Studies. Papers present an interesting background into the historical and contemporary theological and sociological agendas of the pentecostal movement.

Key Words
Bible, cultural profile, dispensationalism, women's ministry, healing ministries, early pentecostalism

1983 "Spirit-Baptism and the 1896 Revival in Cherokee County, North Carolina," in *Pneuma: The Journal of the Society for Pentecostal Studies,* William W. Menzies, Editor. Volume 5, Number 2 (Fall).

Hunter, a minister in the Church of God of Prophecy, provides valuable bibliographical sources and good resources on "xenolalia" which played a part in early pentecostal missions.

Key Words
Charles Parham, W.J. Seymour, A.J. Tomlinson, Homer A. Tomlinson, Schearer Schoolhouse revival, "akolalia"

Ingram, J.H.
1938 *Around the World with the Gospel Light.* Cleveland, Tennessee. The Church of God Publishing House. 132 pages.

A brief autobiography of the author (to 1938) and a pictorial review of 33 years and 300,000 miles of world travel as an itinerant missionary for the Church of God (Cleveland).

Key Words
Cincinnati, pioneer missions, amalgamation

Janes, Burton K.
1982 *The Lady Who Came, The Lady Who Stayed* (two volumes). St. Johns, Newfoundland, Canada: Good Tidings Press. 298 pages.

The biography of Alice Belle Garrigus, "Newfoundland's first Pentecostal pioneer." Produced by the Pentecostal Assemblies of Newfoundland.

Key Words
Frank Bartleman, Christian and Missionary Alliance, persecution, power encounter, Bethesda Mission, healings

Johnson, Harmon A.
1969 *Authority Over the Spirits: Brazilian Spiritism and Evangelical Church Growth.* Pasadena: Fuller School of World Mission. 136 pages. SWM thesis.

See Chapter 5 on pentecostals.

Key Words
anti-polemical, demon activity, Christ the Victor, power encounter, exorcism

Johnson, Norbert E.
1970 *The History, Dynamic, and Problems of the Pentecostal Movement in Chile* (unpublished Masters thesis). Richmond, Virginia. Union Theological Seminary. 131 pages.

In addition to this broad survey of Chilean pentecostalism, a behind-the-scenes look at the spiritual founder of the Chilean movement, Willis C. Hoover. Of interest is Hoover's spiritual experience in 1895 while on furlough in Chicago. (Good bibliography for those interested in Latin American pentecostalism.)

Key Words
Hoover, Methodism, laity, church splits, leadership styles, indigenous Pentecostalism

Jones, Gwen, Ron Rowden, and Mel Surface, Editors
1978 *Higher Goals: National Church Growth Convention Digest.* Springfield, Missouri: Gospel Publishing House. 346 pages.

A condensation of plenary sessions and seminars conducted at the Assemblies of God National Church Growth Convention in August, 1978.

Key Words
evangelism, goals, church growth, biblical principles, outreach

Jones, James W.
1974 *Filled With New Wine.* New York: Harper and Row. 141 pages.

1975 *The Spirit and the World.* New York. Hawthorn Books, Inc. 150 pages.

Casual observations by a not-too-well-informed outsider. Very scattered references to pentecostals.

Key Words
independence, individualism, "autonomy of the spirit," dispensation

Jones, Richard
1976 "Renewal and an American Mission" in *The Spirit and the Church* compiled by Ralph Martin. New York: Paulist Press. 341 pages.

This article, pp 271-279 relates an incident in which the Catholic charismatic renewal spread cross culturally to the Sioux Indians in South Dakota (1971-1972).

Key Words
prayer meeting, Bible study group, language barrier, team, singing

Juillerat, L. Howard
1919 *Gems of Religious Truth.* Cleveland, Tennessee: Church of God Evangel Press. Ca. 180 pages.

Written by the son of F.L. Juillerat, a pentecostal pioneer missionary who went to Switzerland in 1909. Charles Conn says of young Juillerat, ". . . one of the greatest agitators for a vigorous missions program the Church as ever had." See "The Spirit of Missions."

Key Words
missionary spirit, baptism of the Holy Ghost, cities, ripe fields

Kane, J. Herbert
1975 *A Global View of Christian Missions: From Pentecost to the Present* (Revised Edition). Grand Rapids: Baker Book House. 590 pages.

Scattered references to pentecostal missions, mostly indexed by denominational or personal name (see index). Grouped according to continent and country.

Key Words
extraordinary growth, indigenous leadership, power, charismatic gifts, Bible schools, leadership training

1981 *The Christian World Mission: Today and Tomorrow.* Grand Rapids: Baker Book House. 294 pages.

A short but very significant analysis of pentecostals by a veteran missiologist. See Chapter 18 and the index under Assemblies of God and penteostals.

Key Words
Assemblies of God, Holy Spirit, signs and wonders, producing church growth, charismatic movement

Kay, Richard W.
1972 *Church Growth and Renewal in the Bahamas.* Pasadena: Fuller School of World Mission. 282 pages.

SWM thesis. Short section (p. 100ff) on three pentecostal groups: Church of God, Church of God of Prophecy, Assemblies of God.

Key Words
splits, R.M. Evans, A.J. Tomlinson, Edmond S. Barr, blacks and whites

Kelsey, Morton T.
1981 *Tongue Speaking: The History and Meaning of Charismatic Experience.* New York: The Crossroad Publishing Company. 252 pages.

See Chapter 4 "The Pentecostal Churches," and Chapter 6 "What Can This Mean?"

Key Words
rapid growth, tongues, Christian and Missionary Alliance, Assemblies of God, Full Gospel Business Men's Fellowship

Kendrick, Klaude
1961 *The Promise Fulfilled: A History of the Modern Pentecostal Movement.* Springfield, Missouri: Gospel Publishing House. 237 pages.

Written by an Assemblies of God historian and scholar, most of the book is given to the AOG. See p. 95ff. for a brief history, philosophy and methodology of the AOG foreign missions department.

Key Words
1915 missionary policy, administration, indigenous methods, promotion

Kessler, J.B.A.
1967 *A Study of the Older Protestant Missions and Churches in Peru and Chile.* Goes, Holland: Oosterbaan & le Cointre.

Kennedy, Neil L.
1980 *Dream Your Way to Success.* South Plainfield, New Jersey: Bridge Publishing Inc. 248 pages.

The authorized biography of Paul Yonggi Cho, pastor of the Full Gospel Central Church in Seoul, Korea.

Key Words
Buddhist, war, communists, healing, miracles, church growth

Klaiber, Jeffrey
1970 "Pentecostal Breakthrough," in *America.* 122 (January 31): 99-102.

Klassen, J.P.
1975 *Fire in the Pararno* (unpublished master's thesis). Pasadena: Fuller School of World Mission.

Kliewer, Gerd U.
1975 *Das Neue Volk der Pfingstler: Religion Unterwicklung und Sozialer Wandel in Lateinamerika.* Bern: Herbert Lang. 229 pages.

Knight, Cecil, B., Editor
1984 *Sermons From the Word: Twentieth Anniversary Sermons for the Church of God in Korea.* Seoul, Korea: Church of God Publishing Department. 232 pages.

Anniversary sermon collection of twenty-one sermons. Some are related to world evangelization.

Key Words
mission, international, Holy Spirit, good news, hope, second coming

Knight, Herbert V.
1972 *Ministry Aflame.* Carlinville, Illinois: Illinois District Council of the Assemblies of God. 219 pages.

A history of the Illinois District Council of the Assemblies of God. Two interesting stories are "The Cunningham Healing" (p. 160) and "Pioneer Work in South China" (p. 184), which reveal pentecostal mission practices.

Key Words
healing, power encounter, idols, 1924

Kulbeck, Gloria Grace
1958 *What God Hath Wrought.* Toronto. The Pentecostal Assemblies of Canada. 364 pages.

A history of a mainline Canadian pentecostal organization. Chapters 14-22 deal with foreign missions.

Key Words
trail-blazing, the islands, East Africa, Rhodesia, China

Kydd, Ronald
1983   "The Contribution of Denominationally Trained Clergymen to the emerging Pentecostal Movement in Canada," in *Pneuma: The Journal of the Society for Pentecostal Studies.* Volume 5, Number 1 (Spring). William M. Menzies, Editor.

Key Words
Canadian pentecostalism, leadership training, prayer, revival, anointing, organization

La Berge, Agnes N.O.
n.d.   *What God Hath Wrought.* Privately published by the author. 127 pages.

Life and work of the former Agnes Ozman.

Key Words
Bible school, camp meetings, itinerant preaching

Lalive d'Epinay, Christian
1967   "The Training of Pastors and Theological Education: The Case of Chile," *International Review of Missions* (April).

Laurentin, Rene
1977   *Catholic Pentecostalism.* Garden City, New York: Doubleday and Company. 237 pages.

See Chapter 2 "From Pentecostalism to Neo-Pentecostalism."

Key Words
origins, Parham, the poor, neo-pentecostalism, Catholic reactions, Pope Paul VI

Lawrence, Bennett F.
1916   *The Apostolic Faith Restored.* Springfield, Missouri: Gospel Publishing House. (Out of print).

Lindsay, Gordon
1968   *The Pentecostal Ministry.* Two Volumes. Dallas: Christ for the Nations. 141 pages.

Lindsay, Gordon, Compiler
1972   *They Saw It Happen.* Dallas, Texas: Christ for the Nations.

1972   *John C. Lake—Apostle to Africa.* Dallas: Christ for the Nations. 58 pages.

The story of a healing evangelist who went to Africa in 1908 and later moved to Portland, Oregon in 1920.

Key Words
calling, healing, revivals, deliverance, demon possession, power encounter

Los Angeles Times
1906 "Weird Babel of Tongues," *Los Angeles Times* (April 18).

The first secular news story in Los Angeles to report the events at the Azusa Street Mission.

Key Words
religious sect, tumble-down shack, weird doctrine, fanatical rites, tongues, prayer

Lovett, Leonard
1978 "Black Holiness-Pentecostalism—Implications for Ethics and Social Transformation." Unpublished doctoral dissertation. Emory University. 183 pages.

Although writing for other agendas, this Church of God in Christ (pentecostal) author gives an interesting insider's view on the dynamics of black pentecostal growth. See "From Azusa Street to the World" (p. 52ff).

Key Words
scripture, theology, experience, Baptism in the Holy Spirit, Black Power, Adventism

Luce, Alice Eveline
1950 *Pictures of Pentecost.* Springfield, Missouri: Gospel Publishing House. 238 pages.

Written by a missionary from England who began under the Episcopal Missionary Soceity (India) and later associated with the Assemblies of God in 1915. Later she worked in Mexico and subsequently established the Latin American Bible Institute in La Puente, California.

Malaska, Hilkka
1970 *The Challenge for Evangelical Missions to Europe: A Scandinavian Case Study.* South Pasadena: William Carey Library. 178 pages.

SWM thesis. Very brief, but informative, section on Scandinavian pentecostals and their early American connections.

Key Words
T.B. Barratt, Lewi Pethrus, responsive areas, leadership, felt-needs, G.O. Smidt.

Marshall, June Glover
1974   *A Biographical Sketch of Richard G. Spurling, Jr.* Cleveland, Tennessee: Pathway Press. 29 pages.

Massih, Bashir Abdol
1978   "The Incarnational Witness to the Muslim Heart" in *The Gospel and Islam.* Monrovia: MARC.

McClung, Floyd
1982   "Urban Missions: Reaching the City of Amsterdam" in *Unreached Peoples, '82,* Edward R. Dayton and Samuel Wilson, editors. Monrovia: MARC. 400 pages.

Urban missiology from a pentecostal missionary with Youth With A Mission.

Key Words
Biblical perspectives, biblical models, Youth With A Mission, urban missionaries

McClung, Grant
1983a   "An Assessment of the Church of God European Bible Seminary, 1973-1983" (unpublished research paper for Leadership Training Models). Pasadena: Fuller School of World Mission. 149 pages.

Analysis of a pentecostal Bible school which has problems and opportunities typical to others like it in the movement. Copy on file with Dr. Robert Clinton at SWM and with the author.

Key Words
history, training program, Holland's Two-Track Analogy, Clinton's Adapted Systems Model, strengths, weaknesses, recommendations

1983b   "Signs and Wonders in the Life and History of the Church of God (Cleveland, Tennessee): An Introductory Survey." Fuller Seminary School of World Mission. Unpublished research paper for Signs, Wonders, and Church Growth. Pasadena: Fuller School of World Missions. 49 pages.

An overview of signs and wonders (mostly healings) in a classical pentecostal denomination. On file in SWM research library and with the author.

Key Words
early beginnings, divine healing, God's nature, faith and healing, "demonization," church growth, power encounter

1983c   "A Preliminary Feasibility Study for Planting Urban Ethnic Churches of God in the Los Angeles Five-County Area" (unpublished research paper for Techniques of Planting New Churches). Pasadena: Fuller School of World Mission. 76 pages.

Pentecostal strategizing for an urban area. On file in SWM research library and with the author.

Key Words
Dayton and Fraser, planning, people-centered evangelism, church planting, urban ethnics, goals, means and methods

1983d "Improving the Missions Training Curriculum at the Church of God School of Theology and Broadening its Scope to Include Training in All Cross-Cultural Ministries of the Church of God (Cleveland, Tennessee)" (unpublished research paper for Implementing Change in Christian Organizations). Pasadena: Fuller School of World Mission. 67 pages. Perspectives on missionary training.

Key Words
client system, in-service and interrupted-service personnel, Havelock's principles, missions department, national leaders, solutions, curriculum, culture

1983e "Analysis of Growth" (interview with Donald A. McGavran) in *The Pentecostal Minister*. Volume 3, Number 3 (Fall).

Key Words
Theology of church growth, signs and wonders, secularism in America, receptive people, faith projections, reaching ethnics, future of the Church Growth Movement

1984 "Readings in the Church Growth Dynamics of the Missionary Expansion of the Pentecostal Movement" (masters thesis). Pasadena: Fuller School of World Mission.

SWM thesis articles on key pentecostal missions topics. Ninety percent of the 25 articles are written by pentecostals.

Key Words
(Chapters) history, theology, practices, strategy, future, pentecostals and the church growth movement

McCracken, Horace
1943 *History of Church of God Missions.* Cleveland, Tennessee: Church of God Publishing House. 173 pages.

An early compilation of Church of God missions history.

Key Words
financial organization, 1926 General Assembly, faith missions, World War II, missionary calls

McCurry, Don
1978a "A Time for New Beginnings," *The Gospel and Islam.* Monrovia: MARC.

1978b "Resistance/Response Analysis of Muslim People," *The Gospel and Islam.* Monrovia: MARC.

McGavran, Donald A., John Huegel, and Jack Taylor
1963   *Church Growth in Mexico.* Grand Rapids: Eerdmans. 136 pages.

An early Church Growth study from the Institute of Church Growth in Eugene, Oregon. Note Chapter 11 ("The Pentecostal Contribution") and the index under "Pentecostal Churches."

Key Words
Holy Spirit, spontaneous action, denominations, responsive action, denominations, responsive populations, training, indigenous, masses, resistant classes

McGavran, Donald A.
1960   "Of Churches, Sects and Denominations," in *The Christian* (February 21, pp. 8, 9, 25).

1965   *Church Growth and Christian Mission.* New York: Harper and Row. 252 pages.

Three chapters from pentecostal missiologist Melvin L. Hodges include, "Creating Climate for Church Growth," "Developing Basic Units of Indigenous Churches," "Administering for Church Growth."

Key Words
theological base, "power-filled churches," prayer, living local churches, training, laymen, leadership, grassroots

1969   *Church Growth Bulletin,* First Consolidated Volume. South Pasadena: William Carey Libarary. 401 pages.

See index under "pentecostals," "Assemblies of God," and "Brazil." Note McGavran's favorable statements on pentecostals on p. 277 and a lead article by a pentecostal missions executive on pp. 42-44.

Key Words
spiritual motivation, signs and wonders, leadership training, Pentecostal World Conference, notable growth

1970   *Understanding Church Growth.* Grand Rapids: Eerdmans Publishers.

1976   "Then The End Will Come" (interview) in *Church Growth Bulletin.* Volume 13, Number 1 (September).

1977a"Let's Get Serious About the Three Billion," in *Church Growth Bulletin.* Volume 13, Number 5 (May) Third Consolidated Volume.

1977b *Church Growth Bulletin,* Second Consolidated Volume. South Pasadena: William Carey Library. 526 pages.

Note the index under such references as "Assemblies of God," and "pentecostals."

1977c "What Makes Pentecostal Churches Grow?" in *Church Growth Bulletin* (January).

Key Words
faith healing, church planting, urban mission, people movement, indigenous

1979 "Impressions of the Christian Cause in India: 1978," in *Church Growth Bulletin.* Volume 15, Number 3 (January). Third Consolidated Volume.

1980 *Understanding Church Growth,* Revised Edition. Grand Rapids: William B. Eerdmans Publishing Company. 480 pages.

See index under "Pentecostal, Assemblies of God, Foursquare."

Key Words
revival, Brazil, common Christians, new congregations

McGavran, Donald A., James H. Montgomery, and C. Peter Wagner
1982 *Church Growth Bulletin,* Third Consolidated Volume. Santa Clara, California: Global Church Growth. 312 pages.

See index for references to Assemblies of God, pentecostals, and charismatics. Note: The January, 1977 issue (p. 97) for McGavran's article "What Makes Pentecostal Churches Grow?" and two recent pentecostal case studies. (See also the first and second consolidated volumes.)

Key Words
spiritual gifts, power, church planting, signs and wonders, power encounter

McGee, Gary B.
1983 "Early Pentecostal Missionaries: They Went Everywhere Preaching The Gospel" in *Assemblies of God Heritage* (Summer), Volume 3:2.

1984 "This Gospel Shall Be Preached: A History and Theology of Assemblies of God Foreign Missions: 1914-1959" (unpublished doctoral dissertation). St. Louis: St. Louis University.

Author is Associate Professor of Theology and Church History, Assemblies of God Theological Seminary.

Key Words
Division of Foreign Mission, missiology, missions administration, leadership, personnel, finances, Noel Perkin, organization, training

1986   *This Gospel Shall Be Preached.* Springfield, Missouri: Gospel Publishing House. The published version of McGee's 1984 dissertation.

McPherson, Aimee Semple
1923   *This Is That: Personal Experiences, Sermons, and Writings.* Los Angeles: Echo Park Evangelistic Association. 800 pages.

Autobiographical with photos.

Key Words
tent meeting, healing, preaching overseas crusades, Angelus Temple, sermons

1973   *The Story of My Life.* Waco, Texas: Word Books. 255 pages.

Meloon, Marion
1974   *Ivan Spencer: Willow in the Wind.* Plainfield, New Jersey: Logos International. 234 pages.

Biography of a pioneer in the Latter Rain movement which spread to some foreign fields.

Key Words
Genesee Wesleyan Seminary, Elim Bible Institute, revival, India

Menzies, William W.
1971   *Anointed to Serve: The Story of the Assemblies of God.* Springfield, Missouri: Gospel Publishing House. 436 pages.

The fundamental thesis of this authorized history is that "the Assemblies of God represent a microcosm of the Pentecostal Movement." See Chapter 10 and the statistical charts on missions in the appendices.

Key Words
coordination, J. Roswell Flower, Noel Perkin, J. Philip Hogan, indigenous missions, faith support, April 1943 conference, training, "Global Conquest" program (cities), Good News Crusades, MAPS

1979   The Holy Spirit in Christian Theology" in *Perspectives on Evangelical Theology,* Kenneth S. Kantzer and Stanley N. Gundry, Editors. Grand Rapids: Baker Book House, 189 pages.

Assembly of God author. One of the papers from the thirteenth annual meeting of the Evangelical Theological Society.

215

Key Words
mission of the Spirit, experience of the Spirit, historical survey, community faith

Miller, Elmer S.
1967   *Pentecostalism Among the Argentine Toba.* Unpublished doctoral dissertation (University of Pittsburgh). 277 pages.

Mills, Watson E.
1973   *Speaking in Tongues: Let's Talk About It.* Waco, Texas: Word Books. 162 pages.

Primarily written about tongues by Southern Baptist theologians; some discussion is related to glossolalia and missions. See "The Place of Glossolalia in Neo-Pentecostalism" by Assemblies of God theologian William G. MacDonald.

Key Words
glossolalia and mission, xenoglossolalia, supernatural powers

1974   *Speaking in Tongues: A Classified Bibliography.* Franklin Springs, Georgia: Society for Pentecostal Studies. 66 pages.

A valuable tool for researchers of the pentecostal-charismatic movement.

Key Words
glossolalia, books, essays, articles, theses, reports and papers, popular magazines, etc.

Mitchell, Robert Bryant
1982   *Heritage and Horizons: The History of Open Bible Standard Churches.* Des Moines, Iowa: Open Bible Publishers. 414 pages.

See Chapters 8, 23, 24, and Appendix D.

Key Words
Jacob O. Lehmans, Hazel C. Forrester, North India, Burma, women, youth

Monterroso, Victor M.
1967   "Interview: Church Growth in the Americas," *Latin America Evangelist* (May-June).

Montgomery, Jim
n.d.   *Why They Grow: The Foursquare Church in the Philippines.* Fuller Theological Seminary School of World Mission. 322 pages.

Excellent field study with a number of church growth insights. Good prognosis at the end.

Key Words
graph of growth, church multiplication, people movements, growth through families

1975 *Fire in the Philippines*. Carol Stream, Illinois: Creation House. 140 pages. Former title: *New Testament Fire in the Philippines*.

Foursquare denominational study. Widely quoted as area case study.

Key Words
pioneer evangelism, families, Baptism of the Holy Spirit, divine healing, lay leadership, women preachers

1979 "Why Strategy? A Study in Contracts," in *Church Growth Bulletin*. Volume 15, Number 4 (March). Third Consolidated Volume.

Strategy insight from a case study of a Filipino pentecostal church planter.

Key Words
prayer for the sick, worship services, homogeneous unit, training for ministry, rigor of life style, social action, financing, media, vision

Moore, Everett LeRoy
1954 *Handbook of Pentecostal Denominations in the United States*. Pasadena Nazarene College. 347 pages.

Master's thesis which highlights the major classical pentecostal denominations. Each church has a section on "missionary activities." Good bibliography.

Key Words
organization, Bible schools, indigenous

Moore, Sidney
1973 *5,000 Arrows*. Pico Rivera; California: CFM Press. 80 pages.

Foursquare missions in Papua, New Guinea. Good area case study.

Key Words
Eastern Highlands, highland people, medical work, missions compound

Moree, Christopher, Editor
1983 *SOW (Save Our World)*. Cleveland, Tennessee: Church of God World Missions. Volume 22, Number 3 (Summer).

Reports from all regional areas of Church of God World Missions indicate interesting events and trends.

Key Words
revival, young people, unreached people, coming of the Lord, urgency, hope, leadership training

Musk, Bill A.
1978   "Popular Islam: The Hunger of The Heart," *The Gospel and Islam,* Don McCurry, Editor. Monrovia: MARC.

Myland, D. Wesley
1910   *The Latter Rain Covenant.* Chicago: The Evangel Publishing House (Reprinted by A.N. Trotter, P.O. Box 26, Billings, Montana 65610).

Nelson Amirtharaj
1974   *A New Day in Madras: A Study of the Life and Growth of the Protestant Churches in Madras City, India After 1950.* Pasadena: Fuller School of World Missions. 327 pages.

SWM dissertation. Historical and theological backgrounds of various denominations in Madras, a city of two million. See Chapter 2 for information on pentecostals.

Key Words
witnessing, fasting, indigenous, music, open-air evangelism, cottage prayer meetings

Nichol, John Thomas
1966   *Pentecostalism.* New York: Harper & Row. 264 pages.

One of the best-known surveys, written by the son of a pentecostal minister. Note: Chapters 4, 5, 10, and 11 for the international spread of the movement. Excellent bibliography.

Key Words
revivals, T.B. Barrett, Donald Gee, Azusa Street, mass meetings, pioneering

Nickel, Thomas R.
1962   *In Those Days.* Monterey Park, California: Great Commission International. Whitaker Books, Monroeville, Pennsylvania. 72 pages.

n.d.   *The Amazing Shakarian Story.* Los Angeles: Full Gospel Business Men's Fellowship International.

Niklaus, Robert L.
1982   "Brazil: Pentecostal Invasion," in *Evangelical Missions Quarterly.* Volume 18, Number 2: 117-118 (April).

An update on pentecostal growth in Brazil which stood at 8.5 million in April, 1982.

Key Words
literal, interpretation of the Bible, 26,000 churches, Sao Paulo, urban, radio

Olila, James Howard
1968 "Pentecostalism: The Dynamics of Recruitment in a Modern Socio-Religious Movement." (unpublished master's thesis.) University of Minnesota. 57 pages.

Written by a colleague of Gerlach and Hine.

Key Words
nature of recruitment, types of recruiter-recruit relationships, techniques and appeals of recruitment, inner dynamics, primary and secondary recruitment, face-to-face situations, kinsmen and friends

Oliver, Dennis M.
Church Growth: Canada. Canadian Theological College. 4400 4th Avenue, Regina, Saskatchewan, S4T OH8, Canada. Volumes I-III (March, 1974-Fall, 1976).

Subsequent volumes under new name, *His Dominion* (Volume IV, 1977-).

Key Words
Canadian pentecostals, church growth, fastest growing, Pentecostal Assemblies of Canada, lay evangelism, evangelists

Olsen, Walther A.
1977 *The Dynamics of Religious Conversion in France: Research in Progress.* Pasadena: Fuller School of World Mission. 200 pages.

SWM thesis. Short section (p. 66ff) on the pentecostal church and charismatic movement in France.

Key Words
1930 beginning, evangelistic drive, church planting, Normandy, gypsy movement, charismatic movement

Orr, J. Edwin
1973 *The Flaming Tongue: The Impact of Twentieth-Century Revivals.* Chicago: Moody Press. 241 pages.

Oosthuizen, Gerhardus Cornelis
1975 *Pentecostal Penetration Into the Indian Community in Metropolitan Durban, South Africa.* Pretoria, South Africa: Human Sciences Research Council. 356 pages.

An excellent study of conversion and growth among the Hindu Indian population of South Africa. Reference is made to all Indian pentecostal churches and denominations. Very good bibliography.

Key Words
organization, theology, healing, sociological assessment

1975 *Moving to the Waters: Fifty Years of Pentecostal Revival in Bethesda, 1925-1975.* Durban: Bethesda Publications. 239 pages.

Bethesda is the name used for the branch of the Full Gospel Church of God in the Indian community of South Africa. This work, one of the largest of its kind, was pioneered by J.F. Rowlands.

Key Words
J.F. Rowlands, visions, healing, Durban Indian Community, *Moving Waters,* signs and wonders, training

Ostling, Richard
1982 "Counting Every Soul on Earth," in *Time* (May 3).

The story of Dr. David B. Barrett's *World Christian Encyclopedia* which documents 51 million worldwide pentecostals plus another 11 million in more traditional denominations which "follow Pentecostal practices."

Key Words
statistics, Christians, demography, global analysis, comprehensive lists, major spiritual changes

Palmer, Donald G.
1974 *Explosion of People Evangelism.* Chicago: Moody Press. 191 pages.

The original title is "The Growth of the Pentecostal Churches of Columbia," a master's thesis for Trinity Evangelical Divinity School. A good case study primarily conducted in Bogota, Pereira, and Palmira. See Chapters 4-5, the illustrations, and tables.

Key Words
pentecostal distinctives, healing, prophecy, persuasion, preaching themes, separation from the world, Assemblies of God, leadership training, home Bible study, Foursquare Church, United Pentecostal Church

Patterson, Joseph, German R. Ross and Julia M. Atkins, Editors
1969 *History and Formative Years of the Church of God in Christ with Excerpts from the Life and Works of Its Founder, Bishop C.H. Mason.* Memphis: Church of God in Christ Publishing House.

Paul, George Harold
1965 *The Religious Frontier in Oklahoma: Dan T. Muse and the Pentecostal Holiness Church.* Unpublished doctoral dissertation (The University of Oklahoma). 302 pages.

See Chapters 11 or 12 on the world outreach of the Pentecostal Holiness Church.

Pedatto, Jack
1983 "The Kingdom of God Theology as It Relates to Power Encounters and the Advance of the Gospel During the Azusa Street Revival." Pasadena: Fuller School of World Mission. Unpublished research paper for Healing Ministry and Church Growth. 13 pages.

A survey and classification of power encounters during the early days of the pentecostal movement. On file in SWM Research Library.

Key Words
secret encounters, open encounters, personal attack, powers of darkness, victory

Pedersen, Janice L., Editor
1982 *Foursquare World Advance.* Los Angeles: International Church of the Foursquare Gospel.

The official Foursquare missions magazine. Articles since 1981 have focused on unreached peoples.

Pentecost, Edward Clyde
1974 *Reaching the Unreached: An Introductory Study on Developing an Overall Strategy for World Evangelization.* Pasadena: Fuller School of World Mission.

SWM dissertation. Look under each country for history, location, and size of pentecostal groups.

Pentecostal Evangel
1936 "The Purpose of the Pentecostal Enduement," in *Pentecostal Evangel* (December 5) XXIV. (1, 10, 11).

Perkin, Noel and John Garlock
1965 *Our World Witness.* Springfield, Missouri: Gospel Publishing House.

History and survey of Assemblies of God foreign missions.

Perez-Torres, Ruben
1979 "The Pastor's Role in Educational Ministry in the Pentecostal Church of God in Puerto Rico." Unpublished doctoral dissertation. School of Theology at Claremont, California. 111 pages.

A view of pentecostal pastoral theology in Puerto Rico and its relationship to the working dynamics of the local pentecostal church.

Key Words
church, pastor, educational ministry

Petersen, Philip Lee
1958 "The Teaching Ministry of the Holy Spirit: The Meaning of The Concept of the Holy Spirit as The Great Teacher of Christian Teachers." Pasadena: Fuller Theological Seminary (unpublished master's thesis). 68 pages.

Written by a pentecostal minister in the Open Bible Standard Churches.

Key Words
Holy Spirit, paraclete, teacher, spiritual gifts, illumination

Planter, Josephine
1936 *Book of Remembrance.* (Third Edition) Los Angeles: D.C. Wetty, Printer. 144 pages.

Experiences of Josephine Planter, missionary to Tunis, North Africa.

Key Words
healing, visions, Baptism of the Holy Ghost, Islam, spiritual warfare, World War I

Plymire, David V.
1959 *High Adventure in Tibet.* Springfield, Missouri: Gospel Publishing House. 225 pages.

Foreword by Noel Perkin.

Polen, O.W., with Jim O. McClain
1983 "Tentmaking and Future Plans for World Missions" (Interview). *Church of God Evangel* (October 10).

Pomerville, Paul Anthony
1982 *Pentecostalism and Missions: Distortion or Correction?* Pasadena: Fuller School of World Mission. 381 pages.

SWM dissertation written by an Assemblies of God missiologist. Primarily theological and theoretical in nature. See Chapter 2 (pp. 28-61), the appendix (statistics), and the bibliography.

Key Words
rapid growth, "The Third Force," missionary phenomenon, rate of growth

1986 *The Third Force in Missions.* Peabody, Massachusetts: Hendrickson Publishers. The published version of Pomerville's 1982 dissertation.

Price, Charles S.
1972 *The Real Faith.* Plainfield, New Jersey: Logos International. 125 pages. Originally printed in 1940. Pentecostal teaching from an early pioneer.

Key Words
faith, Word of God, prayer, Holy Spirit

1972   ... *And Signs Followed.* Plainfield, New Jersey: Logos International. 145 pages.

Prien, Hans-Jurgen
1978   *Die Geschichte des Christentums in Lateinamerika.* Gottingen, West Germany: Vandenhoeck & Ruprecht. 1,203 pages.

See index under "Pfingsten" (Pentecostals) and "Pfingstkirchen" (pentecostal churches).

Key Words
Amerikanische Heiligungsbewegung, Erweckungen, Lateinamerika Chile, Brasilien, "Assembleias de Deus no Brasil," Hollenweger, Pfingstbewegung

Quebedeaux, Richard
1983   *The New Charismatics: The Origins, Development and Significance of Neo-Pentecostalism.* Revised Edition, Garden City, New York: Doubleday. 252 pages.

Pages 42-51 provide a good overall view of the international diffusion of classical pentecostalism. Pages 59-71 discuss the international spread of the charismatic movement ("Rapid Spread to Other Parts of the World"). Good bibliography.

Key Words
agressive evangelism, preaching, Azusa Street, World War II, North and South America, Europe, Africa, Asia

Ratz, Calvin C.
1970   *They Call Him Pastor Wheat.* Toronto. The Pentecostal Assemblies of Canada. 113 pages.

The story of Ken McGillivray in China.

Key Words
Kalgan, World War II, Japanese, Mongolia, Communists, Taiwan

Read, William R.
1965   *New Patterns of Church Growth in Brazil.* Grand Rapids: Eerdmans Publishing Company. 240 pages.

See Chapters 1, 4, 5, 6 and 10 for the story of pentecostal growth. The bibliography is also valuable.

Key Words
Congregacao Christa no Brasil, Assemblies of God, *Brazil Para Cristo,* "The Bright New Pattern"

1980   *Brazil 1980: A Tool for the Evangelization of Brazil.* Pasadena: Fuller
        School of World Mission. 351 pages.

        SWM dissertation. Use of computer programming for measuring
        Church Growth. See Appendixes 10-13 for pentecostal statistics in
        Brazil.

        Key Words
        Church Growth, statistics, computer analysis

Read, William R., Victor M. Monterroso, and Harmon A. Johnson
1969   *Latin American Church Growth.* Grand Rapids: William B. Eerdmans
        Publishing Company. 421 pages.

        A major Church Growth study commissioned by the School of World
        Mission. McGavran calls it "a monumental study." The Pentecostal story
        is woven throughout the book. See "pentecostals" under each country
        division. "Pentecostal Beginnings" (p. 41), and "Pentecostals" in the
        Index. Chapter 21 is an analysis of pentecostal growth.

        Key Words
        Brazil, Congregacao Crista, Assemblies of God, Church of God, amazing
        multiplication, independent pentecostals, lower class, urbanization,
        ministerial training, healing, worship, spontaneous, lay ministry

Reed, Jerold F.
1974   *A Componential Analysis of the Ecuadorian Protestant Church.*
        Pasadena: Fuller School of World Mission. 219 pages.

        SWM dissertation. See p. 21ff for historical growth patterns of
        pentecostal denominations and movements.

        Key Words
        largest church, 1963-1973

Reeder, Hilda
1951   *A Brief History of the Foreign Missionary Department of the Pentecostal
        Assemblies of the World.* Indianapolis: Pentecostal Assemblies of the
        World. 76 pages.

        Denominational missions history of one of the early Black pentecostal
        movements (a "Oneness" organization). This group had missionaries as
        early as 1913.

        Key Words
        organization, China, South Africa, women, white missionaries

Rees, Seth C.
1897   *The Ideal Pentecostal Church.* Cincinnati, Ohio. M.W. Knapp,
        Publisher. 134 pages.

Early literature from "The Revivalist Office." Foreword by John Pennington.

Key Words
clean, powerful, a demonstrative church, power, the fullness of God, a missionary church

Richards, W.T.H.
1972 *Pentecost Is Dynamite*. Nashville: Abingdon Press. 95 pages.

Reflections on the nature and dynamics of the pentecostal movement by an insider.

Key Words
revival, leadership, evangelism, pentecostal, characteristics, zeal

Richardson, Carl
1974 *Exorcism: New Testament Style*. Old Tappan, New Jersey: Fleming H. Revell Company. 128 pages.

Popularly written on exorcism, Satan, demonology, and the occult. The author is a Church of God (Cleveland, Tennessee) minister.

Key Words
the Devil, Black Magic, Zodiac, exorcism, occult, New Testament

Robeck, Cecil M., Jr., Editor
1983 *Theology, News and Notes*. Volume 30, Number 1 (March). Fuller Theological Seminary

Special issue on pentecostals and charismatics.

Key Words
James D.G. Dunn, David J. du Plessis, David Allan Hubbard, Peter Hocken, Russell P. Spittler, David Watson, Cecil M. Robeck, Jr.

Roberts, W. Dayton
1963 "Pentecost South of the Border," *Christianity Today* (July 19).

Robertson, Pat
(with Jamie Buckingham)
1972 *Shout It From the Housetops*. South Plainfield, New Jersey: Bridge Publishing, Inc. 255 pages.

The story of "The 700 Club," a pentecostal-charismatic sodality which has spread to many foreign countries.

Key Words
Pat Robertson, miracles, broadcasting, Canada, Columbia, satellites, Costa Rica, conversions

Romero, Joel Eladio
1970 *Church Planting Evangelism: An Argentine Case Study.* Pasadena: Fuller School of World Mission. 238 pages.

SWM thesis. Pages 155-163 discuss the work of U.S. pentecostal missionaries and the subsequent growth of the national church. See also the graph comparing all denominational growth on p. 188.

Key Words
Assemblies of God, Italian immigrants, Marcos Mazzucco, Church of God, J.H. Ingram, Tommy Hicks, whole family conversions, Toba Indians, L.W. Stokes, Buenos Aires, Chilean pentecostal immigrants, church planting evangelism

Sargunam, M.E.
1973 *Multiplying Churches in Urban India* (unpublished master's thesis). Pasadena: Fuller School of World Mission.

Samarin, William J.
1972 *Tongues of Men and Angels.* New York: The Macmillan Company. 277 pages.

One of the first comprehensive studies on speaking in tongues. Written by a professor of anthropology and linguistics. Note the bibliography, appendices, and index under the names of key pentecostal leaders and writers.

Key Words
xenoglossia, cryptomnesia, "Prayed, Prophesied, and Interpreted," social factors, samples

Saracco, Noberto
1977 (article) *International Review of Missions.* (January).

Amazing pentecostal growth.

Schoomaker, Violet
1957 *Light in India's Night.* Springfield, Missouri: Gospel Publishing House. 237 pages.

Reflections of an Assemblies of God pioneer who went to India in 1902, serving for nearly fifty years.

Key Words
visions, miracles, Gandhi

Scism, Harry E.
1978 *The Foreign Missions Story.* Hazelwood, Missouri: United Pentecostal Church International. 48 pages.

General survey of the foreign missions program, staff, and statistics from the United Pentecostal Church.

Key Words
organization, personnel

Shakarian, Demos (as told to John and Elizabeth Sherrill)
1975   *The Happiest People on Earth.* Old Tappan, New Jersey: Fleming H. Revell.

Sherrill, John L.
1964   *They Speak With Other Tongues.* New York: McGraw-Hill Book Company. 165 pages.

One of the most popular accounts of the American pentecostal-charismatic movement through the eyes of a reporter who himself was drawn into it by his own personal experience.

Key Words
Baptism of the Holy Spirit, xenolalia, pentecostal literature, David du Plessis, Full Gospel Business Mens' Fellowship International, Dennis Bennett

Shinde, Benjamin P.
1974   *The Contribution of the Assemblies of God to Church Growth in India.* Pasadena: Fuller School of World Mission. 218 pages.

SWM thesis. The beginning of the worldwide pentecostal movement is related to the birth of the Indian pentecostal churches. Church growth study with future projections.

Key Words
regional conference (districts), growth factors, healing, Bible training institutes, literature, construction of church buildings, obstructions to growth

Shumaker, John Timothy
1972   *Church Growth i. Paraguay.* Pasadena: Fuller School of World Mission. 158 pages.

SWM thesis. See p. 96ff for history and growth patterns of pentecostal churches.

Key Words
early erratic growth, slow progress

Simmons, E.L.
1938   *History of the Church of God.* Cleveland, Tennessee: Church of God Publishing House. Also the manuscript of an unpublished Revised Edition. 156 pages.

See Chapter 13 on "Church of God Missions."

Skinner, J.W.
1974 *Ripening Harvest.* Toronto, Canada: The Pentecostal Assemblies of Canada. 64 pages.

Informative booklet giving worldwide outreaches and developments of this denomination. Chapters are arranged alphabetically according to the fourteen fields, mostly African.

Key Words
Kenya (large field), Uganda, South Africa

Smith, Henry J.
1979 *Development of the Educational System of the Church of God, As It Relates to Ministerial Preparation, 1918-1978.* Unpublished doctoral dissertation (California Graduate School of Theology). 183 pages.

Spittler, Russell, P. Editor
1976 *Perspectives on the New Pentecostalism.* Grand Rapids, Michigan: Baker Book House. 268 pages.

Papers from the 1972 meeting of the Society for Pentecostal Studies. Note Part Two, "Theological Viewpoints."

Key Words
classical viewpoint, neo-pentecostal viewpoint, Roman Catholic viewpoint, "experience-certified theology," spiritual gifts

1983 "Bar Mitzvah for Azusa Street: Features, Fractures, and Futures of a Renewal Movement Come of Age" in *Theology, News and Notes,* Fuller Theological Seminary. Volume XXX, Number 1 (March).

Stark, Pearl M.
n.d. *History of the Work in Angola.* Cleveland, Tennessee. Church of God World Missions. 71 pages.

Personal accounts of an early Church of God missionary to Angola.

Stetz, John
1976 "Biggest Little Church in the World," in *Church Growth Bulletin.* Volume 13, Number 1 (September). Third Consolidated Volume.

A look at the organization of the Full Gospel Central Church in Seoul, Korea.

Key Words
"Church in the home," shepherds, training, organization

1978   "Korean Students Plant Churches," in *Church Growth Bulletin,* Volume 14, Number 3 (January). Third Consolidated Volume.

Insightful report of church planting efforts by students in the Full Gospel Bible College in Seoul, Korea.

Key Words
"upper room" method, prayer and fasting, vision

Stone, James
1977   *The Church of God of Prophecy: History and Polity.* Cleveland, Tennessee: White Wing Publishing House and Press. 310 pages.

Denominational history. Brief sections (pp. 67-69, 184-187) on the history and polity of their world missions efforts from 1910.

Key Words
Bahamas, Foreign Missionary Committee, second Sunday offerings, Foreign Language Department

Sumrall, Lester with J. Stephen Conn
1977   *Run With the Vision.* Plainfield, New Jersey: Logos International. 161 pages.

Autobiography of a pentecostal evangelist with foreign mission outreach.

Key Words
vision, preaching, healing, China, spontaneous guidance, South Bend, Indiana, Manila, *World Harvest* magazine, Hong Kong, Brazil, schools

Synan, Vinson
1971   *The Holiness-Pentecostal Movement in the United States.* Grand Rapids: William B. Eerdmans Publishing Company 248 pages.

Though not directly related to pentecostal missions, this is one of the most quoted sources on the theological, historical, and social roots of the American pentecostal movement. Insights into the thinking of early pentecostal pioneers.

Key Words
Wesleyan tradition, holiness movements, Azusa Street, south, Black pentecostals, denominations

1973   *The Old-Time Power.* Franklin Springs, Georgia: Advocate Press. 296 pages.

Commissioned by the Pentecostal Holiness Church as their official history through 1973. Chapters 12-14 are the most profitable although written from a social-historical rather than missiological point of view.

Key Words
Oral Roberts, Argentina, Chile

Synan, Vinson, Editor
1975 *Aspects of Pentecostal-Charismatic Origins.* South Plainfield, New
    Jersey: Bridge Publishing, Inc. 251 pages.

    First two chapters have interesting elements in the early movement
    but do not reflect at length on evangelism/mission. (See pages
    25-35.)

    Key Words
    phases, developments of pentecostalism, fast-growing denominations

Tate, Francis Vincent
1970 *Patterns of Church Growth in Nairobi.* Pasadena: Fuller School of
    World Mission. 210 pages.

    SWM thesis. Pentecostals are cited among ten representative churches
    for a church growth study. See index under "pentecostals."

    Key Words
    Pentecostal Assemblies of Canada, poor and less educated classes,
    emotional, Luhya, monotribal churches, house churches

Thomas, E.C., Editor
1983a *The Pentecostal Minister.* Volume 3, Number 3 (Fall). Church of God
    Publishing House, 1080 Montgomery Avenue, Cleveland, Tennessee
    37311. Entire issue devoted to Church Growth.

    Key Words
    articles on such topics as: Pentecostal Leaders Look at Church
    Growth, interview with Donald A. McGavran, the Holy Spirit, church
    planting, the Church Growth pastor, case studies of growing pentecostal
    churches

1983b "International Congress on World Evangelism." Cleveland, Tennessee:
    Church of God. 100 pages.

    Conference outlines from plenary sessions, seminaries, and workshops
    held during the August 10-12, 1983 meeting.

    Key Words
    world evangelism, ministers, laity, youth, world vision, opportunities for
    service, cross-cultural ministries, international church

1983c "Pentecostal Leaders Look at Church Growth" in *The Pentecostal
    Minister.* Volume 3, Number 3 (Fall).

    Key Words
    pentecostal denominations, long-term pastorates, denominational
    structure, leadership, the charismatic movement, ethnic groups

Tinney, James S.
1978 "William J. Seymour: Father of Modern Day Pentecostalism" in *Black Apostles: Afro-American Clergy Confront the Twentieth Century.* Randall K. Burkett and Richard Newman, Editors. Boston: G.K. Hall & Company. 283 pages.

Interesting essay linking the black contribution to the rise of the pentecostal movement. Biographical insights on William J. Seymour.

Key Words
Africa, Los Angeles revival, "Evening Light Saints," Black pentecostals

Tippett, Alan R.
1967 *Solomon Islands Christianity.* London: Letterworth Press.

1973 *Verdict Theology in Missionary Theory.* (Second Edition) South Pasadena: William Carey Library.

Tomlinson, A.J., Editor
1918 *The Church of God Evangel.* Volume 9, Number 49 (December 14).

Headline of this older issue of the *Evangel* reads "Pray For a World-Wide Revival to Follow the World War."

Key Words
revival prayer, prevailing prayer

Underwood, B.E., Compiler
1984 "Self-Study Report." Oklahoma City, Oklahoma: World Missions Department of the International Pentecostal Holiness Church. 267 pages.

A self-study report presented to the Evangelical Foreign Missions Association (EFMA).

Key Words
structure, personnel, finance, church relations, goals

Van Dusen, Henry P.
1958 "The Third Force in Christendom," in *Life* (June 9).

See pp. 113-124 for Van Dusen's famous article which gave pentecostals a new appraisal.

Vaters, Eugene
1983 *Reminiscence.* St. Johns. Newfoundland, Canada: Good Tidings Press. 164 pages.

The autobiography of Pastor Eugene Vaters, the second General Superintendent of the Pentecostal Assemblies of Newfoundland.

Wagner, C. Peter
1968 *A Preliminary Study of the Origin and Growth of the Protestant Church in Bolivia.* Pasadena: Fuller School of World Missions. 285 pages.

SWM thesis. See Table of Contents for history and growth patterns of the Swedish Free Mission (Pentecostal). International Church of the Foursquare Gospel, and the Assemblies of God.

Key Words
Foursquare-1920, statistics

1970 *The Protestant Movement in Bolivia.* South Pasadena: William Carey Library. 240 pages.

Wagner's revision and printing of his earlier master's thesis (see Wagner 1968).

1973 *What Are We Missing?* Carol Stream, Illinois: Creation House. 196 pages.

Formerly titled *Look Out! The Pentecostals Are Coming,* this popular work surveys the dynamic growth of the pentecostal churches in Latin America and discusses the contributing elements. Good bibliography.

Key Words
body life, church planting, ministerial training, Holy Spirit, Church Growth

1982 "Characteristics of Pentecostal Church Growth," in *The Pentecostal Minister.* Volume 2, Number 2 (Summer), pp. 4-9.

Key Words
rapid growth, reasons for growth, rates of increase, purity, prayer, power, the poor, dangers of respectability, redemption and lift

Walker, Alan
1968 "Where Pentecostalism is Mushrooming," in *Christian Century* (January 17).

Walker, Paul L.
1981 *The Ministry of Worship.* Cleveland, Tennessee: Pathway Press. See Chapter 9, "The Church, A Commissioned Community."

Key Words
worldwide witness, fellowship of faith, evangelize, occupy, preaching, Psalm 67

Walker, Jr., John Herbert
1950   *Haiti.* Cleveland, Tennessee: Church of God Publishing House. 68 pages.

General survey of Haiti and the history and polity of the Church of God.

Key Words
organization, financial system, literature, schools, system of evangelization

Warner, Wayne
1978   *Touched by the Fire.* Plainfield, New Jersey: Logos International. 163 pages.

Eyewitness accounts of the early days of the pentecostal revival

Key Words
healings, prayer, living by faith, miracle, worship, revival.

White, Robert, Compiler
1978   "New Directions in World Evangelism." Cleveland, Tennessee: Church of God World Missions. 50 pages.

Collected essays from the 1978 Pre-General Assembly Missionary Conference of the Church of God.

Key Words
new era, goals and strategies, world missions board, pastoral care of missionaries, educational program, interpersonal relationships, lay ministries

Wigglesworth, Smith
1971   *Ever Increasing Faith,* Revised Edition. Springfield, Missouri: Gospel Publishing House, 176 pages.

Written by the twentieth-century "Apostle of Faith." A collection of eighteen messages which the author preached in different parts of the world.

Key Words
faith, deliverance, power, healing, Baptism in the Spirit, spiritual gifts

Wilkerson, David
1963   *The Cross and the Switchblade.* New York: Geis Associates. 217 pages.

The story of Assemblies of God minister, David Wilkerson, and the rise of Teen Challenge, a youth rehabilitation ministry which has now spread to numerous countries.

Key Words
David Wilkerson, Nicky Cruz, deliverance, New York, youth, Holy Spirit

Williams, J. Rodman
1972   *The Pentecostal Reality.* Plainfield, New Jersey: Logos International. 108 pages.

See Chapter 5 "The Holy Spirit and Evangelism."

Key Words
power, Book of Acts, evangelism, prayer

Willems, Emilio
1967   *Followers of the New Faith.* Nashville: Vanderbilt University Press. 290 pages.

Case study of Protestantism in Brazil and Chile. Willems is cited in most any survey of Latin American pentecostalism.

Key Words
Pentecostal sects, Hoover, Chile, Brazil, the functions of pentecostalism

Wilson, Everett A.
1983   "Sanguine Saints: Pentecostalism in El Salvador," in *Church History,* 52.

See pages 186-198 for a pentecostal educator's view of pentecostal church growth in El Salvador.

Wilson, R. Marshall
1971   *Youth With A Mission.* Plainfield, New Jersey: Logos International, 170 pages.

Dynamic story of the early years of one of the largest pentecostal-charismatic mission sodalities in the world today.

Key Words
Loren Cunningham, young people, Summer teams, Discipleship Training Schools, Schools of Evangelism, frontiers, worldwide

Winehouse, Irwin
1959   *The Assemblies of God: A Popular Survey.* New York: Vantage Press. 224 pages.

One of the earlier histories. See Chapters 6-8 for insights into their foreign missions work.

Key Words
Noel Perkin, missionary biographies, worldwide report, mission village

Wogen, Norris L., Editor
1973   *Jesus, Where Are You Taking Us?: Messages from the First International Lutheran Conference on the Holy Spirit.* Caral Sream, Illinois: Creation House. 250 pages.

Of particular interest are addresses from Mel Tari, "Hand of God in Indonesia," and David du Plessis, "Holy Spirit in Ecumenical Movement."

Key Words
Holy Spirit, miracles, raised from the dead, Bible, second coming, movement, World Council of Churches, Catholics

Womack, David A.
1968   *The Wellsprings of the Pentecostal Movement.* Springfield, Missouri: Gospel Publishing House. 96 pages.

Written in cooperation with the Committee on Advance for the General Council of the Assemblies of God.

Key Words
apostolic patterns, New Testament patterns, history, revelation, future, prescriptions

1973   *Breaking the Stained-Glass Barrier.* New York: Harper & Row. 167 pages.

Pentecostal style missions strategy written by a former missionary and Home Secretary of the Assemblies of God Foreign Missions.

Key Words
strategy, team concept, mass communications, training national leaders, Ephesus model

Woodside, Kenneth L.
1960   *The Great Awakening.* New York. Privately published by the author. 32 pages.

Written to commemorate the "golden jubilee" of the Church of God (Cleveland, Tennessee) in the Bahamas.

Key Words
R.M. Evans, Carl M. Padgett, Edmond S. Barr

Woodworth-Etter, Marie B.
1916   *Signs and Wonders God Wrought in the Ministry for Forty Years.* Indianapolis, Indiana. Privately published by the author. 584 pages.

First-hand experiences of an itinerant evangelist.

Key Words
signs and wonders, sermons, healing, visions, manifestations

Worsfold, J.E.
1974   *A History of the Charismatic Movements in New Zealand.* West Yorkshire, England: Puritan Press, Ltd. 368 pages.

Interesting area study with a number of biographical insights.

Key Words
Smith Wigglesworth, Wellington, crusades, healing, Assemblies of God, ecumenism

Zechariah, C.
1980   *Factors Affecting the Growth of the Protestant Churches in Tamil, Nadu and Kerala.* See pp. 122-123, 162-165 for power encounter.

Zimmerman, Thomas F.
1975   "The Reason for the Rise of the Pentecostal Movement," in *Aspects of Pentecostal-Charismatic Origins,* Vinson Synan, Editor. South Plainfield, New Jersey: Bridge Publishing Inc.

Reflections of an insider who has been one of the most prominent pentecostal leaders in contemporary times.

Key Words
revivals, Word of God, holiness, worship, evangelistic zeal, fulfillment of prophecy

1982   "Conference on The Holy Spirit." Springfield, Missouri: Assemblies of God. 232 pages.

Conference outlines from plenary sessions, seminars, and workshops held during the August 16-18, 1982 meeting.

Key Words
Holy Spirit, Word of God, Baptism of the Holy Spirit, church growth, healing, evangelism, supernatural, world missions, prayer and fasting, charismatic, pentecostals

Index

Index

Day of Pentecost, 13, 77, 83
decentralized training, 76
"Declaration at St. Louis," 167
deliverance, 86
Delong, Lambert, 53
demographic trends, 75
"demon of respectability," 132
demon possession, 74
demonic powers, 94-95
demonic spirits, 92
Denmark, 73
denomination, 12, 14-15, 18, 50, 53
desire for respectability, 142
devil, the, 143, 161
devils, 40-42
De Wet, Christiaan, 161
Dispensationalism, 8, 51
dissertations/theses at SWM, 114
divine destiny, 52, 53
divine healing, 6, 48-49, 74-75, 110
Dollar, Harold, 162
Dominican Republic, 87
Dowie, Alexander, 141
dreams, 11, 72
Duff, Alexander, 29
Du Plessis, David J., 4, 38, 47, 50, 77, 138

East Bengel, 30
Easton, Susan, 28, 35
ecumenical, 38, 47,
Ecumenical Missionary Conference, 35
Edwards, Leland, 144
EFMA, 156
Egypt, 8
El Salvador, 83, 87
Elim Pentecostals, 29
End of the Ages, 70
"End Time Message," 8
enduement with power, 7-8, 33
England, 74, 129, 139
Enns, Arno, 75
Episcopal, 126
Episcopalians, 4, 64
eschatology, 5, 8, 51, 61, 88
eschatological factor, 9
"eschatological intensity," 51
eschatological urgency, 8, 137
eschatological worldview, 8
eschatos, 157
ethnic group, 157
ethnos, 157
Europe, 17, 53, 73, 138, 142
Evangelical Missions Quarterly, 49
evangelism, 50, 54, 63, 65-66, 74-75, 88, 111,

evangelism (continued), 129, 152-154, 159-160, 166, 170
"evangelistic door-opener," 74
evangelistic mandate, 152
evangelistic priority, 78
evangelistic zeal, 7, 10, 14, 60, 74
Evans, Sister, 77
Evans, R.M., 17
evil spirits, 122, 163-164
exclusivism, 6
exorcism, 130, 163-164
experience, 4, 5-7, 40-41, 83, 154-155
Eye of the Storm, 82

faith healing, 113
faith mission, 16
Far East, 138
Felch, Margaret, 35
felt-needs, 6
finances, 12, 14-15, 18
Fire-Baptized Holiness Church, 18
Fire in the Philippines, 114
Flint, Marguerite, 35
Flower, J. Roswell, 20
"Focus for the 80s." 145
force for evangelism, 146
Foreign Missions Board, 17, 18
Foursquare Church, 12, 114, 128, 144, 146, 156
Foursquare World Advance, 114, 156
Fourth Dimension, The, 99
Fox, George, 4
Frodsham, Stanley H., 10, 14, 50-51, 74, 79
Frontier missions, 17
fruit of the Spirit, 67, 111
Full Gospel Central Church, 73, 101, 103, 126
Fuller School of World Mission, 109, 114-115, 121, 125, 151, 160
future cautions, 140
future challenges, 144
future commitment, 137
future issues, 144
"Future of the Pentecostal Movement, The," 140

Garr, Alfred G., 27, 34
Gaver, Jessyca Russell, 57
Gee, Donald, 4, 8, 10, 14, 16, 42, 49, 62, 141
General Study Commission, 143
Gentiles, 83, 92
Germany, 51, 214
gifts of the Spirit, 67, 94
Glasser, Arthur, F., 74, 113
Global Church Growth, 98, 109, 115, 117

239

Index

Index

U.S. ethnics, 112
unknown tongue, 8, 24
Unreached Peoples, 158
unreached peoples, 17, 144-145, 147, 163
upward mobility, 153
urban evangelism, 146
"urban heritage," 78
Urban Missions, 145
urban strategies, 78
"urban targets," 145
urbanization, 78
urgency, 8, 15, 34
urgent missiology, 47

Vision of the Disinherited, 141
visions, 11-12
voice of God, 11

Wagner, C. Peter, 71, 109
Waldron, Vivian, 17
Walther, Grace, 35
Ward, A.G., 14
Warner, Wayne, 27
Wead, Doug, 31
Welsh revival, 59
Wesley, John, 4
West Africa, 79
West Indies, 83
What Are We Missing? 71, 114, 124
What God Hath Wrought, 52
What Meaneth This, 67
When the Fire Fell, 9, 59
William Carey Library, 78, 109
Wilson, Aaron A., 8
Wind and Flame, 63
winnable, the, 75, 142
Winter, Ralph D., 77, 113, 144
witch doctor, 162
With Signs Following, 14
Womack, David A., 48, 140, 143
women in missions, 35, 76
Woodford, L.F.W., 54, 110
Word and Witness, 19
Word and Work, 79
Word of God, 7-8, 50, 58-60, 66, 73, 86, 100-101, 127, 138, 167
working class, 129
"world Christian," 172
World Christian Encyclopedia, 3
World Dominion, 110
world evangelism, 8, 64, 141
World Missionary Council, 110
World Presbyterian Alliance, 67
World War II, 126, 130, 142

worldly respectability, 79
worship, 5, 10, 14, 60, 71, 73, 85, 90, 93, 153, 167

xenoglossia, 13
xenoglossolalia, 13-14
xenolalia, 9, 13-14
"Xenolalia and The Resulting Urge to Open Foreign Missions," 13-14

Yearbook of American Churches, 42
young people, 139
Your Church Can Grow, 125
Your Church Can Be Healthy, 125
Youth With A Mission, 145-147

Zimmerman, Thomas F., 57, 72, 138
Zurich, Switzerland, 42